Essays on New France

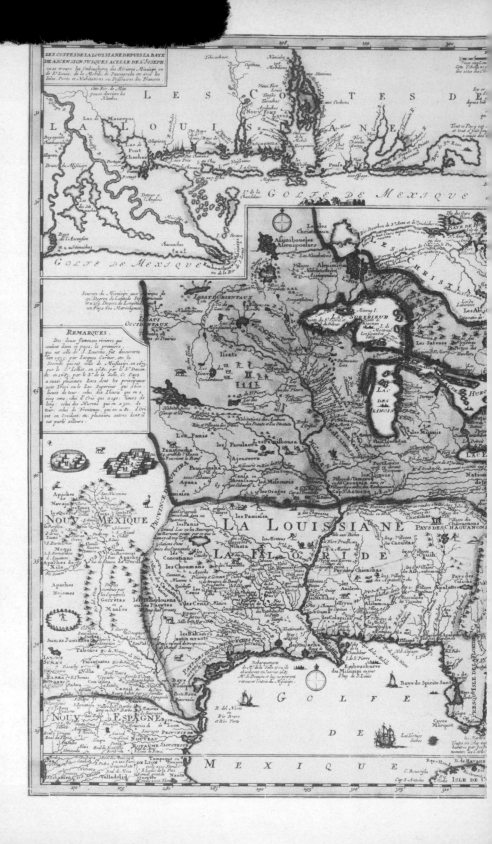

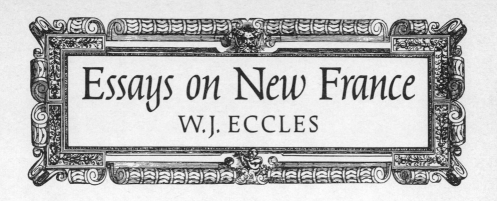

Essays on New France
W.J. ECCLES

TORONTO Oxford University Press 1987

CANADIAN CATALOGUING IN PUBLICATION DATA

Eccles, W. J. (William John), 1917–
Essays on New France

Includes bibliographical references and index.
ISBN 0-19-540580-3

1. Canada—History—To 1763 (New France). I. Title.

FC305.E27 1987   971.01   C87-093506-2   F1030.E27 1987

© Copyright Oxford University Press Canada 1987

OXFORD is a trademark of Oxford University Press
1 2 3 4—0 9 8 7
Printed in Canada by Webcom Limited

TO THE MEMORY OF
Michael
AND FOR
Robin and Peter

Contents

Acknowledgements

'Forty Years Back' from *The William and Mary Quarterly*, 3rd series, vol. XLI, July 1984. Used by permission.

'The History of New France According to Francis Parkman' from *The William and Mary Quarterly*, 3rd series, vol. XVIII, April 1961. Used by permission.

'The Role of the American Colonies in Eighteenth-Century French Foreign Policy' from *Atti del I Congresso Internazionale di Storia Americana* (Genova, 26–29 Maggio 1976) Tilgher-Genova, 1978. Copyright Casa Editrice Tilgher-Genova s.a.s.

'Social Welfare Measures and Policies in New France' from *XXXVI Congreso Internacional de Americanistas España, 1964 Actas y Memorias*, vol. 4, Sevilla, 1966.

'New France and the Western Frontier' from *Alberta Historical Review*, Spring 1969. Used by permission of the author.

'A Belated Review of Harold Adams Innis's *The Fur Trade in Canada*' from *Canadian Historical Review*, December 1979. Reprinted by permission of the University of Toronto Press.

'The Fur Trade and Eighteenth-Century Imperialism' from *The William and Mary Quarterly*, 3rd series, vol. XL, July 1983. Used by permission.

'La Mer de l'Ouest: Outpost of Empire' from *Rendezvous: Selected Papers of the Fourth North American Fur Trade Conference 1981*, edited by Thomas C. Buckley. Copyright 1984 by the North American Fur Trade Conference.

'The Social, Economic, and Political Significance of the Military Establishment in New France' from *Canadian Historical Review*, March 1971. Reprinted by permission of the University of Toronto Press.

'The Battle of Quebec: A Reappraisal' from *The French Colonial Historical Society Proceedings of the Third Annual Meeting*, edited by Alf Andrew Heggoy. The French Colonial Historical Society (Athens, Georgia 1978).

'New France and the French Impact on North America' from *The American Review of Canadian Studies*, vol. III, no. 1, Spring 1973. Used by permission.

'The Role of the American Colonies in Eighteenth-century French Foreign Policy' from *Atti del I Congresso Internazionale di Storia Americana* (Genova, 26–29 Maggio 1976) Tilgher-Genova, 1978. Copyright Casa Editrice Tilgher-Genova s.a.s.

'Sovereignty Association, 1500–1783' from *Canadian Historical Review*, December 1984. Reprinted by permission of the University of Toronto Press.

Preface

This selection contains essays on New France written over a period of twenty-five years. Some of them have been reprinted in anthologies of one sort or another, and requests were received for permission to have photocopies made for libraries or for teaching purposes; too often, it was discovered, this last was done without permission. Moreover, a few of the articles first appeared in rather obscure journals. It thus appeared worthwhile to undertake the present work.

Primarily the essays were, for the most part, an attempt to drag the history of New France out of its narrow, all-confining, parochial context and into three broader streams of history: those of continental North America, European culture and imperialism, and the stream, far too long neglected, of the indigenous peoples. To a degree the book also reflects the strengthening over time of certain concepts, advanced by a historian working in a relatively small but by no means insignificant area of history. Some early hypotheses had to be revised and, in the odd instance, totally rejected as further research dictated. An example of the latter was the notion, widely subscribed to, that in the fur trade some Indian nations served, or sought to serve, as middlemen, in the European sense of the term; that is, they were capitalist entrepreneurs in moccasins, seeking to intervene between producer and consumer to buy cheap and sell dear in order to garner a profit. This concept I now believe to be false, completely alien to the mores of the Indians of the seventeenth and eighteenth centuries.

Since it was clearly out of the question to rewrite the articles, they stand as they first appeared, apart from a few minor revisions and changes in syntax made at the behest of the relentless editors—for which last I am more than grateful. In the articles that were published in Canadian journals quotations in French were printed in that language. This time it was decided that I should translate them into English.

Over the years grants in aid of research were received from several institutions, without which the work could not have been done. In particular my sincere thanks are extended to the Canada Council, its successor the Social Science and Humanities Research Council of Canada, the Ewart Foundation at the University of Manitoba, the Killam Foundation, and the University of Toronto Humanities and Social Sciences Committee of the Research

Board. In addition my sincere thanks must be expressed to the archivists of the Archives Nationales, Bibliothèque Nationale, and of the Archives du Ministère des Affaires étrangères in Paris, the Public Archives of Canada, Archives Nationales du Québec à Montréal, Archives du Séminaire de Québec, the State Archives of New York and Massachusetts, and the staff of the Robarts Library at the University of Toronto.

Finally, I must acknowledge that it was the collection of essays by a friend and colleague, James Axtell's *The European and the Indian. Essays in the Ethnohistory of Colonial North America*, that first gave me the idea to put together a batch of my own.

INTRODUCTION

Forty Years Back

This paper was one of seven, forming a symposium, commissioned by the editor of The William and Mary Quarterly. *They appeared in the issue of July 1984 (Volume XLI). The contributors were asked to look back over their careers as historians of colonial North America and give their personal recollections along with their appraisals of the field and discipline in the years since the Second World War. My paper appears here in a slightly expanded form—actually an early draft that had to be cut, with a few minor revisions.*

The last forty years have seen as many changes in the approach of historians to their study of the past as have been seen in science and technology. Time appears to have been telescoped, condensed, accelerated. In the field of North American colonial history we have gone from the romantic, chauvinist, but felicitous prose of Francis Parkman to history contrived with the aid of the computer. Indigenous peoples and social groups, hitherto ignored, are now to the fore. It has been a very interesting, and at times aggravating, period in which to practise the craft. Intellectual historians some years hence will have a rich field to winnow.

When I returned to Montreal and university after the Second World War, and chose New France as my field of specialization, I dutifully reread Parkman's epic series *France and England in North America* and found nothing in those works with which I could disagree. I read all the other secondary sources, French and English, and found that the latter were, for the most part, little more than paraphrased Parkman. The only difference was that they lacked his literary style. Most of the works in French showed a marked pro-clerical bias. The only recent writings of any value were the articles by E.R. Adair, a specialist in early modern British and European history with an international reputation. This was, of course, before the magisterial works of Guy Frégault and Marcel Trudel began to appear.

Upon moving to McGill from the University of London, Adair had turned his attention to seventeenth- and eighteenth-century Canadian history. With his depth and breadth of knowledge of the age he quickly put things in a new context and destroyed some hoary old myths in the process, greatly to the

1

dismay of the old guard in both English and French Canada. His family background went a long way to explain his irreverent attitude, his inability to suffer fools gladly. He was the son of one of the younger colonels—he claimed the youngest—in the army of the Confederate States of America who had refused to take the oath of amnesty at the end of the war, removed to England with his Spanish Florida Creole wife, and there lived the rest of his long life. When England went to war in 1914 and the senior Adair had to register as an alien, he did so as a citizen of the Confederate States of America. It was under the direction of his son Robin—a proud, brilliant, arrogant man who made the strongest of impressions on all who knew him—that I elected to work.

Among the history graduate students, Adair enjoyed a fearsome reputation as an extremely demanding teacher, never satisfied with whatever they did, but most painstaking in his criticism. They warned me that I would surely regret my decision. Yet, I thought, during my four long years overseas the Kriegsmarine and the Luftwaffe had failed to cause me serious harm; hence it was difficult to see what pain an elderly professor of history could inflict. Subsequently I came to suspect that I had made a serious error in judgement on that score.

When the time came to select a topic for my M.A. thesis Adair wanted me to study the intendancy of Gilles Hocquart, but to show him that I had a mind of my own I chose another intendant of New France, Jean Bochart de Champigny, who had served in the colony during a particularly lively period, 1686 to 1702. War then raged with the Iroquois and the English colonies; flamboyant characters abounded—Louis de Buade de Frontenac, Pierre Le Moyne d'Iberville (scourge of the English and founder of Louisiana), René-Robert Cavelier de La Salle, and a host more—while in the background Louis XIV and Jean-Baptiste Colbert made their vital decisions.

An entire summer I spent in sultry, dreary Ottawa poring over the transcripts of the French documents twelve hours a day, seven days a week, at the Public Archives of Canada. Incredible though it may seem today, researchers then were allowed to walk into the stacks and help themselves to volumes of transcripts as they needed them, while the archivists were in attendance. History quickly assumed an entirely new dimension as the men of that age seemed to speak to me directly. It later became emotionally disturbing to read the letter of a young Canadian officer, relating what he planned to do some months hence, knowing as I did, from other sources, that he would be killed a week later.

Before long a view of events and personages at the end of the seventeenth century began to emerge that was markedly at variance with the accepted interpretation. This was particularly true of Frontenac who had been made a legendary, heroic figure, first by Parkman, then by the anticlerical French historian Henri Lorin. Up to that point no one had disputed their view of events; it had become conventional wisdom. To dispute it clearly spelled trouble. Yet not to write the thesis as the evidence dictated would, it seemed to me, be an exercise in futility. I made my decision, knowing full well what to expect.

During the ensuing seven months I had to endure several exasperating sessions in Adair's study, beside the fireplace at his house on University Avenue, over tea and sandwiches—cucumber for Adair, peanut butter for me as for his other students—as he tore my chapters to ribbons. Arguing with him, I found, was akin to arm wrestling with a chain saw. He always insisted that the historian had consciously to strive to be fair in his judgements—yet he could be unfair in his criticism of his students' work, even cruel at times. He seemed to enjoy reducing female students to tears, and they, it seemed to me, took masochistic pleasure from the experience; at least they always came back for more. He demanded that every statement, judgement, conclusion be backed by irrefutable evidence and convincing argument—which, nevertheless, he never failed to dispute. This may not be the best way to train a scholar, but it can work. A day after his destruction of one key chapter, Adair encountered me on the campus; I suspect that I must have glowered at him. With the faintest suspicion of a smile he halted and asked me: 'Well, Eccles, does it still sting? Never mind, we'll make a historian of you yet.' The intimation that I might conceivably one day make a historian was, in my case, the closest he ever came to praise.

With some manifest misgivings Adair and the examiners agreed that I should be granted the degree of *Magister in Artibus* and go on to strive to be admitted *Doctoris in Philosophia* if I desired. I desired, and I had already chosen a thesis topic: Frontenac. Adair told me that I was rash, then told me to take myself off to the archives in France. There were extremely few scholarships available for post-graduate work in those days (a situation that has, mercifully, changed for the better in the past three decades), but the French government accorded McGill a scholarship each year to enable a graduate student to attend a French university. By incredible serendipity it fell to me that year. The actual amount of money was extremely modest, yet it got me there and back, kept body and soul together, and the red identity card of a *boursier du gouvernement de France* opened many doors.

In 1951 Paris was a grim, unhappy city. France had not then recovered from the war. Bitter recriminations between those who had supported the Vichy government and quondam members of the Resistance still flared in the press. At one end of the inner courtyard of the Sorbonne there was a vast mural depicting King Philippe Auguste, on horseback, handing the royal charter to the rector of the university in the year 1200. A German bullet had shattered the glass over the breast of the king. One day as I was about to go through the entryway I saw the courtyard packed with shouting, gesticulating students; two factions, the inevitable left versus right. Fists flew, then I saw shoes whipped off and bodies go down from a blow to the head from a steel capped heel. I squirmed back and out across the street just in time to escape the baton charge of the very tough CRS riot squad.

The franc fell steadily on the 'free market'. Living quarters were almost impossible to find; the city badly needed a coat of paint; and the hordes of *fonctionnaires*—their numbers having been swollen, I was told, by Pierre Laval to keep as many Frenchmen as possible from being dragooned into forced labour in Germany—seemed bent on making life as difficult as possible for all. Politically the country appeared headed for chaos as government followed government every few weeks. This was, in fact, more apparent than real. The politicians were playing musical chairs with a variation to the rules: when the music stopped they added a chair. During that unusually cold, bleak winter I was given a ticket to attend a session of the National Assembly. As luck would have it a vote of confidence in Edgar Faure's government had been called for and two days had to elapse before the vote could be taken to give time for sober reflection. Thus the session I attended began at one minute past midnight. Faure defended his policies, then deputy after deputy mounted the rostrum to attack them. One who did was Edouard Daladier, bald and very obese, bearing no resemblance to the dapper little man who accompanied Chamberlain to Munich in 1938, but he spoke well. (He had, of course, once been a professor of history.) Most of the others did not. The speeches droned on and on until dawn. A Communist deputy almost emptied the Chamber. Then I felt a light tap on my shoulder, and turned. A young man of obvious Algerian appearance seated behind me whispered in my ear: 'Do you think they are ready for self-government yet?'

Yet the things that make Paris the most beautiful and interesting city in the world were still there to be enjoyed, and the Sorbonne was a startling revelation. One impressive course was that given by the courtly, aristocratic Paul Vaucher. It was a rather old-fashioned but fascinating study of eighteenth-century diplomatic history. The lectures of Professor Ernest Labrousse revealed an entirely new, to me, dimension to the study of history. His tart comment that the first task of the historian was to learn to count left me sucking a hind tooth. My introduction to the methods of the *annales* school in Professor Jean Meuvret's seminar at the *seizième section* of the Ecole des hautes études made me realize that the French historians were a light-year ahead of those practising the craft in North America. I did not see until later that the exclusion of war and political strife from their study of a past society, particularly that of the seventeenth century, could result in a rather warped overview.

At the Collège de France I attended Professor Marcel Giraud's weekly lecture on society in the Confederate States of America; he held the chair in North American history. Those lectures opened my eyes to what could be squeezed from the most disparate scraps of evidence. They also had their amusing side. They were not well attended: I was the only student. The French students were too concerned with the requisite papers for the *license*, the *aggrégé*, or the *docteur ès lettres* requirements to waste time on such exotica. Retired generals and *haute bourgeoise* ladies from Neuilly or the Île St-Louis dropped in occasionally. Apparently it was the thing to do. As the weather turned colder, *clochards* left their quarters beneath the bridges of the Seine and crept quietly into the shelter of the Collège lecture halls, there (wrapped in their peculiar, rich aroma) to doze. All told a rather motley assembly, which did not seem to worry Giraud in the least. I am sure that even if no one had attended he would still have given his well-organized, noteless lectures as required by decree of the Emperor Bonaparte.

Most of my time was spent at the Archives Nationales and the Bibliothèque Nationale, with forays to other depositories in Paris and the provinces. At first it seemed that the French archivists took a perverse delight in creating difficulties and putting obstacles in one's path. Later I realized that they merely sought to ascertain if one were a serious scholar. Satisfied on that score they would then provide every assistance. Sometimes, however, outside intervention was required. Rather foolishly, I had left the Affaires Étrangères archives to the last and then discovered that the number of volumes of bound documents one could consult each day was severely restricted. It was clear that I would not have time to go through all that I should before leaving France. In some agitation I mentioned this to Professor Giraud, who smiled and said quietly, 'Calmez-vous Eccles (Ek-lez), calmez-vous.' When next I entered the Quai d'Orsay a rather discomfited *présidente de la salle* informed me that since I was pressed for time I could have as many volumes a day as I wished.

It was with considerable reluctance that I took ship back to Montreal in the fall, there to begin hammering the great mass of accumulated notes into some sort of meaningful order. I also wrote letters to every history department in the country, offering my services. Some chairmen replied, some did not bother. There were no openings. The inflated enrolments engendered by the influx of war veterans were over and everywhere had begun to decline. Finally, when hope had just about vanished I received an offer of a locum tenens appointment for one year at the University of Manitoba. My telegram of acceptance was sent within the hour. I was not then to know that one academic year would stretch to four, and then elsewhere down to the present.

At the end of August 1953 I took the train to Winnipeg—two nights and nearly three days. Until then I had seen virtually nothing of Canada outside the province of Quebec. After a few weeks in Winnipeg I came to realize that Montreal, and Quebec in general, were not really part of Canada. They belonged to Europe, although separated by an ocean. The motto of the Quebec I had left was 'Je me souviens'. That of Winnipeg was 'Prudence, Commerce, Industry'. The latter did not pluck at my heart strings. Winnipeg has, I am told, changed greatly in the intervening years. Then it was an absolute horror: no bookstore, not a single decent restaurant, liquor laws drafted by the temperance movement. Aesthetically the city was enough to reduce one to tears. Some friends in Montreal had formed a select little society, the Oh Canada Club. The members, in their perambulations about the country, took photographs of the most hideous buildings they encountered. The most horrendous example submitted each year earned the congratulations of the members and a splendid dinner at the University Club. I submitted a photograph of the old Winnipeg City Hall—I was torn between it and the Administration Building on the University campus. I was vexed when my entry was rejected on the grounds that it had to be a *maquillage*: there could not possibly be, it was claimed, a building anywhere that ghastly.

The climate, in my view, rendered the city uninhabitable. When I arrived the temperature was in the upper 90s Fahrenheit. Five months later it was 40 below, where it remained for weeks on end. The university campus at Fort Garry had been located, by decision of some political genius, about ten miles from the edge of town on the bald prairie. The Red River made an impressive, sweeping U-turn at the site but every building had its back to the river. Standing on a windswept corner before daybreak in January waiting for a bus, as the students swept by in their automobiles, tried me sorely. When the sun did appear above the horizon there would frequently be not one but three, or five, (once there were seven) suns close together in a horizontal line. This was the 'sun dog' phenomenon, caused by the refraction of ice crystals in the intensely cold lower atmosphere. I learned to hate the sight of it, spectacular though it was.

That first year of teaching full time: sheer hell. Preparing lectures for three courses and a graduate seminar occupied all my waking hours—academics have all been through it. The lectures in modern European and American history presented no problem. The works of Andrews, Wertenbaker, Lavisse, Renouvin, *et al*. were swiftly rendered into fifty-minute segments. It was my half of the Canadian survey course that reduced me to despair. Lectures based on my own research, dealing with topics not found in any textbook, baffled the students. All too frequently at the end of a lecture, students would approach and ask where I was in the assigned text; they could not find what I had been talking about anywhere. One was expected to stick to the text, merely annotate it, not wander away. There was, however, the odd lighter moment. I had early adopted the unconscious nervous habit—

long since mastered—of pacing up and down in front of the class. One morning as I began my pacing I suddenly saw a broad chalk line on the floor and, in large letters, the world HALT. Somewhat startled, I looked up and there on the wall in front of me was ABOUT TURN. Somehow I finished the lecture and for the rest of the term continued my practice of pacing in order not to disappoint the students.

My nemesis was not the students' somewhat irreverent but charming attitude, but the lectures I had to prepare for Canadian history post 1791. There I found myself really in trouble. The available secondary sources were so excruciatingly dull that I found it impossible to contrive anything resembling an interesting, meaningful lecture. The questions that I thought should have been asked had not been, and too many of those that had seemed to me perverse or of little significance. For the most part the history of nineteenth- and twentieth-century Canada then consisted of little more than what one politician had said to another: the struggle for responsible government, the march to Confederation, then on to the Statute of Westminster. What could be more dreary? When I asked colleagues how much bread these political enactments had put in the mouths of the poor, they looked at me in consternation. The condition of society was then of no concern for the practising Canadian historians. As it was, the lectures I contrived bored me to tears and, I fear, had the same effect on the students. They must have sighed with relief as I departed the lecture hall at the end of term, but their sighs could not possibly have matched mine in intensity.

In the spring of that first academic year, 1953–4, the Canadian Historical Association was to meet at the University of Manitoba. The chairman of the program committee kindly put me down for a paper. On the appointed day, in a large, crowded lecture hall, an eminent University of Toronto professor gave an eminently forgettable paper on the perennial topic: Canadian nationalism. Every other eminent professor in the audience then had to offer his comments and contradict those of his colleagues, *in extenso*. Eventually I was allowed to give my paper, 'Frontenac: New Light and a Reappraisal'. The reaction of that audience was stunned disbelief. The reputation of one of the country's legendary heroes had been assailed, even sullied, and, as I was later acerbically informed, heroes were in short supply in Canada. Fortunately the audience was, by that time, more anxious to discover if a pre-lunch bar was open somewhere on the campus than to deal with me as they seemingly felt I deserved. Thus the discussion from the floor was mercifully curtailed.

June 1954 must, obviously, have been an extremely tranquil time in the wider world. The *Winnipeg Tribune* made a four-column front-page story of the article, the *Winnipeg Free Press* did likewise, and *Time* magazine gave it two columns, quoting the author of the high-school textbook used in

Manitoba: 'It's going to be tough to write textbooks if every character in history is going to be debunked.' The tougher the better, I thought.

During the ensuing summer I finished writing my thesis, all but the final chapter. Everything I write seems to go through four or five drafts. That last chapter must have gone through ten, but in the late winter of 1955 the thesis was sent on its way. When I returned to McGill for the defence two old friends took me to lunch at the University Club before the examination and insisted on my downing a double brandy with the coffee to steady my nerves. I felt as though the firing squad awaited me: 'No blindfold. Just a cigarette.' We need not have worried. The external examiner was Professor Guy Frégault of the Université de Montréal, then the leading historian in the field. Fortunately for me, a decade earlier Frégault had published a rather hagiographic biography of Pierre Le Moyne d'Iberville, who had been one of Frontenac's *bêtes noires*; thus anything critical of Frontenac delighted him. When one of the examiners accused me of being prejudiced and my conclusions of going beyond the evidence, Frégault waded in before I could reply: 'Ridicule. Tout à fait ridicule.' He defended the thesis for me, dismissed all such criticism summarily, cowed them all, and so I emerged unscathed, the thesis accepted magna cum laude.

That out of the way, I began revising the thesis for publication, which necessitated trips every summer to the archives in Quebec, Ottawa, Albany, and Boston. At Albany it was disconcerting to ask for a particular volume and be handed a small canvas bag containing some charred, blackened scraps of paper, all that remained of the documents after a disastrous fire.

During those years, 1953 to 1957, Professor W.L. Morton, chairman of the department, kept my head above the academic waters by sending the other three members of the department off on sabbatical leave one after the other so that my locum tenens appointment could be renewed. In late May 1956 I was at the archives in Ottawa and Professor Tryggvi Oleson had still not received word that he had been granted a fellowship. I was just about to accept an appointment at Brandon College to teach French when a telegram arrived from Morton; Tryggvi had been granted a Guggenheim on reversal. And so I survived.

During my second year at Manitoba, Professor Morton decided that a new general history of Canada embodying the most recent research was badly needed. His initial notion was that some ten historians would each write a 50-page section. Upon being approached, the outstanding but ever-reckless Toronto publisher, Jack McClelland, agreed to take on the project. Then Morton, mulling it over, became convinced that 500 pages would not suffice. One day he announced that he was going to put it to McClelland that two volumes would be needed—and, he rather despondently added, most likely that would be the end of it.

When Morton returned from Toronto a few days later he was in a state of euphoria. McClelland's reaction had been: Why just two volumes? Why not ten or fifteen if need be? A volume for each author would eliminate the problems of deadlines and division of royalties. So, with that decision made the Canadian Centenary Series History of Canada began its period of gestation. Morton and McClelland then blithely assumed that the entire series would be published by 1967, Canada's centennial year. At the time of writing the series is still not completed and some of the volumes that have appeared, including my own, are now so dated that they should be allowed, mercifully, to go out of print.

Meanwhile I finished *Frontenac: The Courtier Governor* and sent it to Jack McClelland, who had rashly agreed to publish it after one of his editors had read the first draft of a few early chapters. His firm, I incline to think, had then had little experience, likely none, in publishing scholarly works, let alone one as controversial as mine appeared to be. The manuscript was sent to a host of readers, few of whom appeared to know anything about the history of the period depicted. After reading the manuscript they read the previously published works on Frontenac and his age, noted that my interpretation was markedly at variance, and therefore advised rejection. The work was regarded as heresy. Typical was the comment in one such appraiser's lengthy report: 'It is a pity that painstaking research should be marred by so much prejudice and so much illogicality.' Only the critiques of two French-Canadian historians, Marcel Trudel and the Reverend A. d'Eschambault, offered anything constructive.

Although I did not have a written contract with McClelland and Stewart—a detail that we had overlooked—and despite the hostile reaction to the work, Jack McClelland declined to go back on his word. In 1959 the book duly appeared. To my, and I suspect everyone else's, surprise the reviews were generally favourable, even eliciting an editorial in the Montreal *Gazette* of 28 March, 'How Such a Book Was Possible'. The editor sought to make the point that research funds should be made available to ensure the publication of more such revisionist works.

In 1957 I had departed Winnipeg to accept an appointment at the University of Alberta in Edmonton. I was sorry to leave my colleagues at the University of Manitoba and its associated colleges, but I was certainly not sorry to see the last of Winnipeg. Edmonton proved to be a much pleasanter place to live. Even so, the summer still had to be spent at the archives in the east. The four-to-five day drive across the Prairies and through muskeg, moose-pasture, and black-fly country north of the Great Lakes convinced me that Canada stood sorely in need of some judicious editing.

During those summers I met and came to know well the historians at the Université de Montréal and Université Laval: Guy Frégault, Michel Brunet,

Marcel Trudel, Fernand Ouellet, and Gustave Lanctot the retired Dominion Archivist. They were always courteous and helpful. There was never, from them, the slightest hint that they resented an English Canadian invading their national scholarly domain—just the reverse, in fact. In the decades of the sixties and seventies the history of New France and pre-Confederation Quebec was being turned inside out and completely rewritten, with the emphasis on social and economic history. I was regarded by them as just another toiler in the vineyard. English-Canadian historians, on the other hand, for the most part tended to look askance at my choice of field. As one of them remarked at a meeting of the Canadian Historial Association in Toronto, loud enough to be sure that I overheard, 'Why bother with that lot? Aren't there enough good topics left in Ontario history?' I, obviously, was letting the side down. During those years I was continually asked what had caused me to choose 'that field'.

In January 1958, out of a clear blue sky, I received an invitation from Professor Ray A. Billington to write the history of the frontier of New France for inclusion in his projected Histories of the American Frontier Series. It was welcome news indeed that an interest in things Canadian actually existed south of the border, although it then did not extend beyond the French regime. That, however, was a selective interest that I freely shared. Thus began a pleasant, if distant, editorial relationship. Ray Billington was truly the gentleman scholar. With me he was always helpful, encouraging, and very patient. He had to wait for my volume in the Canadian Centenary Series to be finished before I could begin to work for him.

Billington placed far more emphasis on the environment as a determining factor in history than I did; he sought on occasion to persuade me to his way of thinking but he never attempted to enforce his views. He firmly believed that in American history the environment had, to a large degree, dictated how people would conduct their lives. I could agree that the environment had influence, but the institutions brought from France were to my mind of far greater signifiance. The St Lawrence River and the harsh Canadian climate determined certain terms; but the cultural baggage the settlers brought with them—the Roman Catholic religion, the *Coutume de Paris*, the despotic but paternalistic framework of government, the mores and language of northern France—rather than the environment, in my view, really dominated the lives of the Canadians.

With what I sought to do in *The Canadian Frontier, 1534–1760*, as in everything I have written, Billington had no quarrel whatsoever. That was—as R.G. Collingwood put it in his influential work, *The Idea of History*—to make the past live in the present, to recreate it and make the reader see, in his mind's eye, past events, past scenes, past ways of life as though he or she were sharing them, and thus to understand why the people behaved as they did. Everything becomes grist to that mill. What always has to be guarded against is the imposing of present-day values on the past.

I am not sure—since we never discussed it—that Billington agreed with me that the historian has to begin with a question, then seek the answer. Frequently the search reveals new, more significant questions and has to turn in a different direction for the evidence that will provide convincing answers. Unfortunately in Canadian history, historians have too often begun with an a priori answer, then sought evidence to support it, ignoring or brushing aside evidence that did not. As one colleague was informed by the very eminent director of his thesis before he left for the archives, his task would be made much easier were he first to decide what his conclusions were going to be.

The same year, 1958, that I received Ray Billington's invitation I was asked to give a paper at the meeting of the Canadian Historical Association. At that time I was working on a critical appraisal of Francis Parkman's view of New France that I had promised to submit to *The William and Mary Quarterly*. The editor of that journal readily agreed to my reading the paper at the meeting; and the CHA program committee agreed, with rather dismaying alacrity, to forgo publishing it in the Association's annual report.

The paper, entitled 'The History of New France According to Francis Parkman', sought to make the point that his epic work had outlived its usefulness and that a quite different approach was now needed. One staunch member of the old guard, possessed of a notoriously inflated opinion of his own importance, took sharp exception and denounced both the paper and its author from the floor. Many years ago he had, he declared, read Parkman's entire works while snowbound in a north-country log cabin and in his view they could not be improved upon. A stop had, he declared, to be put to this iconoclasm. Guy Frégault, the commentator, reacted strongly, declaring that the historian who was not an iconoclast was nothing; but since he spoke in French his remarks were largely lost on the audience at Queen's University. In retrospect that outburst appears to have been the last gasp of those who regarded the history of Canada as a litany brought down the mountain engraved on stone tablets.

In 1963 I accepted the offer of a professorship at the University of Toronto, much closer to the archives in Quebec. Before leaving Edmonton I managed to finish the final chapter of *Canada under Louis XIV, 1663–1701* for W.L. Morton's series. Credit for its being completed then and not later must, to no small degree, go to the University of Alberta, which sanctioned a light second-term teaching load and put an exceptionally competent typist at my disposal. From December to June I was thus able to write for ten hours a day, seven days a week. Those years at Edmonton went quickly. They were pleasant years and it was not without sincere regret that I left Alberta.

Toronto in 1963 was just about to begin shedding its well-earned reputation as the dreariest city in North America, dominated as it had been for generations by the Orange Lodge and the Methodist chapels. It is a city virtually without a history. Nothing happened there except for the civil disturbance, known as the Rebellion of 1837, a quarter-century after the American forces burned the place during the War of 1812. (That last, of course, provided the British with an excuse to put the torch to Washington the following year. There are perhaps some, in both countries, who wish we could have a repeat performance.) During the sixties and seventies, however, waves of immigrants from southern Europe, Asia, and the Caribbean swept in and swiftly transformed Toronto into a quite civilized and colourful city.

That same year I received an invitation from Professor Woodrow Borah, of the University of California at Berkeley, to give a paper at a colloquium on poor-law legislation in colonial North America to be held at the meetings of the Congreso Internacional de Americanistas in Spain the following summer. Fortuitously, in the Archives judiciaires at Montreal I had some months earlier stumbled upon the minutes of the local Bureau des Pauvres, established in 1688. There clearly was a worthwhile article to be carved out of that, and other, evidence. I approached the Dean for travel funds. He appeared taken aback by my request, but he agreed to it. At the University of Alberta, then striving to gain international recognition, funds for such purposes as mine were to be had for the asking; but, as I later discovered, at the University of Toronto—where parsimony had long been a finely honed administrative exercise—my request and its being granted quite flummoxed my colleagues. Some of them are to this day still a trifle bitter. The Dean debited the department's very meagre travel budget, thereby leaving my colleagues bereft for the year.

After the conference, which met first at Barcelona, proceeded to Madrid, and ended at Seville, I went to Paris to seek in the archives at the Quai d'Orsay the answer to the question: why had France so readily agreed to the cession of Canada to Britain in the peace negotiations that ended in the Treaty of Paris, 1763? The answer was, to my surprise, easily found in the correspondence of the French foreign minister, the duc de Choiseul, with the French ambassador at Madrid. Choiseul's policy—in which Canada was totally expendable—raised a whole range of new questions for me.

Those few weeks in Paris were indeed pleasant. The difference between the France of 1964 and the one I had last seen twelve years before was astounding. The old rancour and bitterness were gone. Even the *fonctionnaires* were now polite and tried to be helpful. Peace and prosperity obviously agreed with the French.

Two years later I accepted two invitations. One was to spend the ensuing academic year at my old university, McGill, as visiting professor at its French

Canada Studies Centre. The other, rather rashly accepted, was to offer a course in early Canadian history at the University of Chile at Santiago in their autumn term, March to July. Since I had next to no Spanish, it was stipulated that I would teach in French. At my favourite restaurant the Jacaranda, the waiters were at first somewhat taken aback when, during my first few weeks, I ordered such delicacies as marinated squid for dessert. All told it proved to be an interesting if sometimes frustrating experience, but it did allow me to see parts of Chile, Peru, and Brazil that I would not likely have ever visited otherwise. It was also, I am sure, the first time that a course in the history of Canada was offered in South America.

Two things in particular impressed me during that adventure. One was the tremendous gap between rich and poor, and the attempts then being made to narrow it. The other was that two of the historians and their team of research assistants at the Centro de Investigaciones de Historia Americana, to which I was attached—Professors Rolando Mellafe and Alvaro Jara—were, in their work on the colonial period, employing research methods and techniques, those of the French *annales* school, that were far in advance of anything then being done in Canada or, I venture to suggest, in the United States. Particularly was this true in the field of demography.

In Montreal the following autumn I settled down to writing the tardy volume for Ray Billington. The French Canada Studies Centre required me to give only a graduate seminar and two public lectures. In return I was provided with a splendid office in a fine old Edwardian house on the fringe of the campus. I was spoiled outrageously by the Centre's secretarial staff. No sooner was the first draft of a chapter finished in my pencilled scrawl than it was snatched away; the next day a neatly typed copy was on my desk ready for revision. Thus I managed to finish the book before returning, reluctantly, to Toronto. Despite that city's improving ambiance, Montreal was then still a far more interesting place to be.

At long last unencumbered by commitments, I decided that it was time to begin serious work on the mainstays of the economy and society of New France: agriculture, the fur trade, and the military establishment. The role of, and relations with, the Indian nations were also, I felt, long overdue for study. Those were the things, it seemed to me, that had made New France so different to the English colonies, and the Canadians a very different breed to the Anglo-Americans. A trial balloon, with the long-winded title 'The Social, Economic, and Political Significance of the Military Establishment in New France', that eventually appeared in the March 1971 issue of the *Canadian Historical Review* seemed to indicate that a major study would be worthwhile.

At that juncture of events Richard B. Morris, co-editor of the New-American Nation Series, intervened. He asked me to write the volume to

supplant Reuben Gold Thwaites's *France in America* in the original series.
I did not really want to take on the task, but for reasons that need not be
discussed here I did. At the same time I promised myself that I would not
accept any more such commissions, with their deadlines and editorial
importuning. Fortunately my application to the Canada Council for one of
the recently instituted Senior Killam Fellowships was successful. For the
ensuing three years I taught half-time and was free from December to September to do the research and writing.

The galley proofs reached me in Paris in the spring of 1972. They had
been sent to me, poste restante, at the Montparnasse post office. I collected
the bulky package and headed for the Métro but then, at the corner of the
Rue de Vaugirard, found myself in front of the Café Dome: shades of
Hemingway and Fitzgerald. It being almost noon and a warm spring day,
what better place, I thought, to lunch and begin my proof-reading. The bill
came as a bit of a shock, but it seemed worth it at the time.

The page proofs followed in June with the stern admonition that they had
to be back in New York by a date that gave me a bare two days to go through
them. All went well until noon of the second day when I began to wonder if I
had erred in referring to the *Compagnie d'Occident* at a certain point in
time: was it not, in fact, then the *Compagnie des Indes*? It had to be checked.
To have gone to the Bibliothèque Nationale would have taken far too long,
so I dashed over to the Presses Universitaires bookshop to consult a copy of
Marcel Giraud's *Histoire de la Lousiane*, only to find the shop closed until
two o'clock. I knew that a bookshop on the quay at the foot of the Boul Mich
also had the book, so there I sprinted. The pages of the book were, of course,
uncut, so as unobtrusively as possible, holding the book endwise to the light, I
pried the pages apart far enough to scan them and found what I wanted in the
index, replaced the book, and rushed back to my quarters in the rue Jacob.
There is no telling the demands that research can make.

In the ensuing years, from that Paris summer of 1972 to the present, the
changes that had already begun to take place in the study of North American
colonial history developed and blossomed out in a most fecund manner.
Some American colonial historians began to adopt the methods of the
annalistes, while others proposed to quantify everything in sight. A few
Canadian historians followed suit. Professor Ernest Labrousse, if made
aware of this trend, would likely have shaken his head in bewilderment:
'L'historien doit compter, bien sûr, mais cela, c'est ridicule.' In Quebec,
major demographic studies were underway and everywhere social history
and economic history were to the fore. The early volumes of the *Dictionary
of Canadian Biography* necessitated a great deal of research that otherwise
would not have been done. Women's history began to raise its rather per-
plexed head, and the Indians as a major subject for investigation at long last

captured the serious attention of historians who were now willing to make use of the findings of scholars in other disciplines. Here the influence of the ethnohistorians in the United States began to have a strong effect. The old division, dominant since Parkman's day, of English and French colonial history began to break down as historians studied the period from the viewpoint of the Indians. This obliged them to view both the French and the English in a more detached fashion and in a new light.

Some thirty years ago, when in my lectures I tried to discuss the role of the Indians in Canadian history, I quickly became aware that I had lost my audience. Up to that point they were scribbling their redundant notes, then the pencils went down, heads began to turn, and the chatter began. On one occasion I overheard a student remark to his seatmate, 'Here he goes again—chasing the Indians through the woods.' That is not the reaction today. No essay topics are more popular than those dealing with the Indians; on every examination paper, at least one question on them has to appear. A few lectures do not suffice; now courses on the Indian peoples are required. It would not surprise me were Cree to rank with French and English, a few years hence, as one of Canada's official languages.

So that is the state of the art at present in this country. To have moved from Parkman's interpretation of the age, viewed through whig-coloured spectacles, to history as interpreted by demographers, quantifiers, *annalistes*, and ethnohistorians in one generation shows that there has been rapid change. In 1947, when I began my work, Parkman's magisterial depiction of events had ruled for the better part of a century. No historian today can, or should, expect to have such a long run. We are, however—and of this I feel sure—with our new materials and tools obtaining a far richer and truer view of past societies than ever before.

The History of New France According to Francis Parkman

The initial negative reaction to this 1958 paper by a leading Canadian historian is discussed in the Introduction: 'Forty Years Back'. It soon became apparent that his view was not shared by many of the younger historians. In the United States the new breed of colonial historians, ethnohistorians, rejected Parkman's works out of hand. One of the more eminent, Francis Jennings, published articles attacking Parkman's unscholarly treatment of evidence, his twisting of it to prove a dubious point, and his blatant prejudice against the Amerindians. Colonial historians have long since rejected Parkman's works. Students also, now show marked antipathy to his interpretations of events and his florid prose. Yet, as shown by the recent publication of a new edition of his epic series France and England in North America *and the glowing reviews it received in both Canada and the United States, too often written by persons knowing little or nothing of the history of the period, his work clearly still has appeal. It rises from the scholarly ash heap like the proverbial phoenix.*

Between the years 1951 and 1892 Francis Parkman wrote his epic series, *France and England in North America*. From the date of their first appearance these eight volumes have continued to influence the interpretation of the early history of Canada. Recently, however, some few historians have begun to study the history of New France not in the works of Parkman, but in the original documents, and their depictions of events and portrayals of the more important personages are markedly at variance with his. This departure cannot be accounted for by the discovery of much new evidence; rather, it arises from the fact that the historian today selects and evaluates historical evidence in the light of values and basic assumptions that differ from those in vogue in Parkman's time.

For example: Parkman, in company with the other Whig historians, always used the concept of Progress to judge the past. He was convinced that the onward march of Progress was inevitable; it might be hindered by reactionary forces, but eventually all opposition would be overcome. It seemed to him that this was as natural a law as that water must run downhill; a river might have to twist and turn, seep slowly through swamps, or it might be dammed, but its onward course could not be halted for long. This was the basic premise that underlay his study of the history of New France. To him it was simply a conflict between the forces of light and the forces of darkness, between the nation of Progress and the nation that stood opposed to it; between Anglo-Saxon Protestant liberty—which was the hallmark of Progress—and French Roman Catholic absolutism. This he made very plain in the final volume of the series when, in writing of the French and Indian War, he declared: 'This was was the strife of a united and concentrated few against a divided and discordant many. It was the strife, too, of the past against the future; of the old against the new; of moral and intellectual torpor against moral and intellectual life; of barren absolutism against a liberty, crude, incoherent, and chaotic, yet full of prolific vitality.'[1]

Thus Parkman regarded the final war not as a war of conquest but as a war of liberation. The Canadians were not conquered, they were finally liberated from absolutism. The 'English conquest,' he wrote, 'was the grand crisis of Canadian history. It was the beginning of a new life. With England came Protestantism, and the Canadian Church grew purer and better in the presence of an adverse faith. Material growth; an increased mental activity; an education, real though fenced and guarded; a warm and genuine patriotism, —all date from the peace of 1763. England imposed by the sword on reluctant Canada the boon of rational and ordered liberty . . . A happier calamity never befell a people than the conquest of Canada by the British arms.'[2]

Though his basic theme is, to say the least, debateable, it did enable him to select and organize his material in a simple, coherent framework, which makes the completed works very readable. As literature they rate very highly indeed. By means of this device they are endowed with the epic qualities of Greek tragedy. We have the colony of New France, an outpost of French absolutism, struggling heroically against tremendous odds, coming very close to final victory, but eventually, and inevitably, brought low because it has been foreordained that Progress will win out. In the final analysis French Catholic absolutism cannot, by the very nature of things, prevail against Anglo-Saxon Protestant liberty. As history, however, Parkman's works are of considerably less value because, owing to this frame of reference his approach was essentially uncritical. There was no need to seek very far to discover why New France was defeated, the reasons were obvious. Nor was there need to discover what society was really like in New France; it was enough to indicate that it compared very unfavourably with that of the English colonies.

In his description of Canadian society Parkman made extensive use of his source material, relating incidents from the original documents that convey a clear, albeit superficial and distorted, impression of the social environment. He also used commendable critical judgement on occasion—rejecting, for example, the rather scurrilous tales of La Hontan concerning the morals of the emigrant girls sent to Canada.* It is clear, however, that his opinion of this society was strongly influenced by the prevailing concept of his own day, that of Social Darwinism. Thus he wrote: 'One of the faults of his [Louis XIV's] rule is the excess of his benevolence; for not only did he give money to support parish priests, build churches, and aid the seminary, the Ursulines, the missions, and the hospitals; but he established a fund destined, among other objects, to relieve indigent persons, subsidized nearly every branch of trade and industry, and in other instances did for the colonists what they would far better have learned to do for themselves.'[3] The latter-day historian, accustomed to the social philosophy of the welfare state, would, of course, be less likely to see anything wrong with all this.

Again, in commenting on justice Parkman stated that it 'seems to have been administered on the whole fairly; and judges of all grades often inter-posed in their personal capacity to bring parties to an agreement without a trial. From head to foot, the government kept its attitude of paternity [*sic*].'[4] Intervention by the intendant to protect the *habitants* from extortion by their seigneurs he described as 'well-meaning despotism'.[5] Similarly, Canadian economic activity suffered from the inexcusable lack of nineteenth-century *laissez-faire* concepts: 'The besetting evil of trade and industry in Canada was the habit they contracted, and were encouraged to contract, of depending on the direct aid of government. Not a new enterprise was set on foot without a petition to the King to lend a helping hand.'[6] This last statement was pure supposition on Parkman's part; it may be true, but he could never have proved it. Moreover, although there can be no doubt that Canadian economic activity was nowhere near as flourishing as that of the English colonies, less state aid would not have caused it to thrive; just the reverse, more likely.[7] In any event, this particular yardstick gives very inaccurate measurements.

Parkman's belief in the inevitability of Progress also explains, in large measure, his Olympian attitude. He had only to select the evidence to prove the obvious; he was never beset with doubts in his interpretation of the

---

* Frances Parkman, *The Old Regime in Canada*, Century edn (Boston, 1922), 281–2. Yet one might question Parkman's technique here; he quoted La Hontan's sketch of emigrant girls at length, then stated: 'As regards the character of the girls, there can be no doubt that this amusing sketch is, in the main, maliciously untrue.' If it be untrue, why quote it in this context? He here deliberately created an impression, then made a rather feeble attempt to remove it. Parkman was much given to this device; see, for example, ibid., 275 and *n* where, in eulogizing Jean Talon, Parkman wrote 'so far as I can discover, he is nowhere accused of making illicit gains, and there is reason to believe that he acquitted himself and his charge with entire fidelity.' In the footnote he then proceeded to contradict this statement, to wit: 'Some imputations against him, not of much weight, are, however, made in a memorial of Aubert de la Chesnaye, a merchant of Quebec.' Contrary to Parkman, the present writer considers La Chesnaye's imputations to have considerable weight.

evidence; there are none of those cautious, qualifying phrases that are the crutches of many latter-day historians who fear the hostile reviewer. The absence of such weakening phrases gives Parkman's writing strength and clarity, lends it the ring of conviction. This is, of course, greatly strengthened by his use of primary source material. His familiarity with the documents is most praiseworthy; unfortunately, however, lengthy sections of his volumes were put together with scissors and paste, being little more than translations of long passages from the documents. This is particularly true of *The Jesuits in North America* and the two volumes of the inaptly titled *A Half Century of Conflict*. Both works would have been much improved by the liberal use of a blue pencil.

In his treatment of the clergy in New France, it is quite apparent that Parkman was anticlerical, and, more particularly, anti-Jesuit; but his prejudice was based squarely on political grounds. That it was what the clergy represented that caused him to go to extremes is evidenced by his denunciation of the Puritan regime in New England in terms almost as strong as those used against the Jesuits, accusing the Puritans of having established 'one of the most detestable theocracies on record'.[8] The clergy in both New France and New England were the enemies of liberty, of conscience, of Progress. This was their mortal sin. The Jesuits were, Parkman was convinced, far more the political agents of French and Papal absolutism than they were the agents of God. He had great admiration for them as men—their fortitude in the face of terrible hardship, and their superhuman courage when tortured by the Iroquois, he depicted in glowing passages—but he could never forget that they espoused the wrong cause.

> Liberty may thank the Iroquois [he wrote], that, by their insensate fury, the plans of her adversary were brought to nought, and a peril and a woe averted from her future . . . The contest on this continent between Liberty and Absolutism was never doubtful; but the triumph of the one would have been dearly bought, and the downfall of the other incomplete. Populations formed in the ideas and habits of a feudal monarchy, and controlled by a hierarchy profoundly hostile to freedom of thought, would have remained a hindrance and a stumbling block in the way of that majestic experiment of which America is the field.
>
> The Jesuits saw their hopes struck down; and their faith, though not shaken, was sorely tried. The Providence of God seemed in their eyes dark and inexplicable; but, from the standpoint of Liberty, that Providence is clear as the sun at noon. Meanwhile let those who have prevailed yield due honor to the defeated. Their virtues shine amidst the rubbish of error, like diamonds and gold in the gravel of the torrent.[9]

Such tributes to the Jesuits are rare; diatribes against them, all too frequent. Parkman went to extreme lengths to make the religious climate of New France appear to be one of superstition and ignorance. The description of the life of

Mademoiselle Jeanne Le Ber was clearly contrived to arouse feelings of repugnance in the reader.[10] Education in New France, being under the clergy, was obviously of little value; at the parish schools the children 'were taught a little Latin, a little rhetoric, and a little logic; but against all that might rouse the faculties to independent action, the Canadian schools prudently closed their doors'.[11] After citing the rules of conduct at the school attached to the Quebec Seminary, he commented: 'What is chiefly noticeable in it is, that truth is allowed no place. That manly but unaccommodating virtue was not, it seems, thought important in forming the mind of youth.'[12] Although this fault was noticeable to Parkman, from the evidence available it would not be to those lacking his strong prejudices.

The aims of the Jesuits he succinctly described as: 'The Church to rule the world; the Pope to rule the Church; the Jesuits to rule the Pope,—such was and is the simple programme of the Order of Jesus. . . .'[13] Thus, when discussing the choice of Laval as bishop at Quebec, he made the appointment appear to be a sinister Jesuit plot, stating: 'The Jesuits, adept in human nature, had made a sagacious choice when they put forward this conscientious, zealous, dogged and pugnacious priest to fight their battles. Nor were they ill pleased that, for the present, he was not Bishop of Canada, but only vicar apostolic; for such being the case, they could have him recalled if on trial they did not like him, while an unacceptable bishop would be an evil past remedy.'[14] Parkman cited no evidence to support the imputing of these motives to the Jesuits; it was pure supposition on his part.[15] The nature of the evidence, however, lent itself to such hostile interpretations. Since Colbert was notably anticlerical and particularly so of the Jesuits, those in the colony who wished to pay their court to the great minister found a receptive audience when they accused the Jesuits of all manner of crimes. In the letters and dispatches of Jean Talon, Frontenac, La Salle, and La Mothe Cadillac, Parkman found much ammunition, and he invariably accepted their statements at face value. Those of the Jesuits and Bishop Laval, on the other hand, he regarded as inadmissible. Not satisfied with all this, however, he quoted from a sermon delivered by a Jesuit in Montreal on November 1, 1872, to condemn the Jesuits of two centuries earlier.[16] This, one is inclined to think, is carrying prejudice a little too far.

In his characterization of Bishop Laval also, Parkman used rather dubious methods. To introduce this 'tool of the Jesuits' he first of all devoted over five pages to the Hermitage at Caen where Laval resided for a time. The description, dwelling at great length on the religious fanaticism of the inmates, was well calculated to stimulate revulsion in the reader. Having thus damned Laval with guilt by association, he rather lamely concluded that although the excesses described 'took place after Laval had left the Hermitage, they serve to characterize the school in which he was formed; or, more justly speaking, to show its more extravagant side'.[17] Unfortunately the character of Laval established in the unwary reader's mind by the preceding five pages of vivid description would not likely be altered by this last brief, qualifying statement. Moreover, Parkman went on to negate this qualification by stating: 'In vindicating the assumed rights of the Church, he invaded the rights of others, and used means from which a healthy conscience would have shrunk. . . . He was penetrated by the poisonous casuistry of the Jesuits, based on the assumption that all means are permitted when the end is the service of God. . . .'[18] The Jesuits Parkman could admire as men, but in Laval he could find no redeeming features. Laval had never endured the hardship of life in an Indian village, or withstood torture at the hands of the Iroquois as the Jesuits had. He represented clerical absolutism incarnate, the worst of all the enemies of Progress. Laval, he wrote, 'was one of those who by nature lean always to the side of authority; and in the English Revolution he would inevitably have stood for the Stuarts; or, in the American Revolution for the Crown. . . . His life was one long assertion of the authority of the Church, and this authority was lodged in himself.'[19] There can be no doubt that Laval was possessed of a strong character—and considering the magnitude of his task, he needed it—but the evidence will not sustain the Laval depicted by Parkman. There are no shades of grey in this portrait, it is all black; in fact it is nothing more than a very hostile caricature.

Parkman's delineation of lay figures is also coloured, to a considerable degree, by the theme of Progress; but there are other influences at work as well. Parkman fully subscribed, as one would expect, to the Great Man concept of history—witness his eulogies of Pitt,[20] Frederick II,[21] and Washington[22]—and the romantic outlook is also much in evidence. His two full-length studies of outstanding figures, Frontenac and La Salle, illustrate these influences very clearly. There were other men in the history of New France of equal or even greater stature than either of these: Champlain, Charles Le Moyne, Iberville, Maisonneuve, Gilles Hocquart, Champigny, to mention a few. Perhaps the main reason why he chose Frontenac and La Salle was that there was so much evidence readily available. La Salle's supporters were prolific writers, and Frontenac was certainly a very skilled advocate on his own behalf. They had, in fact, virtually written the books for Parkman; he had merely to edit them. Moreover, both men had fought persistently against the clergy in New France; therefore, if they were not exactly on the side of the Angels of Progress, they at least were lending them a hand. Both men had suffered adversity, both had occupied the centre of the stage—the one in New France, the other in the West. They were made to order for Parkman. All that was needed, then, was to accept at face value what Frontenac and La Salle said of themselves and refute or disregard evidence that conflicted with their statements. Thus it is that in these volumes

Parkman was at his weakest as a historian and at his best as a writer of romantic epic literature.

Frontenac was on one occasion actually made to appear as an apostle of Progress. Of his convoking of the meeting of the four estates at Quebec, Parkman declared: 'Like many of his station, Frontenac was not in full sympathy with the centralizing movement of the time, which tended to level ancient rights, privileges, and prescriptions under the ponderous roller of the monarchical administration. He looked back with regret to the day when the three orders of the State—clergy, nobles, and commons—had a place and a power in the direction of national affairs.'[23] There is not a shred of evidence to support this statement; in fact, Frontenac specifically denied that he had ever had any such intention,[24] but Parkman chose to ignore evidence not in accord wth his views. Similarly, when Frontenac was finally dismissed from his post and recalled to France in disgrace, Parkman claimed: 'he left behind him an impression, very general among the people, that, if danger threatened the colony, Count Frontenac was the man for the hour.'[25] On the contrary he left just the reverse impression, and Parkman was clearly ignoring all the evidence.[26] Worse still, the reader is led to believe that since Frontenac did return to New France when the colony was in grave danger, he was sent back to retrieve the situation. Though the evidence denies any such conclusion, several eminent historians have stumbled blindly into the pitfall set by Parkman; and so the myth of Frontenac, the Saviour of New France, has been perpetuated. In his final estimate of Frontenac, however, it is clear that it was the turbulent Governor's colourful character that most appealed to him; despite the fact that he had consistently depicted Frontenac as a great man, he declared at the end that 'greatness must be denied him'.[27] Why this should be, he does not explain. One can guess that it was because Frontenac had been engaged on the wrong side in the struggle between absolutism and Progress, and in the final analysis Parkman could not condone this.

In the volume on La Salle, however, Parkman's sympathies were completely engaged for his subject. Any evidence that might have detracted from the lustre of this 'great man' was swept aside. Perhaps it would be demanding too much to expect Parkman to have ferreted out all the evidence concerning La Salle's connection with the Bernou, Renaudot, Villermont clique of court intriguers, as Jean Delanglez was later to do so admirably;[28] but one could expect him to take into account the obvious. And the most obvious thing about La Salle was that he was mentally deranged; moreover, his malady grew markedly worse towards the end of his career. Indeed, the evidence for this is so strong that even Parkman was obliged to mention it, but he did so as the only alternative to admitting that La Salle was a scoundrel. After describing La Salle's actions, which had convinced those associated with him that he must be mad, Parkman stated: 'It is difficult not to see in all this the chimera of an overwrought brain, no longer able to distinguish between the possible and the impossible.'[29] With this matter dismissed, La Salle was thereafter treated as though no doubts about either his sanity or his probity had ever existed. La Salle, in Parkman's final assessment, was possessed of the 'Roman virtues' and, 'beset by a throng of enemies, he stands, like the King of Israel, head and shoulders above them all'.[30] There is the Great Man concept; and along with it goes the final and even greater tribute: 'America owes him an enduring memory; for in this masculine figure she sees the pioneer who guided her to the possession of her richest heritage.'[31] Here, in the eyes of Parkman, lies the true greatness of La Salle for which all else must be forgiven. He was, after all, the herald of Progress.

In his attitude towards the North American Indians, Parkman shed all his romanticism. 'The English borderers', he wrote, 'regarded the Indians less as men than as vicious and dangerous wild animals. In fact, the benevolent and philanthropic view of the American savage is for those who are beyond his reach: it has never yet been held by any whose wives and children have lived in danger of his scalping-knife.'[32] To Parkman the Indian was not the noble savage, but a treacherous, murdering fiend incarnate, existing in filth and squalor—an opinion perhaps influenced by his close contacts with the Plains Indians at a time when the Americans were bent on exterminating the remnants of this Stone Age civilization. But there is more to it than that. To Parkman the Indians were nothing more than a stumbling block in the path of Progress. Of the Iroquois, the best that could be said was that they had aided the English colonies in their wars against French absolutism and had foiled the Jesuit schemes to create a native theocracy in Huronia. But for the other tribes, particularly those that fought against New England, there could be little justification for their existence. Of one such tribe he wrote: 'Far worse than wolves or rattlesnakes were the Pequot Indians,—a warlike race who had boasted that they would wipe the whites from the face of the earth, but who, by hard marching and fighting, had lately been brought to reason.'[33]

In depicting the raids by the Canadians and their Indian allies on the frontiers of the English colonies, Parkman gave us his most vivid writing. Reading his description of the Deerfield massacre, or the attacks on the western frontier during the Seven Years' War, makes one feel almost like a participant—but always on the English side. These raids were invariably treated as savage, unprovoked aggressions against innocent English colonial settlers, and gory details were presented to strengthen the case; to the Deerfield raid alone he devoted thirty-nine pages.[34] He was quite unable to conceive that the Indian tribes were fighting desperately against overwhelming odds to retain their ancient hunting grounds in the face of English encroachment. He could not view the struggle from the other camp, that of the Indian. Nor did he ever ask himself why the Indians should have been expected to fight according to

European rules of warfare. That it may, at bottom, have been the English colonials who were the aggressors and the Indians the victims never occurred to him. They had dared to stand in the path of Progress; this made their eradication both essential and inevitable.

If Parkman was, to say the least, severe in his judgement on the Indians, he was virulent in his condemnation of the French for aiding and inciting them against the English colonies. That these same colonies incited the Iroquois against New France was of no account. And when the French most directly concerned happened to be priests as well, the acts committed were clearly beyond the pale. Of Abbé Jean Le Loutre he declared: 'He fed [the Micmacs'] traditional dislike of the English, and fanned their fanaticism, born of the villainous counterfeit of Christianity which he and his predecessors had imposed on them.'[35] Of Father Sebastien Râle, the Jesuit missionary with the Abenaki, he was less censorious, largely because this missionary was killed in a raid by New Englanders on an Abenaki village. Because Father Râle died bravely he was accorded a grudging tribute,'[36] which compares unfavourably with that given to Jonathan Frye, an Andover chaplain killed while accompanying a New England war party against the Pequawket tribe. 'Chaplain though he was,' wrote Parkman admiringly, 'he carried a gun, knife, and hatchet like the others, and not one of the party was more prompt to use them.'[37] In consequence of this raid the hostile Indians were cowed, and Parkman described the results thus: 'In our day . . . farms and dwellings possess those peaceful shores, and hard by, where, at the bend of the Saco, once stood, in picturesque squalor, the wigwams of the vanished Pequawkets, the village of Fryeburg preserves the name of the brave young chaplain, whose memory is still cherished, in spite of his uncanonical turn for scalping.'[38] Again, one who assisted, in however small measure, the march of Progress had to be forgiven much. It is doubtful if Parkman realized how close he came here to the casuistry that he saw so clearly and condemned so vehemently in the Jesuits.

The final picture of New France that emerges from a reading of this series is one that is not altogether unsympathetic. Parkman frequently paid tribute to qualities that he found admirable in the Canadians, although in a rather patronizing manner. He admired, for example, their courage, their fortitude, and the romantic aura of this frontier breed. But he could never really forgive them for being so obstinately French, Roman Catholic, and subjects of a supposedly absolute monarch. 'As a bold and hardy pioneer of the wilderness,' he wrote, 'the Frenchman in America has rarely found his match. [But] his civic virtues withered under the despotism of Versailles and his mind and conscience were kept in leading-strings by an absolute Church. . . .'[39]

Parkman brought to his task the gifts of historical imagination, the willingness to consult all the available source material, and considerable talent as a writer. Thus he was able to create very vivid pictures in the mind's eye of the reader and to enable him to live in the past for a brief spell; but the reader always views this past through Parkman's own Whig-coloured spectacles. Most of his faults were the faults of his age and these must be forgiven him; but this does not mean that they can be overlooked. The consequences of his books for the study of Canadian history have been disastrous. For too many years they have instilled the belief, among English-speaking historians at least, that Parkman had said all that needed to be said about the history of New France, and that there was no need to do any further research.[40]

Clearly this condition cannot endure much longer. It is to be hoped that before too many years have passed, Parkman's works will be relegated to the same shelf as those of his contemporaries—George Bancroft, William Prescott, and John Motley—where they will be consulted more by the student of American literature or historiography than by the student of history.

The Role of the Church in New France

This paper was written for a meeting of the Association for 18th Century Studies held at McMaster University in 1975. It had to be short, hence only a few points that seemed important could be raised. We now need a thorough re-examination of the roles played by the Church and the clergy in New France, including Acadia, Louisiana and the pays d'en haut, as well as Canada. It would be best, however, were the work to await the completion of the magisterial series Monumenta Novae Franciae, *presently being edited by R.P. Lucien Campeau, S.J., before being undertaken.*

When we speak of the Church in the eighteenth century it has to be borne in mind that it consisted not merely of the clergy but of the laity as well. Moreover, the members of the Church, clergy and laity alike, had a dual obligation: to God and to their king. Their obligation to God was so to live in this world that they would be admitted, as belatedly as possible, to the kingdom of heaven. To achieve this end, in the Roman Church, the aid of the clergy was essential. Their duty to the king was summed up in the oath of office of Monseigneur Pontbriand, bishop of Quebec, in 1741:

> I promise His Majesty that for as long as I live I will be his faithful subject and servant, that I will strive with all my strength to serve and to further the well being of his state; that I will not take part in any council, plot, or enterprise that could endanger it, and should anything untoward come to my attention, I will make it known to His Majesty, so help me God, and I so swear on his Holy Gospel.[1]

In New France, from the outset, there was a close alliance between the clergy and the Crown to further their common aims. It was, in fact, the Crown that initiated the work of the clergy in the area. In October 1604 Henri IV, through the agency of a Jesuit, Father Pierre Cotton, asked General Claude Aquaviva of the Society of Jesus to provide two missionaries to accompany the French fishing fleet to the Grand Banks.[2] In that same year the French established a permanent base in the Bay of Fundy. Two Roman Catholic priests and one or two Huguenot pastors accompanied the expedition, but it was not until 1610 that a missionary, the Abbé Jessé Fléché, a secular priest, baptized some twenty-one Indians with what was later regarded by the Jesuits as unseemly haste, for they could hardly have received even the most minimal of instructions: the danger of their falling into apostasy and hence an eternity of hellfire was thus great.[3] Yet the event marked the beginning of the drive by the French Church and Crown to convert all the pagan peoples of the northern segment of the continent to Christianity. It proved to be a far more daunting task than had been imagined. The high hopes of the early missionaries were not to be fulfilled in their lifetime.

There were several reasons for this lack of success, which cannot be gone into here. Suffice it to say that the economic base of the first French settlements in Acadia and on the banks of the St Lawrence was the trade in furs. The Indians were eager to give up their furs in exchange for European manufactured goods but very loath to entrust their souls to the Church of Rome. The French Crown, however, insisted that missionaries had to accompany the fur traders; hence the Indians had to tolerate the obnoxious black robes in their midst.

The capture of the French bases by an Anglo-Scots freebooting expedition in 1628–9, and the ferocious onslaughts of the Iroquois confederacy, caused the Crown, the fur-trade company, and the missionaries to realize that there could be no hope of any of them achieving their aims unless more secure bases were established, bases that would enable them to provide for their own basic material needs rather than depend on food and other supplies brought from France each summer. At this particular time the Crown could provide little aid, being embroiled in the Thirty Years' War. The fur-trade company lacked the capital needed to establish settlers. It was therefore the Church, and more specifically the Society of Jesus, that had to serve as an immigration agency.

The Jesuits succeeded in obtaining sizeable sums of money from wealthy and devout individuals in France, as well as from a powerful secret society, the Compagnie de Saint-Sacrement, which might be described as resembling a blend of the present-day Salvation Army, the Carnegie Foundation, and the Mafia. (For example, it was members of that Compagnie who provided the organization and finances for the establishment of a mission settlement at Montreal.[4]) The Jesuits also brought out labourers to clear land on the seigneuries granted them by the Crown, ready for settlers to put to the plough upon their arrival. Their stated purpose now became to establish 'A New Jerusalem, blessed by God and made up of citizens destined for heaven'.[5] Without this concerted effort by the Church, it is doubtful if New France would have survived until the restoration of peace and stability in France allowed Louis XIV to take the colonies out of the hands of the private companies in 1663 and make them wards of the Crown.

As the number of settlers increased, the role of the clergy became less that of a mission to the Indians and more of a mission to the French colonists. It had been hoped that the establishment of schools and a hospital to care for the Indians would induce them to embrace Christianity. The Indians spurned both. Even when a few Indian families were persuaded to send their children to the schools at Montreal and Quebec, it proved impossible to keep them there. These wild creatures of the forest would not submit to the unaccustomed and harsh discipline. They fled back to their families at the first opportunity. Similarly, they preferred their own medicaments and the ministrations of their shamans to those of the French. (In this they displayed wisdom since only the strong and healthy could withstand the nostrums of current European medical practice.)

But once these schools and hospitals had been established, they were maintained to serve the settlers. Although by 1640 the population of New France was made up of only sixty-four families, and comprised 356 individuals—158 men, 116 women including the religious, 29 Jesuits, and 53 soldiers[6]—yet they had a school, a hospital, and a college for advanced studies. Sizeable towns in France might have envied them, particularly since they paid little or nothing for these institutions. It is a rather cruel irony that the Church, in establishing these firm foundations for European culture and civilization as a means to serve and save the Indians, thereby laid the groundwork for their eventual destruction.

From the outset, a main concern of the Church was to forfend in New France the appalling religious condition that existed in seventeenth-century France, where the mass of the peasantry was more pagan than Christian and most of the rural parish priests were in little better case. Not only was the Church in France faced with the challenge of extirpating Calvin's heresy; it found itself faced with the greater and more urgent task of Christianizing the French people, and this required an educated clergy. In 1637 Father Beurrier, on arriving at his parish of Nanterre, declared that the villagers were ignorant of 'those most common things that one must absolutely understand in order to receive the sacraments and be saved'.[7] A bishop of Autun in the second half of the century informed the pope that in his diocese the people were 'coarse, barely initiated into the primary principles of the faith, living in a dense and inveterate ignorance'.[8] At the same time Father Julien Mannoir wrote that in lower Brittany the people knew so little of the Christian religion that his first task was to establish the rudiments of the faith.[9] Nor were many of the clergy much better. There were continual complaints of their drunkenness and bad morals. Few of them wore clerical garb and they were indistinguishable from the peasants. Non-residence in their parishes was all too frequent; some were seen there only once or twice a year. Many could not understand a word of Latin; they could stumble through the mass but had little understanding of its meaning.[10] The only instruction the vast majority had received was a few lessons from a local curé, either a relative or a close neighbour.[11] This condition had existed for a long time. It was the religious revival, engendered by the Reformation, that threw it into stark relief and, perhaps, exaggerated it. The lingering stirrings of the old rural paganism, which sanctified a spring, an ancient tree, or a wishing stone and required the excommunication of annoying wasps, now was regarded askance by the learned doctors at the Sorbonne.[12] So too was the burning of witches.[13]

In New France from the outset the religious climate was placed on a much higher plane. The clergy who came to the colony were nearly all exceptionally well educated, and highly motivated. This was particularly true of the Jesuits and the Sulpicians, but the secular clergy also were hand-picked by the directors of the *Missions Etrangères* in Paris. The members of the women's orders—The Ursulines, Hôpitalières and the Congrégation de Notre Dame—were drawn from the educated class, and one has only to read the letters of Marie de l'Incarnation to become aware of the extreme fervour that possessed them.[14] Moreover, in New France no purely contemplative orders were permitted; the clergy all had to perform useful social functions.

After the assumption of royal control in 1663, although Church and state worked in close harmony, there was never any question that the Crown was the dominant partner. The bishop was nominated by the king and forty per cent of the funds at the Church's disposal were sparingly doled out by the Crown.[15] The clergy were closely checked by the intendant and the Sovereign Council at every turn.[16] The Crown decided how many clergy there would be and defined their roles. To a considerable degree they were agents of the Crown. There were, it is true, a few spirited conflicts between clergy and royal officials in the seventeenth century, but these were more clashes of personality than conflicts over principle. Some historians, however, have made far too much of them, viewing the seventeenth century through latter-day orange-tinted spectacles. What is much more significant is the degree to which royal officials and senior clergy worked in harmony. The reason for this is that they were, after all, members of the same Church and were agreed on the premises that governed their society, premises so basic that they were unstated and taken for granted.

Nor can it be said—but of course it has been—that the colony was priest-ridden. In 1698 there were 308 clergy in Canada, 2.2 per cent of the population. By 1712 their numbers had increased by four, but they now represented only 1.6 per cent. At the end of the seventeenth century there was one church per 223 souls, and in 1713 one per 246. In 1759 there were fewer than 200 clergymen to serve a population of some 75,000 to 80,000 people.[17] Canada under the French regime was far from being a theocracy. If one seeks a theocracy in America, one should look towards seventeenth-century Massachusetts, not Canada.

Indeed, during the period soon after 1663 when immigrants poured in, raising the population from 3,300 to some 11,000 in less than a decade, the problem was to find enough clergy to serve the people. The few there were were worked to death, travelling winter and summer by canoe and snowshoe throughout the settlements to say mass and administer the sacraments. This proved too much for some of the secular priests; one-third of the first group to arrive gave up after a year and returned to France.[18] As late as 1683 the intendant complained that at least three-quarters of the *habitants* did not hear mass more than four times a year.[19] It was to remedy this deplorable situation that Bishop Laval, immediately upon his arrival at Quebec, had set about establishing a seminary. Its chief aim was to provide a native Canadian clergy, but boys who did not intend to enter the clergy were not excluded. Although the poorer students paid no fees, it cannot be claimed that this seminary enjoyed overwhelming success. The regulations, which were strictly enforced, perhaps explain why. The boys admitted had to be at least ten years old on entry, for the simple reason that few children younger than that had the manual dexterity needed to use a quill pen, which was the only writing instrument available. But at that age children were capable of performing chores on their parents' farms, and, given the desperate shortage of labour in the colony, few *habitant* families could forgo their children's services.

The boys admitted to the Seminary had to have no physical deformity and be of a devout disposition. They rose at 4:00 in the morning during the summer months, slept in till 4:30 in winter. They attended classes and devotions until 8:00 at night, then retired. They wore a distinctive uniform: a blue parka coat with a sash, and a wide-brimmed hat. Their hair was cut short, their meals provided the minimum of food, barely enough to maintain health, and they were permitted to bathe no oftener than was deemed absolutely necessary. Plays and all other amusements had to be shunned, and the young students were obliged to see as little as possible of their own families, to keep them at arm's length to avoid an overly emotional attachment to the secular world.[20] It should, therefore, come as no surprise that of the first 200 students, 135 dropped out, most of them after one or two years. Despite this, or perhaps owing to a subsequent relaxation of this rigorous ascetic regimen, the Quebec seminary over a ninety-year period took in 843 students, 188 of whom were eventually ordained.[21]

By 1760, of the seventy-three parish priests in the colony, four-fifths of them were Canadian born.[22] If Montcalm is to be believed (and on some few matters he can be), by the 1750s the curés were recruited from among the more well-to-do colonial families and, unlike their counterparts in France, were economically well off. He remarked in his journal that they were more respected than the clergy in France, and better housed. The average income of the curés was, he stated, 2,000 *livres** a year, and even the poorer parishes provided a stipend of 1,2000, three times the wages of a Canadian artisan or a curé in France.[23] The Recollet order also attracted Canadians; in 1760 seventeen of the twenty-four were Canadian born. The Jesuits, however, recruited only three, of whom only one served in the colony.[24] It could be that more Canadians would have been accepted into the priesthood had it not been that the authorities, both clerical and secular, came to regard those who had entered with a rather jaundiced eye. The same complaint was made of them as of the laity. They were accused of being proud and independent, lacking in humility, and not at all inclined to recognize, let alone submit to, their superiors. It was for this reason that, in 1726, Intendant Bégon counselled the bishop to have a dean for the cathedral sent from France rather than appoint a Canadian, and the bishop was in complete agreement.[25]

In the field of secular education, by the second quarter of the eighteenth century, the colony was quite well endowed. The Sulpicians had a school for boys at Montreal, and one of the main aims of the Hôpital there was to train schoolmasters to serve in the rural areas. It was the aim of both the royal officials and the clergy to have a school in every parish to teach the children 'to pray, to read, and to write'.[26] By the end of the regime about half the parishes had a school of sorts. In 1727, despite the fact that a lay school teacher's salary was only 375 *livres* a year, it became necessary to establish standards. In that year legislation was enacted requiring any would-be teachers to submit to an examination, obtain the sanction of the intendant and the bishop, then submit to the surveillance of the curé in the parish where he or she would teach. Male teachers, unless they were married, could not teach girls without special permission. The same regulation applied to single female teachers where the teaching of boys was concerned. Teachers were also required to set a good example to their students, avoiding taverns, games of chance, the company of those who lived too freely, and persons of the opposite sex.[27]

The Ursulines had schools for girls at Quebec and Trois-Rivières, and the Sisters of the Congrégation de Notre Dame had schools in Montreal and in some of the outlying parishes. As well as mastering the regular curriculum, the girls were expected to learn civility and the social graces, how to converse, how to please. Judging by the comments of the Swedish professor of botany, Peter Kalm, who visited the colony at mid-century, they were eminently successful.[28]

---

*The *livre* had the value of approximately one English shilling in 1700 and 10 pence, or 10*d*, in 1750. It then had the approximate purchasing power of ten to twelve of today's (1987) dollars.

Despite the availability of these schools, few Canadians appear to have taken advantage of them. We have no reliable statistics on the literacy rate, but judging by the contracts in the notarial archives a very small percentage of the *habitants* could read or write. Of a representative sample of twenty-five engagements of *voyageurs* in 1750, only two of those employed were able to sign their names.[29] Moreover, the presence of a signature is not proof of literacy. Some people learned to sign their name quite legibly, but they could do no more than that; it was merely their mark. In any event the vast majority of the *habitants* could live out their lives without any real need for literacy. There was at least one active merchant in Montreal who could not sign his name on a contract. If one member of a family was literate, that sufficed; usually it was a female member who acquired the skill.

The curriculum and the high standards of the schools were likely also factors in discouraging literacy. The schools taught reading, writing, Latin, the catechism, civility, contracts, and arithmetic. They were divided into eight grades for learning the alphabet, learning to spell, learning to form syllables, reading Latin phrases, reading French, learning to write, and learning Latin grammar. No child was to move to a higher grade until he had mastered the work of the lower group, and no student was to begin learning to read French until he was well versed in Latin.[30] It is difficult to see how a curriculum such as this could have had much utility, let alone appeal, for the some three-quarters of the population who spent their lives tilling the soil, paddling a canoe to the Far West, or voyaging on a schooner to Louisbourg.

The curing of bodies as well as of souls was also largely the responsibility of the Church. In Canada, however, this was never the problem that it was in France, where the great mass of the people lived at the subsistence level most of the time, and below it at recurring intervals. There, crop failures were frequent, causing the price of grain to soar; the people then starved to death by the thousands. (This was the reason why the population of France remained stable at nineteen to twenty million throughout the seventeenth and early eighteenth centuries—deaths equalled births.) In seventeenth-century France—unlike in England, where the medieval system of private charity had collapsed and was replaced by a Poor Law (really a law against the poor)—the Church launched a great program of social reform. Father Vincent de Paul, later to be canonized, was its leading protagonist. The aim was to awaken in the rich a sense of their obligation to aid the weaker members of society and thereby save their own souls.[31] *Bureaux de charité* and *hôpitaux généraux* were established by the Church, with bequests from individuals and some state or municipal aid, to care for the indigent, widows, orphans, cripples, and the moribund. The Crown hoped to solve the terrible problem posed by hordes of vagabonds and diseased, starving poor by establishing in every town an *hôpital général* where the indigent could be housed (incarcerated might be the better term), given work to do, and disciplined into leading useful and starkly moral Christian lives. The *bureaux de charité* were intended to assist people who required only temporary help to tide them over a crisis. Neither institution proved to be effective. The problem was far too great for these institutions, with their very limited resources, to resolve.[32]

In New France poverty, and all the ills that accompany it, was never anything like the problem that it was in France. The abundance of arable land, absence of taxation, and the flow of funds into the colony from the Crown and agencies of the Church effectively removed the spectre of starvation. It was generally accepted that a family had to care for its immediate members. Aged parents had to be provided for by their children. If a family failed in this obligation and it came to the attention of the intendant, he quickly issued an *ordonnance* obliging them to make the necessary provision for the indigent member.[33]

Yet there were still some few among the settlers who lacked this source of aid and were unable to provide for themselves: orphans, widows, some of the aged, cripples, and others who had to resort to seeking alms. To cope with this problem the Church and the Crown merely introduced the institutions recently established in France, *hôpitaux généraux des pauvres*. An *hôpital* was established in Montreal in 1688 by Jean-François Charon, a wealthy merchant, who founded the charitable and educational society, Les Frères hôpitaliers de Saint-Joseph de la Croix. The letters patent granted by the king in 1692 stated that the purpose of the community was 'to take in poor orphan children, the crippled, the aged, the infirm, and other males in need, there to lodge, feed, and support them, put them to the work they are capable of doing, teach the said children a trade and give them the best education possible'.[34] In 1747 the institution was taken over by a cloistered women's order, Les Soeurs Grises de la Charité, founded by Madame Youville.[35]

At Quebec, Bishop Saint-Vallier established an *hôpital* on the outskirts of the town in 1692, over the strong opposition of the intendant, Jean Bochart de Champigny, who believed the funds could be put to better use in providing more curés for rural parishes.[36] Saint-Vallier spent 60,000 *livres* of his own funds on the institution and within a few years it was hard pressed to care for all who needed its assistance.[37] In 1707 it had forty inmates. In 1721 the Crown agreed to pay for a separate building to house the insane,[38] and by 1748 the Hôpital housed over eighty incurables and lunatics.[39]

These *hôpitaux* had a dual purpose: to assist the deserving poor, putting a stop to their importuning the rest of society; and to force the undeserving poor, the lazy who preferred begging, to honest toil, to finding gainful employment, of which there was rarely any shortage. In 1688, when the towns became flooded with mendicants as a result of an influenza epidemic that had left scores of families without breadwinners, Intendant Champigny had the Sovereign Council issue a *règlement* establishing *bureaux des pauvres* in the towns to provide assistance for the needy. They were staffed by the local curés and three lay directors and depended on voluntary contributions for support. Once the crisis was over, the *bureaux* ceased to function.[40]

It is not without significance that it was a royal official who took the initiative here. In fact, with all these institutions the Crown maintained a very tight control, auditing the accounts, providing much of their revenue, ruling on the expansion of facilities and the number of staff, which was always kept to a bare minimum.

This same crown control was exercised over the *hôtels Dieu*, which were hospitals as we understand the term today. The three towns had such hospitals when there were only a handful of settlers, at Quebec in 1639, at Montreal in 1642, and at Trois-Rivières in 1702. At the latter town it was again Bishop Saint-Vallier who took the initiative. When he became aware of the pressing need for a hospital he bought a house with his own funds, endowed it with 1,000 *livres* a year, and turned it over to the Ursulines to operate.[41] Here were treated those who could not be cured by their family physicians, but who were expected to recover. Those who could afford it were expected to pay, those who could not received treatment free.[42] The quality of the medical care would appear to have been high. During the Seven Years' War, when epidemics of typhus and smallpox, along with a large number of wounded, strained the *hôtel Dieu* facilities to the limit, Montcalm reported that the troops could not have been better treated. In a dispatch to the minister he stated: 'You will see, My Lord, by the attached troop return that the losses [from sickness] in the four battalions are far below what they would be in peace time in France.'[43]

When these institutions were first established the staffs were recruited in France by their respective houses, but it was not long before they came to be drawn from among the colonial families. In the *hôtels Dieu* and the *hôpitaux* there were three distinct social grades, performing different functions. At the top were the *religieuses de choeur* or chancel sisters, below them the *converses* or lay sisters who took minor vows, and at the bottom the *données*. The *religieuses de choeur* were drawn from among the seigneurial families, and they had to bring with them a dowry of 3,500 *livres*. (Only a few of the very fashionable orders in France demanded a larger dowry than that, and most required much less.[44]) These sisters led a lady-like existence; only in times of urgency did they serve in the wards. The dirty work of caring for the sick was done by the *converses*, recruited from the artisan and *habitant* class, while the *données* performed the duties of domestic servants in return for their keep.[45] A few members of the lower social orders became *soeurs de choeur*, usually because well-to-do families sponsored them. It might be thought that only girls who could not find a husband entered the orders, but this is belied by the fact that the normal age on entry was nineteen. There were even some English girls, from the Thirteen Colonies, who entered the orders. These were girls who had been taken prisoner when children by Indians, ransomed by the French, and cared for by the nuns. After conversion to the Roman faith some of them found they had a vocation and were admitted to an order. In 1712 the governor and intendant reported that Marie Silver and Esther Owelin would not need the letters of naturalization granted by the king as the one had entered the Ursulines and the other the *hôpitalières* at Montreal.[46] Another such girl, Esther Wheelwright of Maine, a ward of the governor-general, entered the Ursulines and eventually became mother superior at Quebec. It was she who greeted Wolfe's officers when they paid a courtesy call after the surrender of the city.

In addition to serving the King indirectly by caring for the physical needs of his decrepit subjects, some of the clergy served him directly as political and military agents. The missionaries with the Indians were required to keep them in the French alliance, to do everything possible to remove or reduce Anglo-American influence. Examples of this activity in the eighteenth century were afforded by the Jesuit, Father Sebastien Râle, missionary to the Abenaki, who was killed by a New England raiding party in 1724—several previous attempts to eliminate him had failed—and by the famous Abbé Le Loutre, missionary to the Micmacs on the border of Nova Scotia. Father Râle exerted his considerable influence over the Abenaki to prevent New England encroachments on the Anglo-French borderlands. The Abbé Le Loutre also employed diplomacy and political manœuvring, but in addition he served as an active partisan military leader, and a highly skilled one.[47] The missionaries were required to keep the governor-general informed of all that transpired in their regions and pass on his orders and instructions to the military commanders of the western posts.[48] In short, they served as couriers and intelligence agents. Similarly, on the eve of war some of them were sent on missions to the English colonies to discover all they could of the enemy's intentions and dispositions.[49] For this task Jesuits were employed, since their order had papal sanction to wear civilian clothes when it would further the work of the church.

In a more peaceful vein the Church served to bind the colonial society firmly together. It was a highly status-ordered society, with a rigid hierarchical framework, modelled on that of France. It was at the church, every week, that these social gradations were made manifest. The ladies vied with each other to show off what they believed to be the latest court fashions, sometimes to the dismay of the curé looking down from his pulpit on rather startling décolletages. At mass social status was made evident by the position of the family pew—the closer to the altar the higher the status. To attempt to lease a pew farther forward than one's social position deemed fit was to create a scandal. The notarized contracts for the leasing of a pew are quite revealing. The exact position was stated, and once leased it could not be raised above the level of the other pews, nor any changes made to it that would incommode the other pew holders. A pew passed from generation to generation, in direct line, on payment of a 10-*livre* mutation fee, and it could not be transferred out of the line without the sanction of the church wardens. In the Montreal parish church the initial charge for a pew close to the altar was 75 *livres*, with an annual rent of 11 or 12 *livres*.[50] In the rural churches the rates were much lower, but the regulations were every bit as strict. The seigneur received the first pew by right; he and the members of his family received communion and all other honours first; the curé had to offer a specific prayer for them by name; and when they departed this vale of tears they could be buried beneath their pew.[51] After the leading families had assumed their places, the rest of society squabbled over points of precedence, especially over the position they could occupy in religious processions—this despite strict rules laid down by the Sovereign Council.[52]

In addition to regulating social status, the churches themselves must have had a beneficial effect on the aesthetic sense of the Canadians. As the eighteenth century wore on, wooden churches were replaced with well-proportioned stone buildings. Unlike the bleak chapels of New England, in those of New France all the physical senses were catered to. The interiors were beautifully decorated with gilded woodcarving, the paneled walls painted cream with blue and silver trim. At mass the incense must have compensated for the reluctance of the people of that age to immerse themselves in water. The church bells governed the hours of labour in the fields, and in the towns the church organ offered the commonalty the pleasure of fine music. As early as 1661 the church at Quebec had an organ, and some years prior to 1721 a master organ builder was at work in Montreal.[53]

Finally, to examine briefly the religious climate of New France, it is virtually impossible to say exactly what their religion meant to the colonists. The vast majority did not discuss religious matters. That the mass of the Canadians were well versed in the tenets of their faith there can be no doubt. Unity of religion in the colony precluded the violent disputes and debates that reveal so much about New England's religious climate. All that we can glean is an oblique view of the situation in the impressionistic comments by visitors, and the complaints of the clergy and royal officials about certain attitudes of the people. Thus we can deduce that until 1663 a distinctly puritanical attitude prevailed that has been mistaken by some for Jansenism. After that date, with the influx of immigrants come to seek their fortune, the climate became much more worldly. Montreal, for example, ceased to be merely a missionary base and became the commercial centre for the fur trade and a military garrison town.

In the eighteenth century there were continual complaints about the way the people behaved at mass and in religious processions; being drunk and disorderly was the least of their sins. More significantly, there was a distinct decline in moral standards, which mirrored that in contemporary France.[54] Proof of this is to be found in the rapid escalation in the number of foundlings, who were all made wards of the Crown and who were all presumed to have been born out of wedlock. The intendant, who had to include an item in his budget for their upkeep, certainly regarded them as illegitimate since he labelled it *Enfants bâtards*. In 1736 it amounted to almost 14,000 *livres*; 1,042 for Trois-Rivières, 4,970 for Quebec, 7,956 for Montreal, where the bulk of the regular troops were stationed.[55]

There is one revealing difference between France and New France regarding these rejected infants. In France many such children, some 40,000 a year, were abandoned, left to die. Infanticide was a form of birth control.[56] In New France this phenomenon was unknown. The royal officials had little difficulty in finding families willing to take legal charge of the foundlings, including the occasional Indian baby, and assume responsibility for them until they reached the age of eighteen.[57] The reason for this difference in attitude is not hard to find. The rapid expansion of the population in mid-eighteenth-century France caused it to exceed the available food supply. Surplus children, legitimate as well as illegitimate, had to be abandoned; otherwise the entire family would have starved. There was no such problem in New France; instead, additional children were welcomed as a future source of labour.

Despite all the superficial indications of a lack of respect for the cloth and a somewhat less than devout attitute towards their religion, there is one piece of evidence to the contrary that is quite convincing. The eminent demographer Jacques Henripin, in his study of the eighteenth-century Canadian population, collated statistics on the dates of conception of children born in the country. When placed on a graph they show a steady line during the winter months, then a very sharp decline in April, followed by a sharp rise to a peak in July, then a decline to the level of the preceding winter months for the remainder of the year.[58] When one asks why there should have been this marked aberration, one is forced to the ineluctable conclusion that the sharp decline in the spring occurred because it was then Lent. Obviously, the Canadians abstained from more than the pleasures of the table at that time, and this could only have come about because they were heeding the precepts of their church.

Social Welfare Measures and Policies in New France

How this article came to be written is discussed briefly in the Introduction: 'Forty Years Back'. There is nothing to add. In the intervening twenty years since it appeared I have found only a few additional scraps of evidence, none of which call for revision of the article. However, the publication of Louis Dechêne's Habitants et marchands de Montréal au XVIIe siècle *in 1974, in which she discusses the distribution of indentured servants among the Canadian population in the 1660s, necessitated the complete rejection of my earlier statement on that subject. The most interesting of the additional pieces of evidence were found in the series 'Documents judiciaires' at the Archives Nationales du Québec à Montréal. The years 1698 and 1699 were harsh for the Canadians. After eight years of savage warfare with the implacable Iroquois and their Anglo-American allies there had manifestly been a crop failure in 1698. Poverty again became a serious problem. The following spring, at the behest of the superior of the Sulpicians at Montreal, Father Dollier de Casson, the Bureau des Pauvres issued two to four bushels of wheat to some fifteen individuals for the spring sowing; this seed grain they were required to repay to the Bureau after the harvest. The Bureau thus acted as a seed bank. In addition to this, Dollier de Casson requested the Bureau, despite its grave shortage of funds, to give fifteen* livres *to the parish church at Verchères and two* écus *to the Hunault family, who were in extreme misery, Hunault* père *having just returned home after a long period in captivity, most likely in Iroquoisia.*

Were I writing the article today I would emphasize that such poverty was a sixteenth-century phenomenon. When it occurred it was dealt with efficaciously. In the eighteenth century there were some who, falling foul of the law for such crimes as selling liquor to the Indians, pleaded poverty as an excuse. The judges of the Montreal Prévoté court were not at all receptive to this argument. Times were certainly better than they had been for the mass of the people in the years 1700 to 1754, until war again engulfed the colony. Economic and social conditions in those years were as different from those of the period 1640 to 1699 as conditions of the 1930s were different from those of 1950 to 1970.

From the first establishment of Royal government in New France in 1663 until the Conquest in 1760 the basic premise, not merely of royal policy but of all the social institutions—indeed the basic premise upon which society in New France rested—was individual and collective responsibility for the needs of all. In the King's official instructions to Jean Talon, the first intendant to serve in New France, dated 27 March 1665, the concept of social responsibility was made plain:

> The King, considering all his Canadian subjects from highest to the lowest as though they were virtually his own children, and wishing to fulfil the obligation he is under to extend to them the benefits and the felicity of his rule, as much as to those who reside in France, the Sieur Talon will study above all things how to assist them in every way and to encourage them in their trade and commerce, which alone can create abundance in the country and cause the families to prosper.[1]

In the instructions given to the intendants who succeeded Talon, this major premise was spelled out in greater detail. Jean Bochart de Champigny, in 1686, was informed:

> His Majesty wishes him to know that his entire conduct must lead to two principal ends; the one to ensure that the French inhabitants established in that country enjoy complete tranquillity among themselves, and are maintained in the just possession of all that belongs to them, and the other to conserve the said inhabitants and to increase their numbers by all means possible.
>
> His Majesty wishes him to visit once a year all the inhabitants between the Gulf and the Island of Montreal to inform himself of all that goes on, pay heed to all the inhabitants' complaints and their needs, and attend to them as much as he possibly can, and so arrange it that they live together in peace, that they aid each other in their necessities and that they be not diverted from their work.[2]

This, then, was the official policy: avowedly paternalistic. It remained, however, for the officials in Canada, the governor-general, the intendant, their subordinates, and the Sovereign Council at Quebec to implement the policy; to cope with the myriad problems that beset the King's subjects in their day-to-day existence.

During most of the seventeenth century the colony existed under virtual siege conditions, with the powerful Iroquois confederacy striving to destroy it. Thus the underlying military basis of French society was, of necessity, emphasized in Canada. Custom and conditions, therefore, required the close regulation by the royal officials of many aspects of day-to-day colonial existence. Dependent on imports from France of essential supplies, and with communications severed during half the year, the colonial officials had to regulate prices and distribution. The number of tradesmen—butchers, bakers, millers, tailors—was closely regulated, and a close check on both the quality and price of their goods was maintained to protect the consumers. In times of short supply, hoarding was penalized and rationing frequently resorted to. When, in 1691, the Intendant Champigny advocated the abandonment of price regulation, claiming that only freedom from restraint could create abundance and with it lower prices,[3] Louis XIV and the people of New France overruled him. The King stated: 'It is a good thing to conserve the freedom that commerce requires, but when the avarice of individuals goes too far and proves detrimental to the well-being of the country it is necessary to curb it by every practicable means, even by legal sanctions, when other means fail.'[4] And two years later, when the intendant declined to regulate the price and supply of meat, the Sovereign Council insisted that a public assembly be called to discuss the matter. At the meeting the consensus of opinion went against the intendant; he thereupon bowed to the popular will.[5] Regulations were duly imposed and the practice continued until the Conquest.

The fundamental institution upon which society in New France rested was the seigneurial system of land tenure. This system, consciously modelled on the ancient Roman *praedia militaria*,[6] was well calculated to settle a great many families on the land and to bring it into production with the minimum of delay. Too intricate to be discussed in all its ramifications, it must suffice to say that the seigneurial system afforded a large measure of social and economic security for the lower ranks of society, and also of social mobility.[7] The relative ease with which persons, originally of the peasant class, who possessed intelligence, ability and initiative, could amass capital in the fur trade, acquire a seigneury, and with it the status of the colonial *petite noblesse*, was a remarkable feature of social development in seventeenth-century New France.

In his plans for the rejuvenation of the French economy, Colbert assigned an important role to New France. One of the prerequisites for the implementation of these plans was a rapid increase in the colony's population; hence, from 1663 to 1672 the Crown sent to Canada each year some 500 men and up to 150 marriageable girls. The original intention was that the men should be given a concession of land on a seigneury, two arpents of which would have been cleared and seeded ready for them, along with tools, seed, food and clothing enough for the first year.[8] It would then be up to them to clear the forest from the remainder of their concession and bring it into production. In practice, however, this proved unworkable. Conditions in the New World were too different from those in France and men thrust onto the land in such a fashion would have starved to death before the first winter was over had they been left to themselves. The Sovereign Council at Quebec therefore decreed, in 1664, that all *engagés* would be required to work for three years for the previously established settlers at wages of 60 to 90 *livres* a year. At the end of this time it was expected that the *engagés* would have garnered the experience needed to cope with Canadian conditions and would then be granted tools, seed, clothing and food enough for a year, and land of their own on an established seigneury.[9] In the distribution of these indentured servants the members of the Sovereign Council, their fellow seigneurs, and the religious orders engaged far more than their share of this labour force, but then few of the *habitants* could, at that time, have afforded a hired hand.[10] Yet three years was not a long time, and it must also be remembered that these were years of war with the eastern tribes of the fierce Iroquois confederacy. The first harsh lesson that anyone in Canada had to learn was how to elude their scalping knives.

Within this social and economic framework the settlers, once established, were expected to provide for themselves and to care for the members of their own families who, for one reason or another, needed help. When parents became too old to work, for example, their children were expected to look after them. The customary procedure here was for a meeting of all members of the family to be held before a notary decide which of the children would care for the parents and how much the others would contribute. The agreement was then given the official seal by the notary, who retained a copy.[11] Occasionally, however, a family failed to accept its obligation to care for an indigent member, or failed to honour a commitment so to do. When this was brought to the attention of the intendant he was quick to intervene. Two examples must suffice. In March 1710 the Intendant Raudot issued an *ordonnance* 'which obliges the children and relatives of François Dussault and Geneviève Mezeray to appear before the Sieur Basset [notary] to deliberate together on the most appropriate ways to care for their father and mother'.[12] And in January 1739 the Intendant Hocquart issued an *ordonnance* 'which condemns Joseph Chapelain, *habitant* of Chevrotière, to care for his mother Leonard Mouillard, according to his undertaking of 21 February 1738, on pain of being constrained so to do by all means'.[13] Yet the truly remarkable thing is that the intendants had to issue very few such *ordonnances*, for as the Intendant Champigny remarked in 1699: 'They help each other in a manner quite different to the way they do in France.'[14]

It was inevitable, however, given the hasty manner in which many of the emigrants had been recruited in France, that some of them would find conditions in Canada too arduous and would abandon the attempt to wrest a living from the wilderness. Thus, within a few years after the establishment of royal government, Quebec was beset by beggars. In all probability Montreal encountered the same problem, but few of the local records have survived for this period. In August 1677 the Sovereign Council issued an *ordonnance* forbidding all begging in Quebec, ordering the mendicants to quit the town within a week and return to their neglected farms. At the same time the colonists were forbidden to grant alms at the door of their homes under any circumstances, on pain of a ten-*livres* fine.[15]

This rather draconian law appears to have had the desired result. But some six years later, in April 1683, Quebec was once again plagued by beggars who refused to work; this at a time when the established settlers were desperately short of labour. Worse still, these vagabonds raised their children in idleness and inhabited a vile collection of huts on the outskirts of the town, making it the site of all manner of scandalous disorder. To remedy the situation, while there was time for those causing it to re-establish themselves on their land before the onset of winter, the intendant ordered them to return to their concessions within a week. Anyone caught begging in future was to be placed in the stocks, and flogged if caught a second time. Once again, no one was to grant alms at the door of his home to beggars on pain of a ten-*livres* fine.[16]

This legislation was clearly designed to cope with the social and economic problem posed by the indolent, the undeserving poor. There still remained the problem of the deserving poor, those who through no fault of their own were unable to provide for themselves. During these years the only recourse they had was the charity of the more fortunate members of society. To maintain some sort of control of this situation, which past experience had shown could all too easily lead to abuse, these unfortunate individuals were required to obtain a mendicant's license, attesting to their need, from their local curé or judge.[17] As long as there were not too many beggars the system sufficed, but when economic conditions worsened then other measures had to be taken.

Such was the case in 1688. Throughout the history of New France, and more particularly in the seventeenth century, the fur trade was the economic life blood of the colony. For the three years preceding 1688 no furs had reached Montreal from the west owing to the Iroquois war. This had hit the colonists hard; not just the fur trading fraternity, but virtually everyone in the colony felt the effects, a great many being reduced to penury. To make matters worse, an epidemic of the tertian ague in the summer of 1684 had resulted in a very heavy death toll, leaving many widows and orphans. In consequence, what appears to have been hordes of people were reduced to seeking alms in the streets of the three towns and throughout the countryside. Moreover, the authorities were convinced that some indolent people were taking advantage of the situation to maintain themselves in idleness by begging, even though work was available for them.

It was clear that the reiteration of the *ordonnances* of 1677 and 1683 forbidding begging and ordering the mendicants to return to work would not suffice. Fortunately the intendant at this time, Jean Bochart de Champigny, was both an efficient administrator and a very humane person. On 8 April

1688 he called a special meeting of the Sovereign Council to deal with the situation. The resulting *règlement*,[18] a lengthy and detailed document, shows the French colonial system in quite a good light. A social problem is seen to exist, it is carefully analysed, and an honest attempt is made to solve it.

In drafting the legislation the intendant and the Sovereign Council had three main aims in view: to see to it that no one starved, to find useful work for all those capable of working, and to put an end to the public annoyance created by the horde of mendicants. In attempting to achieve these aims they distinguished between two types of poor, the deserving and the undeserving; the former were to be helped to help themselves, the latter were to be coerced into ceasing to be charges on, and sources of annoyance to, the other colonists. In the rural areas each seigneury was required to care for its own without calling for outside help; but in the three towns, Quebec, Montreal, and Trois-Rivières, where the situation was the most acute, a new institution, the *Bureaux des Pauvres*, offices of the poor, was to be established forthwith. These bureaux were to be staffed by the local curé and three directors who were to hold meetings once a month, and oftener if circumstances required. One director was to serve as treasurer and keep a careful account of all alms received and dispensed, another was to act as secretary and keep a journal of the office's deliberations and transactions. They were empowered to investigate the need of all applicants for aid, to seek employment for them, and, lest some of them should demand exorbitant wages to avoid being hired, the directors were required to come to an agreement with those offering employment on the wages to be paid, and the poor were to accept the stipulated rate without argument.

The directors who served as secretaries in the three bureaux were required to request two ladies in each town to call on all homes in their respective districts to collect alms in either cash or kind, taking a servant with them to carry whatever they received. These ladies were, however, to be strictly enjoined not to press people to contribute but to allow all to donate as their conscience dictated. The *règlement* then went on: 'The said directors will distinguish between the types of poor; to some they will give only a little money to obtain tools and work material; for others the said directors will themselves buy these things lest the poor should dispense the money unwisely, or spend it on the wrong things. The Sovereign Council will forbid, under pain of an arbitary fine, tavern keepers and all others to purchase from the said poor their tools and supplies, and which the latter may not sell under any pretext whatsoever. And to others they will grant half rations and inform each of them what wages they may ask according to the work they are capable of doing.'

With this legislation enacted, the Sovereign Council felt able to reimpose the earlier stringent measures against unlicensed begging and the practice was once again forbidden on pain of corporal punishment. Only if some exceptional misfortune had descended upon a family could its members ask the curé in a country district or the directors of a town bureau of the poor for permission to solicit alms. The directors were also empowered, when a family overburdened with children requested help, to put the children out to work for as long as was deemed advisable rather than allow them to become a charge on the public, but contracts of service were to be drawn up by a notary and the conditions were to be made as advantageous as possible for the children. In other words, the indolent were not to be allowed to take advantage of circumstances to avoid work, and the circumstances were not to be used by anyone to take advantage of the deserving poor. 'The said directors', the *règlement* stated, 'will exclude the indolent and proud, whom they will put to work; but the deserving poor who are known to have the interests of their families at heart and who are not debauched will be given every consideration. The aged will also be helped, great care being exercised in all cases to give only what is absolutely necessary as the directors may see fit.' This legislation was by no means original, somewhat similar *bureaux des pauvres* having been established in some at least of the French sea ports as early as 1626,[19] yet it is remarkable for the careful attempt that was made to protect and reconcile the interests of both society and the individual.

But the question remains: how well did this poor law function? A document dated 1698, ten years after the bureaux were first established, states that there had been objectionable consequences. Some individuals had taken advantage of the institution and had come to depend more on charity than on their own efforts; thus the bureaux had, in some measure, contributed to the perpetuation of the problem rather than to its removal. Worse still, many *habitants* suspected that the contributions they were called on to make were, in effect, a subsidy to laziness or bad management, hence some of them refused to give anything. These circumstances inevitably led to bad feeling on the part of all concerned; and this, the Quebec authorities felt, was more detrimental to the people's souls than the alms were of benefit to the bodies of the needy.[20]

This same document also indicates that by 1698 the *Bureaux des Pauvres* were no longer functioning. It is possible only to surmise why they had, at this time, a short existence. The main reason for their establishment, dire poverty in the colony, ended a little over a year after the *règlement* was enacted. In August 1689 the fur brigade returned from the West with 800,000 *livres* worth of furs. The colony was prosperous again. Then, too, shortly before these furs arrived at Montreal the colony suffered a ferocious and damaging assault at the hands of the Iroquois, marking the reopening of hostilities with this powerful confederacy and with the English colonies as well. For the ensuing eight years New France was kept fully occupied by these foes, and at the same time the governor of the colony, the comte de Frontenac, embarked on a policy of fur-trade expansion. Each year after 1689 hundreds of men were sent west to trade with the Indian tribes. Doubtless many of the able-bodied poor who had not found work in the colony to their liking were willing enough to embrace the arduous, but profitable and exciting, life of the *coureur de bois*.

By 1698, however, the war was over, the fur trade was in a very depressed state and voyages to the West were expressly forbidden by royal edict. Thus it is not really surprising to find in that year the Sovereign Council grappling once more with the problems occasioned by beggars and vagabonds. In February the council issued an *arrêt* stating that idlers and riffraff were, on the pretext of poverty, causing annoyance to the residents of Quebec by begging from door to door instead of working, as many of them were well able to do. The remedy for this situation, the *arrêt* stated, was easily to be found in the re-establishment of the *Bureaux des Pauvres*, and this was now ordered to be done. The local curés and four other directors in the towns were ordered to see to the nourishment of the deserving poor by conforming to the *règlement* of 1688 in all its particulars.[21]

The *bureaux* were duly re-established and it is known that they functioned effectively for over a year, and likely much longer. In August 1699 a woman at Quebec was fined 6 *livres* by the Sovereign Council for a misdemeanour and the fine was ordered to go to the local *Bureau des Pauvres*.[21] And by rare good fortune the minutes of the Montreal bureau's meetings have survived for the first thirteen months.[23] They are quite revealing. At the first meeting the officials were duly appointed, a meeting-place chosen, and two deserving cases dealt with. In one it was decided to use all possible means to persuade the intendant to grant a needy man a post as town crier, meanwhile he was given three bushels of wheat; and a poor woman was given three yards of cloth. At subsequent meetings similar decisions were made: a bushel of wheat to this person, a little money to that one, 20 *livres* to an Irish woman to help her establish herself in the colony, a quart of milk a day to a needy woman for her children, assistance to a prisoner-of-war just returned from Albany, and so on. There are several cases where wheat, and sometimes bread, was granted for one month only, while the pauper's relatives were located and made to assume their responsibilities. At one of the earlier meetings it was decided to put alms boxes in all the churches, securely attached with strong iron clamps. There are two cases of orphan children, a few months old, whom the bureau sought to have adopted. It is interesting to note the great care that was taken to ensure that they would be given into the care of families that could be counted on to look after them properly.

At the meeting held on 14 July 1698 it was decided, without any reasons being given, that the bureau would meet only once a month in future. At each of the meetings before and after that date some six to eight cases were dealt with; occasionally cases were left over to the ensuing meeting, but none of them appear to have been treated summarily. It is obvious that the directors of the bureau took their responsibilities very seriously. The last meeting for which the minutes have survived is that held on 15 July 1699. There is no hint given that the bureau was suspending its activities. How much longer it continued to function, or how active the other bureaux were, is not known. Further research may well provide the answers.

These *Bureaux des Pauvres* were intended mainly to cope with emergency situations, but there still remained the chronically indigent who could not help themselves and who had no one to care for them. A decade or more of war, along with both the rise in population (approximately 15,000 by 1700) and the aging of the immigrants of the 1660s, had resulted in enough such persons to constitute a distinct problem. This time it was the clergy, aided by the secular authorities, who took steps to solve it. In Montreal, the main theatre of war, the problem was the most acute, and here the colony's first almshouse, the *Hôpital Général*, was founded by Jean-François Charon and a group of lay brothers. Although granted land by the seigneurs of the island in 1688 to establish their house, they did not properly begin to function until near the end of the century. Their early labours, and a sixty-thousand-*livres* endowment, were devoted to the building of a chapel.[24] The Intendant Champigny, in requesting the minister of marine to grant Charon letters of establishment, stated that the founder's purpose was to establish in the colony one or more houses 'to care for the poor and infirm, men and boys, cripples, the aged, and others who were unable to earn their living, also to give instruction to orphan children and the needy that they might acquire skills or a trade and so manufacture saleable goods. This project [the intendant stated] can only be of great benefit to the colony.'[25] That the almshouse was functioning by 1698 we know. In the minutes of the Montreal bureau of the poor there are entries for June of that year stating that M. Charon should be asked if he would accept two indigents in his *Hôpital*. By 1747 only two of the original lay brothers remained alive and the almshouse was in a bad way. It was, however, saved from collapse by a worthy widow, Madame d'Youville, who, with several companions, obtained royal sanction to take charge of it. The institution's liabilities were assumed, necessary and extensive repairs were made to the buildings, and its functions were greatly extended.[26]

Useful though it undoubtedly was, the Montreal almshouse catered only for male indigents, at least while the Charon lay brothers had charge of it. After 1692 older women who could not support themselves other than by begging were sent to Quebec where Bishop St Vallier had, in that year, established an almshouse with an endowment out of his own pocket. The terms of the royal charter granted the *Hôpital Général* at Quebec are of some interest. In the preamble it is stated that as such institutions had proven very useful in the majority of the towns in France, there was every reason to believe that they would have the same utility in Canada. It is made plain that their main purpose was to eradicate the mendicant problem. Those placed in the care of the *Hôpital* at Quebec, both men and women, were to be given work to do in the institution's workshops or on its farm land. Here too the view is expressed that the majority of beggars were mendicants through choice, preferring to beg rather than to seek gainful employment. Consequently able-bodied beggars were to be placed in the almshouse by the authorities and made to help care for the chronically ill, and for those other deserving souls who were unable to maintain themselves by their own efforts.[27] The aim was to solve a social problem as much as, or more than, to provide Christian charity.

One group that received particular attention from the Crown were foundlings. The authorities always made every effort to discover the parentage of abandoned babies. Any woman found guilty of having concealed her condition and given birth to a child clandestinely was dealt with harshly by the courts— the death penalty being invoked in many cases. All too frequently, however, babies were found abandoned on the steps of a church, or of a private home, and it then remained for the royal officials to care for them. In 1726 the Intendant Bégon ruled that such children had to be cared for at the expense of the seigneury where they were found, rather than by the Crown.[28] But by 1736 it had become established practice for the Crown to accept this responsibility. In that year the Intendant Gilles Hocquart decreed that the *procureurs du roi* would in future pay only seven *livres* a month for the care of abandoned illegitimate children between the ages of eighteen months and four years, by which time it was expected private families would be found who would agree to care for them.[29] Twelve years later, in March 1748, Hocquart issued another *ordonnance* which, although dealing only with the situation in Montreal, throws a good deal of light on the manner in which this social problem was dealt with in Canada.

The *ordonnance* begins by stating: 'The King, having been most desirous in the past that foundlings should be nourished and reared at the expense of, and be a charge on, the Royal domain, it is our responsibility to redouble from time to time our attention for their safe keeping, particularly since we have just been informed that a considerable number of the said children have perished in the past.' The intendant then declared that he would not go into the causes of this unfortunate state of affairs and proceeded instead to lay down detailed regulations for the proper care of the *enfants du Roi*. The local Crown prosecutor was instructed to make sure that the wet-nurses to whom the infants were first entrusted were capable of nursing them; a certain midwife was to be engaged to act as consultant in this connexion, be paid a retainer of 60 *livres* a year, and be exempted from the billeting of soldiers for her services. The wet-nurses were to be paid 45 *livres* for the first three months for each child, and ten *livres* a month after that until the child attained eighteen months. Since this was, the intendant declared, more than the townspeople were accustomed to pay for the nursing of their own children, the Crown prosecutor should have no difficulty in obtaining the services of nurses, who were to be paid cash in advance. When the infants were eighteen months old, and before if possible, the Crown prosecutor was required to have them cared for by honest families who would be made legally responsible for them until the age of eighteen or twenty. These foster-parents were to be given a grant of 45 *livres* upon taking a child into their care. Those children who had not been taken by private families at eighteen months were to continue to be cared for by their nurses, who would be paid seven *livres* ten *sols* a month. Every quarter the Crown prosecutor was required to send the intendant a list of all the children being cared for at the Crown's expense, with the date of their birth; another list being of the children being cared for privately, and by whom; and a third list giving the names of any children who had died, along with the date of their demise.

The intendant also made plain his displeasure at the manner in which the Sieur Foucher, Crown prosecutor at Montreal, had discharged his responsibilities in the past. It was pointed out to him that in the last list that he had submitted, four illegitimate children born in 1743, six in 1744, and ten in 1745, were still unadopted, hence still a charge on the Crown. 'We hereby warn the Sieur Foucher,' declared the intendant, 'that if he continues to be so negligent in future, we will cause him to accept in his own private capacity the costs of such a lengthy maintenance.'[30] How well such children fared while wards of the Crown can only be guessed at, but judging by the very indulgent way the Canadians were reputed to treat their own children, once taken into a family the foundlings must have fared well enough. Nor is there any evidence to indicate that they suffered any handicaps owing to their dubious birth.

There now remains only the medical services to be discussed. The colony was relatively well provided with both surgeons and doctors. One of them at least, Michel Sarrazin, as well as being highly regarded as both surgeon and doctor, enjoyed an international reputation as a scientist, being elected a corresponding member of the *Académie Royale des Sciences* along with Sir Isaac Newton.[31] The Intendant Champigny remarked of him that for every patient from whom he received a fee, he treated ten without charge.[32] Some of the more well-to-do citizens insured themselves against mishap by a means that is common today: the pre-paid medicare plan. In Montreal some forty-two citizens contracted with a master surgeon in such a scheme. For a fee of five *livres* each a year they and all members of their families were to receive medical care until completely recovered from all accidents or ailments except the plague, small pox, epilepsy, and lithotomy.[33] Although this is the only private medical contract so far to come to light, there is passing reference to another such in the records of the Sovereign Council.[34] Further research in the notarial records would very likely disclose more.

The more seriously ill were cared for at the colony's three hospitals: the *Hôtels Dieu* established at Quebec in 1639, Montreal in 1659, and Trois-Rivières in 1702. All three, and particularly the *Hôtel Dieu* at Quebec, enjoyed high reputations for the calibre of medical service they afforded to all, regardless of ability to pay. Separate endowments were maintained for the treatment of the poor, and the intendant insisted on a strict accounting of these revenues.[35] At Montreal the *Hôtel Dieu* contracted with two master surgeons to visit the wards every day, each for three months in turn, at a fee of 75 *livres* a year, to care for the charity cases.[36]

This, then, is as much as is presently known of the social-welfare measures in New France. Until a good deal more research is done, only tentative conclusions can be formed. All that presently can be said is that in the paternalistic, hierarchical society of New France, poverty was not regarded as a sin but as socially undesirable and, under certain conditions, as economically reprehensible. The people of the colony were, in many respects, much more fortunate than the mass of the people in Europe. There was an abundance of free land, fishing and hunting were open to all, and both fish and game abounded. Except during the early years of the eighteenth century, the fur trade flourished and brought considerable wealth into the colony, providing a relatively high standard of living to all ranks of society. The Church, in this age of Vincent de Paul, eventually to be canonized, played its traditional role of caring for the sick, and for the aged who had no one to care for them. It was thus left to the royal officials to enact mainly *ad hoc* measures to alleviate hardship resulting from temporary conditions, and to make provision for such special cases as foundlings, who were wards of the Crown.

It was not assumed, as it was in the England of that age, that a sizeable segment of the population would always be paupers. In New France no one starved—and of few parts of the world in that era could this be said. Steps were taken to prevent ne'er-do-wells from being a charge on society, and those unable to fend for themselves through no fault of their own were afforded some measure of security. The Crown accepted this as its proper responsibility and some at least of the colonial officials made sincere efforts to discharge the responsibility.

New France and the
Western Frontier

This paper was written for a conference held at Banff in the spring of 1969, under the auspices of the University of Alberta. As I recall, the audience was made up largely of high-school teachers. It afforded me an opportunity to test the reaction to the theories I had formed that the Canadian frontier had been very different to that of the Anglo-American colonies and the ensuing republic. My paper was a complete rejection of the Turner and Webb concepts of the American frontier and the overpowering influence of the environment on American society. I wondered at the time if it would be treated as heresy and rejected. It was not. Nor, since then, have I seen cause to recant or revise the ideas here expressed. As is so frequently the case, the radical concept soon becomes conventional wisdom.

Before beginning a study of any frontier the question has to be asked: frontier of what? In Canada under the French regime, as in the other European colonies in the Americas, the frontier can be defined as the outer limits of European civilization. It was a manifestation of the so-called expansion of Europe that began in the fifteenth century and continued for over four hundred years, until European civilization succeeded in dominating the world, the first civilization to do so.

This great wave of European expansion is frequently attributed to the new spirit of individualism released by the forces that accompanied the epoch known as the Renaissance. Such may well be so, but to be more specific one has to examine the motives of the Europeans who were willing to venture across uncharted oceans to conquer unknown lands against incalculable odds. These motives can be defined as fourfold: first, the European's avid desire for recognition and fame; second, the European's insatiable curiosity, his thirst for knowledge; third, the European's highly developed acquisitive and competitive instincts; fourth, the marked intolerance of the European's religious beliefs. These, then, were the dominant motives that brought the French to North America to establish, first commercial bases, then missionary outposts, and eventually permanent settlements.

In early Canada it is possible to distinguish four types of frontier; commercial, religious, settlement, and military. Yet they were all part of one frontier, and this one frontier embraced the entire area, not merely the outer fringes, of the territory in North America controlled by France. Thus the Canadian frontier was markedly different, in its nature and historic development, to that of the English colonies to the south. The frontier of these latter colonies, and of the republic that eventually developed out of them, was basically a settlement frontier, which advanced steadily westward in a roughly distinguishable, if very irregular, line marked by cleared land; a frontier line constantly in contact and usually in conflict with the original inhabitants, the Indians. The Canadian frontier, on the other hand, consisted of a main base on a river that gave easy access to the heart of the continent, and several smaller bases or outposts far in the interior but dependent on the main base, which in turn was dependent on the mother country, France. The settlements of the main base along a stretch of the St Lawrence River between Quebec and Montreal were a relatively narrow ribbon backing onto uninhabited virgin wilderness. In only a very limited sense, unlike in the English colonies, could the back areas of these settlements be regarded as a frontier, but they were part of the larger Canadian frontier.

If the Anglo-American frontier be accepted as the norm, then Canada could hardly be said to have had a frontier at all. Rather it can be said to have been a metropolis, dominating the hinterland around it, and with a few incipient metropolises beginning to develop in the west at such points as Detroit, Michilimackinac, and in the Illinois country.[1]

In the English colonies the frontier was perforce the line of settlement, created by axe and plow as settlers moved steadily westward away from the seaboard. In their wake the forest was cut down, the animal and human life, which it sustained, killed or driven farther west. In short, the Anglo-American frontiersman was a potential settler, the enemy and destroyer of the frontier forestland and its denizens. In marked contrast to this development was the Canadian frontier and the relations of the Canadians to it. The St Lawrence and Ottawa Rivers, and the Great Lakes, gave the Canadians easy and direct access to the interior of the continent, a factor denied to the Anglo-Americans by the Allegheny mountains and the Iroquois confederacy. The watershed between the Great Lakes and the Mississippi basin is low-lying, affording no real barrier. The Canadians could travel with relative ease from their main base in the St Lawrence valley all the way to the Gulf of Mexico. Moreover, throughout the lands along these water routes, supplies of food were easily obtained; game and fish abounded, and corn-raising Indian tribes were eager to exchange food and furs for European trade goods. To the northwest the watershed between Lake Superior and Lake Winnipeg was somewhat more difficult to traverse, but it posed no real obstacle. From Lake Winnipeg the Saskatchewan, Assiniboine, Red, and Nelson Rivers allowed easy travel west, south, and north. Here, too, on the northern plains there were adequate food supplies, provided by the great buffalo herds, fish, and wild rice. Along these waterways, then, there was no barrier to the westward progress of the Canadians until the Rocky Mountains were reached. Thus it was that they had reached the shadow of the cordillera before the Anglo-Americans had managed to struggle across the Alleghenies.

Rivers by themselves, however, are not enough. A means of transportation on them is required; and here again the Canadians had a marked advantage over their Anglo-American and English rivals. The Indian's birch-bark canoe was capable of carrying heavy loads, was light enough to be carried around river obstructions such as rapids by one or two men, and was manufactured entirely from materials readily available in the Canadian forest. The larger white birch trees that provided the essential sheets of bark for the outer shell of the canoe grew abundantly in the St Lawrence valley and the lands along the north shore of the Great Lakes, but to the south and north of this region the white birch of adequate size was very scarce.[2] The Iroquois and the Anglo-Americans, when they could not obtain Canadian canoes, had to make do with ones made of elm bark or with dugouts, which were nowhere as serviceable.[3] Similarly the men of the Hudson's Bay Company posts were gravely handicapped by the lack of both canoes and skilled canoe men until well into the nineteenth century, when they devised the York boat.[4]

Another important factor favouring the Canadians was their infinitely better relationship with the Indian tribes. There was nothing accidental or pre-ordained about this; in fact, when the French made their initial attempts to found settlements in the St Lawrence valley in the first half of the sixteenth century, their relations with the resident Indian tribes changed rapidly from friendliness to suspicion to hostility. By the beginning of the 1600s, however, this relationship had changed radically for the better. In the intervening years the Iroquois tribes that had occupied the area between present-day Quebec and Montreal had departed and no other sedentary tribes had settled in the vacant territory. It was, in fact, an unoccupied buffer zone between the Iroquois and Montagnais nations. Thus, when the French founded their settlements in the St Lawrence valley they did not have to dispossess the Indians. Moreover, the northern Algonquin nations welcomed the French, who were able to supply them with European weapons for use against their Iroquois foes to the south and the Sioux in the west.

Thus by the early seventeenth century the French had established a close commercial alliance with the Algonquin nations and their allies, the Hurons. This led, inevitably, to a military alliance, and the French were obliged to commit themselves to the active military support of their commercial partners against the Iroquois, who in turn obtained European weapons from first the Dutch then the English, by this time established along the Hudson River.

Commerce was not, however, the only motive the French had for maintaining good relations with the northern Indians. Religion was also an important factor. Within a few years of the establishment of a small commercial base at Quebec, French missionaries had begun their work far in the interior. Here was a unique type of frontier, a religious frontier of the mind, as these intellectuals, products of a highly civilized age, struggled in a savage wilderness environment to impose their very sophisticated concepts and values on these North Americans of the stone age. At first they sought to assimilate the Indians to French civilization, but in this they failed. Too many of the Indians seemed to acquire only the worst traits from the French laymen they encountered; and conversely, too many of the French showed a marked aptitude for adopting Indian mores that were quite contrary to Christian teaching. The missionaries therefore strove to keep the Indians and French laymen apart in order to protect their charges from the debasing effects of too close contact with Europeans.[5]

Yet missionary activity, commerce, and imperialism inevitably became closely intertwined, since all three were dependent on the Indians to achieve their aims. Among the western tribes, wherever the missionaries established their chapels French fur traders also had their trading posts. Eventually, in order to exercise control over both the French traders and the Indian allies, military commanders with garrison troops were appointed to the main posts.[6] In this fashion French authority was extended over the interior of the continent. By these means the writ of the King of France ran for thousands of miles in the far reaches of the North American wilderness.

Yet it could hardly be said that the French occupied the West. All that they occupied, west of the junction of the Ottawa and St Lawrence Rivers, were these trading and missionary posts, the closest to the central colony being hundreds of miles removed. In between was virgin wilderness. By the eighteenth century a few of these posts, at Detroit and in the Illinois country, had progressed to the point where some of the land was being settled to provide food for the men at the posts and the traders who travelled along the rivers to more distant tribes within the French fur-trade empire. For the most part the trading posts were just that: a few log huts, perhaps surrounded by a stockade, a small garden to grow vegetables, on a river bank near an Indian village.

Referred to as *coureurs de bois* in the seventeenth century and as *voyageurs* in the eighteenth, these men of the West are legendary figures in Canadian history, but in fact we do not know too much about them. A great deal of research needs to be done to discover who they were, the true role they played in the history of the period, the changes wrought on them by their way of life, and the changes they wrought on Canadian society. Many of them, perhaps most, were illiterate, and only a very few committed anything to paper that has survived.* We know them mainly from the comments of their contemporaries, for the most part in the reports of royal officials and missionaries who deplored their way of life, yet found them indispensable at times. We know that by the end of the seventeenth century there were some two hundred of them who did nothing else their entire active lives, returning to the settlements in the central colony only when age and rheumatism, to which their way of life made them all too prone, rendered them incapable of paddling from sunrise to sunset and carrying backbreaking loads over an infinity of portages.

From the comments of contemporary observers, however, a picture emerges of these men as being a unique blend of French and Indian, wearing Indian dress, travelling like Indians, eating the same sort of food, speaking their language, making war in the Indian manner, living off the land and enduring privation with the fortitude of the Indian. Many of them took Indian girls for wives, and in the Indian fashion changed them as fancy dictated; they gambled away their hard-earned profits, as did the Indians, and gloried in their physical prowess. In short, they embodied the antithesis of the middle-class virtues. What the Indians thought of them we can only guess from negative evidence; most likely they accepted them as equals, for that they were. The missionaries, however, were aghast at their adoption alike of Indian virtues and what seemed to them to be vices.[7] Some of the royal officials too, expressed alarm at the effect they had on colonial society. The marquis de Denonville, governor-general of Canada in 1688, wrote: 'The great evil of the *coureurs de bois* is known to my lord, but not to its true extent; it depopulates the country of good men, renders them unmanageable, impossible to discipline, debauched. It makes of them, and their families, nobles wearing the sword and lace, all gentlemen and ladies. They will no longer consider working on the land, and that combined with the fact that the settlements are scattered results in the children of this country being raised like Indians and as undisciplined as them.'[8]

When these men left the seigneuries along the banks of the St Lawrence their families could never be sure they would see them again in this world. The continual wars among the western nations claimed their victims among the Canadians; a broken limb or disease could mean a slower death; and at every portage crosses marked where a canoe had swamped.[9] These Canadian frontiersmen were an entirely different breed to the fabled frontiersmen of the English colonies who advanced slowly, haltingly, westward with axe and plow, destroying the wilderness as they went. The Canadian *voyageurs* made no attempt to destroy the wilderness because their way of life required

---

* Subsequent research has shown decisively that very few of these men could read or write. They had no need to.

its preservation. They were much more akin to the seamen of New England than to the Anglo-American frontier settlers. They voyaged in their frail vessels through the wilderness, carrying their cargoes to the distant posts to exchange for return cargoes of furs, just as New England seamen sailed to ports in Europe, Africa, the West Indies to exchange fish, rum, and timber for sugar, slaves, or manufactured goods.

In contrast to the English colonies, where the frontier became ever more remote from the settled areas along the seaboard, Canada was part and parcel of an all-pervasive frontier, for all the houses in the colony had the river at their doorstep and along it came the men of the wilderness, French and Indian alike, bringing an awareness of the values and customs of the wilderness into most of the homes in the colony. Yet the values and customs, the mores, that the first settlers had brought from France in their cultural baggage remained dominant. In the English colonies, as the frontier of settlement moved ever farther west, on that frontier the restraints of civilized society were weakened to the point of barbarism.[10]

Here again the Canadian experience was different. The Canadian frontiersmen, although frequently out of the colony, many of them for years at a time, did make frequent trips back to the central colony. Thus they always retained some ties with civilization, and while they were in the West the officers at the main posts, and the missionaries, exercised some degree of restraining influence. Many of the *coureurs de bois* paid little heed to authority most of the time, but all were made aware how they were expected to conduct themselves. Moreover, they were always a minority among the Indian nations, dependent on them to a large degree; in their own self-interest they dared not behave in too offensive a manner.

The Anglo-American frontier settler, by comparison, felt no such restraint in his relations with the Indians. To him they were merely savages whom he despised, feared, and wished removed from the lands he coveted. The Canadian needed the Indians to provide goods and services, they were commercial partners; but to the Anglo-American the Indian was merely an obstacle to progress to be exterminated as quickly as possible.

Given this marked difference in frontier experience, what effect did these peculiarly Canadian conditions have on the central colony? In what ways did the Canadian frontier affect French culture and institutions in the settled communities? In studying this question one has first of all to begin with what the French brought with them from France, then note any departure from the culture and institutional practice of France. And here great care has to be exercised, for some quite radical changes were made by the French government in these institutions in Canada. This was particularly true in the administrative machinery and in the administration of justice. Reforms that the government could not make in France, owing to the resistance of powerful vested interests, were made in Canada. Little change occurred in the structure and working of the Church, only minor variations in methods to suit local conditions. In secular society, however, some marked changes occurred, setting the Canadian people apart as quite distinct from people of the same social class in France or the English colonies. In fact a unique form of society had developed by the end of the seventeenth century. To some degree it was environment, the frontier experience, that brought this about.

The main distinguishing features of this society were the military-aristocratic ethos that was all-pervasive, combined with a status-ordered class system that was, to a remarkable extent, an open one. In Canada social mobility was greatly facilitated by the availability of free land, the economic opportunities latent in the fur trade, the presence of a considerable body of regular troops in the colony with the commissioned ranks open to Canadians, and most important, the Royal edict of 1685 which allowed nobles resident in Canada to engage in trade.[11] This particular edict, oddly enough, quickly came to function in a way not envisaged by Louis XIV, for if those who were already of noble status could engage in trade, then there was nothing to prevent merchants and entrepreneurs who were not noble from aspiring to become so, provided they fulfilled the other requirements. Thus a Canadian of humble origin could make his fortune in the fur trade, acquire a seigneury, and hope that one day he, or his sons, would be ennobled for valiant service. Enough Canadians accomplished this feat to encourage a much larger number to govern their lives accordingly.

In this vital matter, the structure and latent values of Canadian society, we have then two prime factors: the social institutions imported from France but modified by the Crown, and the institutions and environment that were peculiar to Canada. Emerging out of this framework the dominant values became those of the noble and the soldier; ambitious men who were not nobles sought to achieve this status, or at least to emulate the way of life and attitudes of the nobility. To such as these the military virtues were held in highest regard, and for the first hundred years of the colony's history, war with the Iroquois or the Anglo-Americans was the normal state. The colony, with its governor and intendant, was organized on military lines. All able-bodied men served in the militia, and men of the seigneurial class provided the backbone of the officer corps in the *Troupes de la Marine*.

When, in the closing years of the seventeenth century, regular officers were appointed as commandants at the main western posts, they were able to avail themselves of their opportunities and make their fortunes in the fur trade. Needless to say, these appointments were eagerly sought after[12] and a goodly proportion of the officer corps served in the West. Similarly, a large number of the *habitants* spent some time there. Whereas the lower classes in France rarely moved far from their place of birth, spending their entire lives in one parish, hence knew little of the outside world—and the upper classes too lived in a circumscribed world, the vast majority never going beyond the confines of France—the Canadians were accustomed to making great voyages and living amongst peoples of a completely alien culture. They thus became a people of very broad horizons; their experience was not confined to a small group in one small region, but encompassed the continent.

In striking contrast to the unfettered life in the West, in the colony proper society existed within the framework of a well-organized, closely regulated welfare state, where order was maintained by officials of high and low degree, from captains of militia and village curés, to the town majors and the ubiquitous intendant. But this authoritarian system was tolerable because it rested lightly on the people: they paid no direct taxes apart from the tithe; their seigneurial dues—if collected at all—were modest, most likely less than ten per cent of their annual income;[13] and were this social framework to become irksome the *habitants* could always escape its confines by going one way or the other along the great river at their doorstep. In other words, the old concept of the frontier serving as a social safety valve likely has some validity here.

This environment and the unique institutions that developed out of it clearly affected the outlook and mores of the colonial people. During the first decade of Royal government, established in 1663, the great wave of immigration to Canada took place. It was during these years that the expansion into the West occurred and that officials newly arrived from France began to comment on the striking difference between the Canadians and their counterpart in France. Inevitably these officials were first of all struck by, what seemed to them, the deleterious social and economic effects of the metamorphosis. Instead of labouring on the land, they preferred to spend their lives in the bush, trading with the Indians, where their parents, the *curés*, and the officials, could not govern them, and where they lived like Indians. 'I cannot emphasize enough, my lord, the attraction that this Indian way of life has for all these youths,' Denonville wrote to the minister. But he then went on to say, 'The Canadians are all big, well built, accustomed when necessary to live on little, robust and vigorous, very self-willed and inclined to dissoluteness; but they are witty and vivacious.'[14]

The contemporary Jesuit historian, Father Charlevoix, wrote in his journal:

> Our Creoles are accused of great avidity in amassing, and indeed they do things with this in view, which could hardly be believed if they were not seen. The journeys they undertake; the fatigues they undergo; the dangers to which they expose themselves, and the efforts they make, surpass all imagination. There are, however, few more disinterested, who dissipate with greater facility what has cost them so much pains to acquire, or who testify less regret at having lost it. Thus there is some room to imagine that they commonly under-

take such painful and dangerous journeys out of a taste they have contracted for them. They love to breathe a free air, they are early accustomed to a wandering life; it has charms for them, which make them forget past dangers and fatigues, and they place their glory in encountering them often. I know not whether I ought to reckon amongst the defects of our Canadians the good opinion they entertain of themselves. It is at least certain that it inspires them with a confidence, which leads them to undertake and execute what would appear impossible to many others. It is alleged they make bad servants, which is owing to their great haughtiness of spirit, and to their loving liberty too much to subject themselves willingly to servitude.[15]

Father Charlevoix's observation on the cupidity of the Canadians, coupled with their spendthrift attitude, is significant, for these same traits were quite pronounced among the Indians. Like the Indian, the Canadian did not see any merit in storing up worldly goods; both looked down on those who did, and up to those who spent their money ostentatiously on good living.[16] It would seem an obvious conclusion that the Canadians had acquired this attitude from the Indians, and were able to do so because the necessities of life were more easily come by in Canada than in France. In other words, this character trait was a product of relative affluence and the frontier environment.

Ironically, until the beginning of the seventeenth century the French government was most anxious to keep the French out of the West. Finding that this was impossible, it sought to reduce the number of *coureurs de bois* by a licensing system whereby not more than seventy-five traders would go to the West each year.[17] This *congé* system enjoyed little success. Using the war with the Iroquois as an excuse, the governors of the colony sent large trading expeditions to the West in the guise of military detachments. In 1696 Lous XIV refused to allow any more trading licences to be issued. Firmer measures were employed to curb illegal trading and the number of men among the western tribes was considerably reduced, but a hard core of some two hundred *coureurs de bois* remained.[18]

These men can be regarded as frontiersmen in the truest sense of the word. When, therefore, Louis XIV decided in 1700, on the eve of the War of the Spanish Succession, to curb the expansion of the English colonies in North America, confining them to the lands east of the Alleghenies, the *coureurs de bois* were pressed into service to weld all the western Indian nations into a commercial and military alliance directed against the English colonies. They now became almost respectable in their new role of agents of French imperialism.

This policy proved to be quite successful for a good half-century, during which the French, with their new colony at the mouth of the Mississippi, and a chain of posts stretching up the valley to the Great Lakes, excluded the Anglo-Americans from the West. Eventually, however, the growth of population in the English colonies, doubling every generation, caused the pressure of their westward movement to increase immeasurably. As long as the French had to contend only with Anglo-American fur traders they could more than hold their own, but in the 1750s a new element was introduced into the struggle, that of Anglo-American land speculators and would-be settlers, greedy for the rich lands in the Ohio valley. Here began the final conflict between the two types of frontier, the fur trade and military frontier of the French and the advancing land settlement frontier of the Anglo-Americans.

When, in the year 1754, hostilities began in the Ohio valley, the French, with their much greater mobility and their alliances with the western nations, were able not only to retain their hold on the West but to carry the war to the English colonies. During the first three years of fighting, the Canadians, supported by French regular troops, brought the northern and central English colonies almost to their knees. Neither in England nor the colonies was there talk of conquering Canada but, instead, of seeking to arrange a peace before the situation in North America became worse.[19] A British army was destroyed in the wilderness by a small force of Canadians and allied Indians. Similar forces ravaged the border settlements of the northern and central colonies continually. The Anglo-American frontiersmen proved incapable of meeting this challenge. But, as we all know, Canada was eventually conquered, when well-disciplined and trained British regular soldiers, supported by the Royal Navy, succeeded in forcing a poorly led and ill-trained army of French regulars to engage it in a set-piece battle at Quebec. In less than an hour the French army was shattered and in full retreat. Ironically the bulk of the casualties suffered by Wolfe's army on that day were inflicted by the Canadian militia fighting from cover in their traditional way.[20] Had no regular troops been engaged on either side during this war, it is unlikely that Canada would have been conquered when she was.

The defeat at Quebec, and the success of the Royal Navy in preventing reinforcements reaching Canada the following year, caused the vast French empire in North America to collapse like a house of cards. This makes very plain how vulnerable that empire had been. Once Quebec was threatened and the Indian allies began to defect, control of the interior vanished. The Canadians in the St Lawrence valley, however, remained and managed to preserve their cultural entity to a large degree; and within a few years the old Canadian frontier was restored, almost as quickly as it had disappeared. The fur trade was taken over by new men from Scotland, England, and the northern English colonies.

These Nor'Westers quickly adopted the techniques and many of the cultural traits of the Canadians. When one compares their attitudes and values with those of both the Canadians and the bourgeoisie in Britain or the English colonies, it is apparent that they resembled the former much more than those of the class whence they had come. The Canadian frontier had, in fact, assimilated them to a remarkable degree.

And so for another half-century the old Canadian frontier continued to exert its influence. But eventually it had to succumb in the Northwest, as it had already done in the south, under the tide of westward-moving settlement. The axe and the plow finally succeeded in destroying the fur-trade frontier; and with it was destroyed a way of life and a peculiar system of values, part Indian. What it meant to the men who had lived this life was expressed, in exuberant fashion, to Alexander Ross at Lake Winnipeg in 1825, by a *voyageur* then over seventy years old:

> I have now been forty-two years in this country. For twenty-four I was a light canoe man . . . No portage was too long for me; all portages were alike. My end of the canoe never touched the ground till I saw the end of it [the portage]. Fifty songs a day were nothing to me, I could carry, paddle, walk and sing with any man I ever saw . . . No water, no weather, ever stopped the paddle or the song. I have had twelve wives in the country; and was once possessed of fifty horses, and six running dogs, trimmed in the first style. I was then like a Bourgeois, rich and happy; no Bourgeois had better dressed wives than I; no Indian chief finer horses; no white man better harnessed or swifter dogs . . . I wanted for nothing; and I spent all my earnings in the enjoyment of pleasure. Five hundred pounds, twice told, have passed through my hands; although now I have not a spare shirt to my back, nor a penny to buy one. Yet, were I young again, I should glory in commencing the same career again. I would spend another half-century in the same fields of enjoyment. There is no life so happy as a voyageur's life; none so independent; no place where a man enjoys so much variety and freedom as in the Indian country. Huzza! Huzza! pour le pays sauvage![21]

A Belated Review of
Harold Adams Innis's
The Fur Trade in Canada

*For years I had been convinced that Innis's 1930 work on the Canadian fur
trade had set scholarship in Canadian history back by some fifty years. When I
ventured to disclose this apparently heretical thought to some of my colleagues
at the University of Toronto, they quickly distanced themselves from me—in
order, I suspect, to avoid being scorched when the lightning struck. As my
own research deepened in the archives at Montreal—the main repository
for fur trade records, which Innis did not appear ever to have visited—I
became more and more convinced that Innis had misunderstood and mis-
represented the way the fur trade had functioned, its role in the policies of
the Imperial government, and its impact on Canadian and Indian society,
not to mention the economies of both. Yet his interpretation was continually
accepted, and repeated, by the authors of secondary sources and text books,
which were then read by university and high-school students year after year,
indeed generation after generation. It seemed high time that a caveat be
issued: hence this article.*

*I anticipated a stormy reaction from some historians and many economists.
A graduate student in economics did write a rejoinder, which evoked a
rebuttal.* His professors and mentors in the economics department at the
University of Toronto kept their silence and did not come to his support.
Some historians asked what all the fuss was about: they had long known that
Innis's work on the fur trade was nonsense; they had just been too busy
dealing with more important issues to bother about his misconceptions. In
short, it was all old hat. But where, I asked myself, was the hat?*

*At present the economists seem divided, rather unequally; some few strive
to give the 'staples theory' the weight of a revealed religion; others reject it
as too simplistic to be taken seriously. What the historians think of this critique of Innis I really do not know. Perhaps silence means assent.*

---

* Hugh M. Grant, 'One Step Forward, Two Steps Back: Innis, Eccles, and the Canadian Fur
Trade', *Canadian Historical Review*, LXII, 3, 1981. This was followed by my 'A Response
to Hugh M. Grant on Innis'.

A reappraisal of the Canadian fur trade is long overdue. For this to be done adequately there are two prerequisites: first, past misconceptions have to be cleared away: then the trade has to be placed in its historic and not just its economic context. This communication addresses itself primarily to the first of these presumptions.

Harold Adams Innis's major work, *The Fur Trade in Canada*, has long been regarded as the definitive work on the subject, an impeccable piece of scholarship, and a landmark in Canadian historiography. Robin W. Winks stated in his foreword to the 1962 edition, 'The book is of the greatest significance because of Innis' fundamental reinterpretation of North American history and because of the effect of that reinterpretation on subsequent scholarship.'[1] The statement is certainly true, but Professor Winks then went on to state that Innis 'never wrote an inadequately researched or thoughtless book'. A little farther on, however, he qualified this encomium with the caveat 'his method of citation was somewhat quixotic,' as indeed it was.[2] The sweeping generalizations and conclusions of this work have been accepted uncritically by too many later historians. Unfortunately, neither his premises, both stated and unstated, his use of historical evidence, nor the conclusions drawn will stand up to close scrutiny, and all too many erroneous interpretations of North American history have been made in consequence.

Innis saw clearly enough that in the early sixteenth century the trade in furs began as an adjunct of the cod fishery and that the coming into fashion of the beaver-felt hat had made the fur trade viable in its own right. His brief studies of the ecology of the beaver and of the manufacture and marketing of felt hats are certainly well done, although the latter study was derivative, being based on the work of French and British economic historians.[3] It was certainly the profits to be made in the garnering of furs from the Indians and their sale in France at a high profit that first enabled the French to establish permanent settlements in Acadia and the St Lawrence valley. Innis, however, took economic determinism to extremes and grossly exaggerated the role of the fur trade in the history of both North America and Europe. He stated, for example: 'The economic and institutional life of France undoubtedly suffered material disarrangement through the importation of furs on a large scale from New France.'[4] He produced no evidence in support of this claim and it is necessary only to examine the volume and value of the fur trade relative to the kingdom's total trade for it to be immediately apparent that the statement is, to say the least, a gross exaggeration.

Statistics are available for the years 1718–61 for furs imported at La Rochelle, the main port of entry for Canadian produce. These imports average out at roughly one million *livres*' worth a year.[5] After 1739 some furs were shipped to Rouen by the Dugard *Compagnie du Canada*, which likely accounts for the decline in the La Rochelle import figures in the ensuing years.[6]

The total amount entering Rouen could not have been very great, and thus the figure of about a million *livres* a year on average is as accurate as the work done to date will allow. A large amount of beaver was smuggled from Montreal to New York, but the participants in this clandestine trade were careful not to provide records. In any event these furs went to England; the Canadian economy benefited thereby but that of France was not directly affected.

These statistics indicate clearly that the furs imported into France from Canada were a minuscule item in the country's trade balance. By 1741 the total value of French trade with the colonies was calculated to be worth 140 millions a year, and the total for all external trade was 300 million *livres*.[7] Compared to sugar, coffee, indigo, chocolate, and fish, fur was of minimal value.[8] Innis's assertion, therefore, that the economy and institutions of France were thrown into disarray by the Canadian fur trade has to be regarded as a figment of his imagination.

Hard on the heels of the quest for furs as a motive for French colonization in Acadia and Canada came evangelism, the desire on the part of the French crown to carve out an empire in North America to rival that of Spain, and, also, the quest for precious metals and a water route through the unknown land mass to the Pacific. The charter of Richelieu's Company of One Hundred Associates states that its main purpose was to convert the Indians to Christianity.[9] The trade in furs was to be pursued to provide funds for this purpose. For the ensuing thirty years it was the French Church that, directly or indirectly, provided the support that saved the colony from foundering. After the destruction of the Jesuit mission in Huronia by the Iroquois and the consequent opening of the western Great Lakes to French fur traders, the role of the Church in the fur trade dwindled. Montreal, founded as a missionary centre, now became the main base for the exploitation of the western fur trade. Innis, however, failed to see the significance of these underlying factors. For him economics was all that counted.

When in 1663 the Crown took over responsibility for the colony from the moribund company, the monopoly on the marketing in France of all beaver pelts was purchased by a Quebec merchant, Aubert de la Chesnaye; then a year later it reverted to Colbert's newly established *Compagnie des Indes Occidentales*. In 1674 Colbert closed the books of that company and obliged a group of French tax-farmers to take over the beaver-marketing monopoly on a yearly lease of 350,000 *livres*. In his brief treatment of these complex arrangements Innis misunderstood what had actually transpired: that the fur trade did not loom as large on the French colonial balance sheet as he imagined.[10] What the new *Compagnie de la Ferme* of Jean Oudiette had wanted was control of the African slave trade and certain West Indies produce. That the beaver trade was not the company's main interest is demonstrated by the fact that it immediately subleased it to La Chesnaye for 119,000 *livres*, thereby taking a loss of 131,000 *livres* a year just to get it off its hands.[11] Similarly, Innis attributed the demise of the *Compagnie des Indes Occidentales* to heavy losses incurred in Canada when, in fact, the real reasons lay elsewhere.[12]

The pursuit of the fur trade for purely economic ends did not endure beyond the end of the seventeenth century. The amount of beaver exported to France had grown astronomically until, by the 1690s, it far exceeded what the market could absorb. By 1696 the French government had to face the fact that the beaver trade was bankrupt, although the trade in other furs continued to be profitable. The immediate reaction of the minister of marine was drastic. He ordered the suspension of the beaver trade and the abandonment of all but one of the trading posts in the west. At the one post to be held, St Louis des Illinois, no beaver was to be traded. It was to be retained solely for military purposes. England and France were then at war, and for the past decade the Canadians had been struggling desperately to repel the assaults of Britain's allies, the Iroquois confederacy. The minister's hasty decision had to be reversed the following year for political and military reasons. The senior officials in the colony were swift to point out to the minister that were France to withdraw from the west in such a fashion the English colonials would quickly take over the trade with the Indian nations. The commercial and military alliances with them would then be dissolved, they would be drawn into the English camp, and New France would quickly be overwhelmed. It is by no means certain that events would have fallen out at that point in time as these officials foretold, but they clearly saw a manifest danger that they believed had to be forfended. The French government thus found itself obliged to continue to support the fur trade even though its current mainstay, beaver, was then an economic liability.[13]

The accession of William of Orange to the English throne in 1689 and of Louis XIV's grandson to that of Spain in 1700 brought about a marked shift in the European balance of power and a prompt renewal of Anglo-French hostilities. From this point on the fur trade was mainly an economic weapon in Anglo-French imperial rivalry. What was now of primary importance to France was not the trade in furs *per se* but the military alliances it made possible with the Indian nations who were a far more important factor in this European power struggle than has yet been recognized. It was they, not the French or the English, who were sovereign in the west, despite the grandiose claims made by the rival powers. Indeed, their respective claims to sovereignty over the interior of the continent had about as much validity as the claims of the English Crown to the throne of France, which were not relinquished until 1802. The French position was that, given their grossly inferior numbers, they had, at all costs, to keep the Indians from contact with the English. This meant they had to supply the Indians with the European goods they could no longer do without. Were the French not to supply them they would, of necessity, go over to the English. With the renewal of Anglo-French hostilities in 1702 fur-trade posts became a chain of garrisoned military forts where furs had to be traded, at a loss if necessary, to retain the Indian nations in the French alliance and bar any attempted expansion of the English colonies west of the Alleghenies. If the fur trade at these posts showed a profit, so much the better. At least it was expected that the trade would help to defray the costs of this ambitious new imperial policy in North America.

This was a political factor that Innis failed completely to grasp. He viewed the events that occurred between 1696 and 1700 from the viewpoint merely of economics. He gives a confused account, including masses of dubious statistics culled from primary sources that are not subjected to critical scrutiny, but the overriding significance of the political decisions made during those years escaped him.[14] He mistakenly assumed that the French military effort in New France was intended solely to serve the economic ends of the fur trade.

In his preface to Murray G. Lawson, *Fur: A Study of English Mercantilism 1700–1775* (ix), Innis states: 'Military and naval efforts to check encroachment on the St Lawrence from the Hudson route and Hudson Bay, and particularly the establishment of posts along the Great Lakes to check the Iroquois from the south and English competitors from the north, involved an enormous outlay of funds on the part of the government and sharp fluctuations in the supplies of varying grades of furs, depending in part on victories and defeats.' The French government's decision in 1696 to abandon the western posts and to curb the trade in beaver indicates clearly enough that the expenditures mentioned here were not made for the sake of the fur trade; neither was the subsequent decision of 1700 to establish a new base at Detroit and the colony of Louisiana to control the Mississippi valley. Innis also overlooked the fact that the British too had to make an enormous outlay of funds for military purposes in North America—for example, Forts Churchill, William Henry, Edward, and Oswego, not to mention Halifax. Nor will his statement that 'an increased burden of taxation to support militaristic ventures' placed the Canadians in a disadvantageous trading position bear scrutiny.[15] The only taxes paid by the Canadians were import and export duties on certain items and they were in no way affected by military expenditures. Those costs were borne by the French government and were certainly not a charge on the fur trade. Similarly, 'The increase in fixed capital which accompanied extension of military control . . .'[16] was not a drain on the fur trade; if anything it had the reverse effect. He also states: 'The vicious circle, in which cheaper English goods and more efficient English traders in the south necessitated greater expenditure on military measures to check competition, and the burden of increasing expenditures falling chiefly on the fur trade reduced the prices offered by the French to the Indians and encouraged competition . . .'[17] There is not a particle of evidence to support those claims but a great deal that refutes them, some of which, ironically, Innis himself cites in other contexts.[18]

A careful and extensive comparison of the prices of English and French trade goods has yet to be made, and so far as the French are concerned it is difficult to see how one could discover the prices they charged the Indians; whatever the market would bear, most likely. What evidence there is available indicates that some English goods were cheaper, some more expensive, but on the whole the difference between French and English prices was minimal. Too often comparisons that have been made are akin to those of apples and oranges and many of the comparisons made by the French in the seventeenth century, showing the prices of goods at Albany to be far lower than those at Montreal, are suspect since their compilers were pleading a case to have the *quart*, the twenty-five per cent export duty on beaver, removed to increase their profits.

English traders to the south were definitely not more efficient than the Canadians. Indeed, the reverse was the case. The fact that the merchants of New York obtained the bulk of their furs clandestinely from Montreal testifies to this.[19] *The American Gazetteer*, vol. II, published in London in 1762, in the entry on Montreal declared: 'the French have found some secret of conciliating the affections of the savages, which our traders seem stranger to, or at least take no care to put it in practice.'[20]

Military measures were neither required nor employed to check English competition in the fur trade; the burden of military expenditures most definitely did not fall on the trade, and there is no evidence to indicate that the French were obliged to reduce the prices they offered for furs for that reason. In fact, in 1754, when the French established Fort Duquesne at the forks of the Ohio, the governor general ordered the commandant of the fort to regulate the prices charged the Indians for goods to put an end to their complaints of overcharging. This was done for political and military reasons. In short, military and political policy led to an increase in the prices offered by the French to the Indians, hence to an improved competitive position: the reverse of what Innis claimed.[21] Again there is not a particle of evidence to support any of these claims, and that which Innis cites refutes them.[22]

A further figment of Innis's imagination is contained in his assertion: 'The military organization which had grown up because of the exigencies of the fur trade, though long effective, eventually collapsed.'[23] One would have thought that if there is one fact in Canadian history that is indisputable it is that New France was conquered, after five years of hostilities, by a British army and the Royal Navy, assisted by the fatal blunders committed by the French commander, the marquis de Montcalm, at the battle of Quebec in 1759.[24] Innis, however, will not have it. He declares, 'The French power in New France collapsed of its own weight,'[25] but he subsequently advances a different reason for the British victory. 'The conquest of New France was largely the result of the efficiency of English manufactures combined with the control of shorter routes to the interior from New York and Hudson Bay.'[26] Wolfe, Murray, and Admiral Saunders would not likely have been in agreement. Moreover, Innis here blithely overlooked the fact that the Hudson's Bay Company men failed to establish themselves beyond the shores of the bay prior to the Conquest, and that the Anglo-American traders who eventually reached the Ohio valley were swiftly driven out.[27]

Two major points that Innis emphasized throughout his work were that the Canadian fur traders could not compete successfully with the Hudson's Bay Company owing to the latter's shorter trade route to the interior, hence lower costs, and the superiority and lower price of British trade goods.[28] He produced no viable evidence in support of these assertions; indeed, some of the evidence he cites contradicts them.[29] To deal first with the issue of the shorter trade route to the interior from Hudson Bay, this is, of course, true. Goods could be landed at the Bay posts much more cheaply than at the main Canadian base at Michilimackinac, but once the goods arrived at the latter base they were only a short journey from the major fur-trade areas. On the other hand, goods landed at the Bay then had to be transported several hundred miles inland to the tribes that produced the furs.[30]

The Hudson's Bay Company lacked the two things required to transport goods to the interior—birch-bark canoes and skilled canoemen. It was not until the York boat was developed in the nineteenth century that the Bay men were able to compete successfully with the Canadians. Prior to the Conquest the Bay Company had to rely on Cree middlemen to transport furs to the Bay posts and the trade goods back to the fur-producing tribes. This was a long hazardous journey through country where game was very scarce, hence supplies of food had to be carried both ways, which reduced the amount of cargo that could be carried. The Cree canoemen undoubtedly expected to be recompensed for their labour, particularly when they could obtain the same goods from Canadian traders in their midst or nearby. Thus Innis's assertion that 'goods were obtained on a large scale, and with access by sea, at much more favourable rates' is, to say the least, dubious, and he produces no evidence to support it.[31]

Another important factor was that the Cree middlemen voyaging to the bay used small three-man canoes having a maximum capacity of 1,000 pounds of goods,[32] whereas the Canadians used five- to eight-man *canots du maître* carrying loads of 4,000 pounds.[33] At one point Innis gives as a reference evidence that contradicts his assertion.[34] The Canadians, in addition to larger canoes, had other advantages over the Bay traders. They had a much longer navigation season, April to October. For the Indians going to the Bay it was a race to get there and back before freeze-up.[35] The Canadians travelled through country where fish and game abounded, in contrast to the hundreds of miles of 'starving country' west of Hudson Bay. Moreover, leached corn, the staple food of the fur brigades, could be obtained at Detroit and Michilimackinac.

When he came to deal with the rivalry between the Hudson's Bay Company and the North West Company, Innis again asserted that the former company had the advantage of a shorter route to the interior for the transport of heavier goods at lower cost, but in a footnote he cites the *Journals of Hearne and Turnor* who stated: 'The Canadians have greatly the advantage . . . in getting goods inland as five of their men with one canoe will carry as much goods as ten of the Honourable Company's servants can with 5 canoes.'[36] Exactly the same condition had obtained during the French regime, but Innis failed to draw the obvious inference from the evidence he cited.

The assertion Innis made that the Bay Company could transport heavier goods into the interior at lower cost than could the Canadians, failing to note that it was Indian middlemen and not company servants who performed the task, was accepted without question by some later historians of the fur trade. It has recently been stated that 'after 1714 the Hudson's Bay Company managed to hold on to the major share of the trade of the subarctic Indians. The company was the primary supplier of bulky, or heavy items such as kettles and guns that were difficult to transport overland in canoes in large quantities.'[37] The first statement is refuted by the tables produced by Murray Lawson, which show a steady decline in Hudson's Bay Company fur receipts from 1713 to 1760 and also by the statistics given by Innis for fur receipts at the Bay during the decades 1738–48.[38] The second statement, that the Bay posts supplied the Indians with the bulk of the heavy goods, is dubious in the extreme. The authors produced no evidence to support the assertion and it defies common sense. It would have been much easier for the Canadians to transport such goods in their eight-man *canots du maître* than it would have been for the Cree middlemen trading at the Bay with their small three-man canoes. Thus the notion that 'a shorter route to the interior' gave the Hudson's Bay Company a marked competitive advantage over the Canadian traders, prior to the introduction of the York boat, has to be regarded as just another Innis myth that came to be accepted as conventional wisdom.

One point that Innis emphasized strongly was his a priori belief that the French were unable to compete successfully with the English in the fur trade owing to the superior quality and lower price of English goods.[39] A typical assertion of the claim occurs in the concluding chapter of the work in question:

'The importance of manufactures in the fur trade gave England, with her more efficient industrial development, a decided advantage. The competition of cheaper goods contributed in a definite fashion to the downfall of New France and enabled Great Britain to prevail in the face of its pronounced militaristic development.'[40] He made the same assertion in his preface to Lawson's *Fur: A Study in English Mercantilism, 1700–1775*, even though the body of that work demonstrated the contrary. Innis, however, never allowed himself to be deterred by a want of evidence, or even conflicting evidence, in making his sweeping generalizations. He cited, for example, a lengthy statement dated 20 February 1765, which declared that the British traders in the west greatly feared the consequences were New Orleans to be ceded to Spain. The quoted writer stated: 'should that city pass into the hands of the Spaniards their allies the French will nevertheless supply them with suitable goods at a cheaper Rate than the English can do by reason of the high price of Labour among our Manufactures to wit, especially in Gunns, course cutlery etc . . .'[41] He also quoted from a letter written by a British trader at Michilimackinac to a gentleman in Quebec, published in the Quebec *Gazette* of 18 August 1768: 'All those who have wintered between this and the River Mississippi, complain of the French and Spaniards, of New Orleans, having undersold them considerably in every Article . . .'[42] That the French and Spaniards of Louisiana were then trading the same goods that the Canadians had used for decades Innis chose to ignore.

It is, of course, impossible to obtain first-hand evidence on the relative quality and price of French and British trade goods. The only available evidence is documentary, what interested parties wrote on the subject. This evidence has to be examined critically—all of it cannot be accepted at face value and the motives of the writers have to be taken into account. Moreover, one has to be reasonably sure, when price comparisons are made, that articles of the same quality are being compared.

Innis produced no evidence in support of his assumed 'growing supremacy of Great Britain in manufactures' in the first half of the eighteenth century. The assumption was, in fact, quite unfounded. Walter L. Dorn, in his *Competition for Empire*, published in 1940, wrote: 'There can be no question that before 1780 France was at least the manufacturing equal of England.'[43] This judgement was subsequently confirmed by more intensive research.[44] Nor should this come as any surprise since France, with a population three times that of England, was then the leading industrial power in Europe.

Had Innis consulted the letters written by the Hudson's Bay Company's traders he would have found a steady stream of complaints year after year, on the poor quality of the goods they received from England. Although the writers may have exaggerated somewhat to drive the point home, there is no reason to suspect that the burden of their complaints was not true. They had no discernible motive to make false statements. These Bay traders reported sadly and sometimes angrily that too much of their merchandise the Indians would not accept. It had to be shipped back and could not be replaced until the following year; meanwhile the Indians went to the nearby Canadian posts. As one disgruntled factor at York Fort commented, the Canadian traders inspected their goods very carefully at Montreal or Lachine before they were shipped west, whereas the Bay traders had to make do with whatever they received.[45]

English gunpowder was notoriously inferior to that of the French and for the Indians this was a vital commodity since they depended on it for the hunting of the larger game that provided the bulk of their food supplies. Poor powder could mean starvation for an entire band. In 1734 the Bay traders at Moose River wrote to the company's governors: 'We cannot but take notice of the badness of the powder and the disservice it does us. It is so foul that in the winter time after firing three or four times it will freeze in the guns, thereby occasioning much danger, and in the summertime it will cause the foul, watery matter to run out both at bore and touch hole. But above all the Indians that sometimes trades with the French and know the difference between theirs and ours, utterly protest against our powder and tell us that they are not able to do any execution with it.'[46]

Samples of French goods were obtained from the Indians and sent to London with the urgent plea that quality be matched.[47] Surprisingly, serious complaints were made of the very items that Innis maintained the British produced of a quality far superior to the French products—cloth and metal goods.[48] Such comments as those of Joseph Isbister at Fort Albany in 1740 are typical: 'The Flannel last year proved but indifferent, and the duffles is altogether useless, it being both thinner and narrower and not fit for either Indians or Englishmen.'[49] The cooking pots sent to the Bay, a major trade item, appear to have been grossly inferior in quality to those supplied by the French. Many of those sent were much larger than was desired by the Indians, being too difficult to transport. There were frequent complaints that the handle lugs were weak and broke after short usage, or that the kettles themselves were as thin as paper, 'fit to be sold only for old brass'.[50] Knives, axes, and the bar iron sent to be made into axes and ice chisels were also often of inferior quality and shattered in sub-zero weather.[51] In 1716 the factor at Albany Fort requested that short-barrelled muskets such as the French supplied be sent in future 'for they are mighty taking with the Indians'.[52]

As for the rum that Innis claimed gave the Bay Company an advantage over the French,[53] the Indians preferred brandy, which was far too expensive at 7s.6d. a gallon for the British traders. They went to great lengths to produce an 'English brandy' from cheap gin with rather alarming additives to make it look and taste something like the French product.[54] In any event,

Canadian traders who were willing to defy the *ordonnances* of the Quebec officials could obtain all the rum they wanted at Oswego.[55]

The burden of the Bay traders' complaints of poor-quality British goods was summed up by Thomas McCliesh at York Fort in 1728. After listing the large quantities of goods that he was sending back to England he declared:

> We have likewise sent home 18 barrels of powder that came over in 1726, for badness I never saw the like, for it will not kill fowl nor beast at thirty yards distance: and as for our kettles in general they are not fit to put into an Indian's hand, being all of them thin, and eared with tender old brass that will not bear their weight when full of liquid, and soldered in several places. Never was any man so upbraided with our powder, kettles and hatchets, than we have been this summer by all the natives, especially by those that borders near the French. Our cloth likewise is almost torn from one end of the piece to the other . . . here came at least forty canoes of Indians this summer, most of them clothed in French clothing that they traded with the French last summer. They likewise brought several strong French kettles and some French powder in their horns, with which they upbraided us with, by comparing with ours, at same time told us that they would give us the same number of beaver as they gave the French, provided our kettles to be strong and clear of soldering.[56]

Evidence such as this makes a mockery of Innis's statement: 'Trade from York Factory to the interior was rapidly developed after 1713, with no competition from the French in the interior.'[57]

Similar complaints of poor-quality woollens were voiced by a leading merchant in New York. In 1731 Cornelius Cuyler complained to his London supplier that the last shipment of strouds was 'almost good for nothing at all . . . I believe they are made of Dogs hair.' The following year he again complained, 'the Strouds which you now Sent me are Course Refuse old musty Strouds good for nothing.'[58] Despite these complaints, which referred to specific shipments and may have been the exception rather than the rule, the burden of the evidence appears to indicate that in this one item the British did indeed produce a superior product.[59] Governor General La Galissonière and Intendant Bigot, however, claimed that the woollens of Montauban were just as good as those of England but that the Montreal smugglers had convinced the fur traders that the product they brought in from Albany was preferred by the Indians. To have admitted that this was not, in fact, the case would have put them out of business.[60] A particularly telling piece of evidence is a *mémoire* of Governor General Vaudreuil, written at the height of the Seven Years' War, wherein he declared that English *écarlatines* were essential to hold the Indians in their alliance with the French. The *Compagnie des Indes* obtained supplies from England by way of Holland, but losses at sea had been heavy; he therefore requested that future shipments be sent on the king's ships. He also reported that the intendant Bigot insisted that the cloth be sold at pre-war prices despite higher costs and the company's demand

for a fifty per cent increase. This makes yet another example of the subordination of the fur trade to political and military ends.[61] In any event, the
question as to whether or not English woollens were superior is an academic one so far as the fur trade is concerned for the simple reason that the
Canadian traders were well supplied by either the *Compagnie des Indes*, or
the Albany merchants; thus the Hudson's Bay Company had no advantage.
Moreover, woollens were only one item of trade goods; linen and cotton
garments, hardware and spirits, made up a far larger proportion of the value
of goods shipped to the west.[62]

The statistics that were available in Innis's day show quite conclusively
that in the eighteenth century down to the Conquest the British share in
the fur trade was in steady decline. Indeed, Innis himself gives figures for
beaver traded at the Bay during the decade 1738–48 showing a decline from
69,911 to 39,505 pounds.[63] The tables compiled by Lawson from the English
customs entries show the value of furs for the years 1700–60, averaged out,
amounted to the equivalent of approximately 400,000 *livres tournois* a year.[64]
By comparison, French fur imports at La Rochelle for the years 1718–61
averaged over a million *livres* a year.[65] In addition, there were the furs
imported at Rouen by Dugard and Company, and the beaver traded clandestinely at Albany, which likely accounted for some twenty per cent of the
furs shipped to England.[66] In the mid-seventeenth century New York had
exported 40,000 beaver pelts a year; by the end of the century the amount
was reduced to 15,000 and almost all of it was obtained clandestinely from
the Canadians.[67] These figures, unreliable though they undoubtedly are,
still point to one inescapable conclusion—that Innis's claim, which he made
over and over again, that the French were unable to compete successfully
with the British in the fur trade is quite erroneous. In fact, the reverse
appears to be much closer to the truth. Had the Seven Years' War not intervened, the Hudson's Bay Company might well have been driven to the wall
by the Canadians.[68]

As for the much-vaunted price differential between Albany and Montreal,
this too appears to have little basis in fact. Sir William Johnson cited prices
for some staple trade goods in New York in 1746 and also immediately after
the Seven Years' War.[69] Fortunately, in the second list he gave prices in
both sterling and New York currency, which indicates that the prices in the
earlier list were in the latter currency. This is not an insignificant point since
the exchange rate at both points in time was approximately £186 New York
to £100 sterling.[70] When the prices of such goods as blankets, shirts, knives,
kettles, muskets, gunpowder, mirrors, vermilion are compared, converting
the *livre* at the current exchange rate of ten pence, the prices are virtually
the same. For example, blankets in New York sold for 14 shillings and 7s.7d.
—quality being the most likely cause of the discrepancy—and in Montreal

the price varied from 9 to 14 *livres*. A musket cost 17s. in New York, 20 *livres* or 16s.6d. sterling in Montreal; knives were a shilling each in New York and 1s.6d. to 11d., depending on size, in Montreal; kettles 2s. in New York, and in Montreal *chaudières* were 2s. 5d. sterling.[71] That the prices of such goods in both colonies were approximately the same should occasion no surprise. There is no discernible reason why they should not be. However, a much more intensive study of trade-goods prices in both colonies is needed before definitive conclusions can be drawn. Had, however, goods at Albany been as cheap and of such superior quality as Innis claimed, compared to goods in Montreal, then it is impossible to see how the Canadians could have garnered the lion's share of the fur trade as the evidence clearly indicates they did.

On one significant aspect of the fur trade—monopolies—Innis appears confused and he has certainly spread confusion. He frequently alluded to the fur trade of New France as being monopolistic; sometimes, however, he qualified this by distinguishing between internal free trade and external monopoly,[72] but he failed to make it clear that after 1665 this external marketing monopoly applied only to beaver and moose hides. From 1700 on beaver represented less than half the total value of furs exported to France; thus this so-called monopoly applied to less than half of the fur traded. This confusion is heightened by Innis's continual failure to distinguish between furs and beaver, which he treats as synonymous.[73] He does, however, make it plain that he considers monopolies to be a bad thing in the case of New France and he attributes much to this. Thus he states: 'Through these organizations—the trading organization of the interior and the monopoly organization of external trade—there developed in the colony a highly centralized system of administration. This centralization was shown in agriculture, in industry, in the church, and in colonial government. The tendency towards centralization was responsible for the development of paternalistic government.'[74] What he implies here is that the fur trade was responsible for the framework and nature of all the colony's institutions, which is absurd. The other French colonies where the fur trade was of little importance, as in Louisiana, or non-existent, as in the Antilles, had the same institutions. The fact that they were modelled on those of France he ignored. As for the one true monopoly in North America, the Hudson's Bay Company, this feature of that company is occasionally mentioned in passing, uncritically. It would appear that a British monopoly was without consequence, an imagined French one baneful.

Another popular fallacy promulgated by Innis was that the fur trade had inhibited the proper economic development of New France. He declared that 'Dependence on the fur trade and a military organization was not compatible with agricultural and industrial development and large external trade.'[75]; that 'The population of New France during the open season of navigation was increasingly engaged in carrying on the trade over longer distances to the neglect of agriculture and other phases of economic development';[76] and, finally, that 'A colony engaged in the fur trade was not in a position to develop industries to compete with manufactures of the mother country.'[77] The unstated premise here is that a colony should have a mixed economy with an agricultural, industrial, and commercial base that fostered a thriving foreign trade. In Innis's view the fur trade had prevented New France from developing its economy in that fashion.

It is true that in the last three decades of the seventeenth century the expansion of agriculture was hampered by a shortage of labour needed to clear virgin forest land and the Crown officials complained vociferously of the large number of men who had left the settlements to engage illegally in the fur trade as *coureurs de bois*.[78] The lure of the fur trade was not alone responsible for this exodus of potential agricultural labourers; the imbalance in the sexes was also a major factor. There were fewer than half as many women of marriageable age as men,[79] and a wife was a necessity to establish a viable farm. Had the fur trade not existed most of the surplus men would, most likely, have returned to France. In any event, early in the eighteenth century the sexes came into balance, the number of men absorbed by the fur trade was limited, and the rapid expansion of the population, doubling every generation, allowed of their periodic absence in the west without other branches of the economy suffering unduly. Moreover, most of the *voyageurs* left the settlements after the spring ploughing and returned in time for the harvest.

What really inhibited the economic development of New France were factors, some of them still operative today, that Innis failed to mention: namely, the harsh winter climate with its short growing season; the colony's inability to produce anything, except furs, that could not be produced more cheaply in Europe or the English colonies; the great distance from available markets; and the prevailing economic policy of the mother country, usually referred to as 'mercantilism'. France would never allow any of its colonies to compete with it in the marketplace. In fact, there was a good deal more industry in New France than Innis realized, at the artisanal level. In Europe the only industries that employed large numbers of men were fishing, shipbuilding, and iron foundries. In New France it was the same, with the exception of the fur trade. Moreover, the iron foundry, the Forges de St Maurice, was first established out of fur-trade profits. Innis was, therefore, quite wrong in asserting that the economic development of New France was hindered by the fur trade.

In treating of the fur trade down to 1760 Innis had a simple, albeit erroneous, theme that gave the work some sort of cohesion—namely, the superiority of

British industry, organization, trade goods, and routes to the interior, which not only made it impossible for the French to compete successfully but also made the conquest of New France inevitable.[80] In part three of the work, dealing with the fur trade from 1760 to 1821, the underlying theme is the rivalry between the Hudson's Bay Company and the North West Company. This presented problems since both were British, and used British goods. One was a monopoly, the other 'private enterprise', and it was the former that won the struggle. What resulted was a scissors-and-paste narrative account with little analysis but a welter of poorly organized detail, the relevance of much of which is not easy to determine. Moreover, the mass of evidence cited does not appear to have been subjected to critical examination. It is all taken at face value. A great deal of useful information is provided, but in a barely coherent fashion.[81] Much of it could have been reduced to tables, or presented more succinctly by means of maps. Occasionally Innis failed to grasp the significance of the evidence he liberally presented. He mentioned in passing the introduction of the York boat but failed to see that this represented a revolution in northern communications and was an important factor in the eventual elimination of the Nor'Westers by the Hudson's Bay Company.[82] In his concluding chapter he made the baffling statement: 'Dependence on the York boat rather than the canoe was symbolic of the increasing importance of Capitalism.'[83] He noted that the amalgamation of the XY and North West Companies made possible a sizeable reduction in wages paid their employees.[84] He mentioned that there was some resentment of this expressed by the clerks, *voyageurs*, and interpreters, but there the matter was let drop; the economic and social consequences were not examined. The chapters end without any conclusions being drawn.

The ensuing section dealing with the Hudson's Bay Company's activities from 1821 to 1869 and the sale of Rupert's Land to the Dominion of Canada also consists mainly of details presented in an inchoate fashion. He manifestly had not digested the material. One sweeping generalization that had been introduced earlier is here discussed in greater depth—the basic conflict, as he saw it, of settlement and the fur trade. Here he took geographic determinism to absurd lengths. In his preface to Lawson's book he stated that after 1713, 'With expansion of trade from New Orleans on the Mississippi, traders from the St Lawrence were pushed to the Northwest, following La Vérendrye from Lake Superior to Lake Winnipeg and the Saskatchewan.'[85] This reveals that he had failed to discover how the fur trade was organized prior to the Conquest. The fur traders of Louisiana could not compete with the Montreal traders who controlled the trade of the Lake Michigan region and on the upper reaches of the Mississippi.[86] The Canadian traders were certainly not pushed north to the Saskatchewan by competition from New Orleans. The Canadian traders moved west on the Saskatchewan because the only other viable route, the Missouri, was blocked by the powerful and hostile Sioux nation. Moreover, the northern route gave access to tribes with greater supplies of the better-grade furs. Innis stated further that 'Competition from the Hudson River drainage basin with the French and from Hudson Bay left only the territory northwest of Lake Superior.'[87] Here he ignored the richest fur region of all, that at La Baye (Green Bay), which included the headwaters of the Mississippi to the height of the land, and the region south and east of Lake Michigan to the Wabash.

He also asserted that 'The present Dominion emerged not in spite of geography but because of it,'[88] and that the fur trade dictated the outcome of the American Revolution and the location of the Canadian-United States boundary.[89] He linked these events to his belief that the fur trade and settlement were incompatible and in continual conflict. In his concluding chapter he states: 'The history of the fur trade in North America has been shown as a retreat in the face of settlement.'[90] Yet two pages later he asserts that 'The area which was crucial to the development of the fur trade was the Pre-Cambrian shield,'[91] Since the Pre-Cambrian shield was eminently unsuitable for agriculture, hence for settlement, it is impossible to reconcile the two statements.[92] The only region where settlement came into conflict with the fur trade was the Selkirk settlement on the Red River, and here the conflict was not directly over furs but for control of the region where the fur brigades obtained the essential supplies of pemmican. Elsewhere he declares: 'To a very large extent the American Revolution and the fall of New France were phases of the struggle of settlement against furs.'[93] The causal connections of these great events to the fur trade he sees as the French occupation of the Ohio valley and the Proclamation of 1763. He failed to grasp the fact that the French did not occupy the Ohio valley for its furs. The Montreal traders had never shown any interest in the area. The French occupied the region, over the objections of the Canadians, for purely political and military reasons.[94] Similarly, the Proclamation of 1763 was a political document enunciating political decisions made to serve political ends. Any connection these decisions had with the fur trade was incidental.

The assertions that 'Canada emerged as a political entity with boundaries largely determined by the fur trade',[95] that 'It is no mere accident that the present Dominion coincides roughly with the fur trading areas of Northern North America',[96] that the North West Company was the forerunner of the present confederation,[97] and that the present boundaries were a result of the dominance of furs,[98] are all further examples of economic determinism carried to the extreme. Significantly, this assertion is the final conclusion of the book.

When the case is subjected to scrutiny it quickly collapses. The present border from the Atlantic to the western end of Lake Superior was in no way connected with the fur trade. In fact, if the fur trade were to have determined the border in the Great Lakes areas then it would presently run from the western end of Lake Erie south of Lake Michigan to the Mississippi. In 1783, despite the strong opposition of le comte de Vergennes, the French foreign minister, Britain ceded to the United States the territory south of the Great Lakes to the Mississippi for political reasons.[99] When, after the Louisiana Purchase, the border west of the Great Lakes had to be determined, it was only in the Columbia territory that the fur trade was a factor in the negotiations. Had the western boundary been determined by the fur trade it would today run along the Saskatchewan river to the Rocky Mountains, rather than the 49th parallel of latitude, for the fur trade country lay to the north of that river, and west of the Rockies it would follow the lower reaches of the Columbia River.

In a critique of a major work a detached, judicious balance has to be maintained in the rendering of judgement. It is, therefore, disturbing that virtually nothing can be found on the credit side of the ledger in this instance, except that Innis's *The Fur Trade in Canada* was a pioneering work that brought the Canadian fur trade to the attention of a wide audience. Unfortunately, it gave a distorted view of the trade and at the same time inhibited further investigation. The work contains a great mass of information, much of it presented in chapters that lack cohesion, and frequently the evidence presented contradicts the book's conclusions. The end result has been the establishment of myths as conventional wisdom.

The basic flaw in the work is that Innis manifestly approached the subject with certain a priori premises and conclusions already formed and he chose to disregard any evidence that pointed to different conclusions. Historians, if not economists, today begin—or at least they should—the study of any topic with a question, or series of questions, and study all the available evidence in search of answers. They may have some notion before they begin as to what the answers will be, but if the evidence subsequently indicates that they were wrong then they have to draw the conclusions that emerge from the evidence. Frequently it happens that the original questions are found to be of less significance than other questions that emerge from the evidence and have to be pursued. Innis, however, began with answers, not with questions, and thereby he went sadly astray. All too often his arguments defy both the evidence and logic, the latter sometimes being akin to asserting that wind is caused by the trees waving their branches.

For half a century this work has been regarded as definitive, and hence historians have, until very recently, shied away from a re-examination of the fur trade. This is most unfortunate since the trade played such an important role, not just in the economy of New France, but in the framing of its social structure, in military affairs, and in the execution of colonial policy that, in the final analysis, determined the fate of both the French and the British empires in North America. All of these aspects of the fur trade are long overdue for thorough investigation.

The Fur Trade and Eighteenth-Century Imperialism

This paper was an attempt to place the Canadian fur trade of the eighteenth century in a broader context than that of merely the striving, on the part of the French, to buy cheap and sell dear. Today the economic tail wags the political dog; then, in the French scheme of things, economics were subservient to political ends. Colonies existed to support France in one way or another. In Canada's case the Canadians, and the allied Indians and their trade in furs, were to be mobilized to check the growing, overweening might of Britain in America. The following article most certainly is not the last word; much, much, more research and thought about the results remains to be done.

The North American fur trade of the seventeenth and eighteenth centuries has usually been viewed, until recently, as merely another commercial enterprise governed by the premise 'buy cheap, sell dear' in order to reap the maximum profit. Of late, the Canadian end of the trade has come to be regarded as having been more a means to a non-commercial end than a pursuit conducted solely for economic gain. As European penetration and dominance of the continent progressed, the trade, which had begun as an adjunct of the Atlantic shore fishery, became a commercial pursuit in its own right. After 1600, when the first Roman Catholic missionaries were sent to New France, it became a means to finance and further that tragic drive to convert the Indian nations to Christianity. This attempt continued until mid-century, when the Jesuit mission in Huronia was destroyed, along with the Hurons as a nation, by the Iroquois Confederacy.[1] For the rest of the century the fur trade of New France went through vexed and troubled times.[2]

Stability was temporarily restored to the trade in 1663, when the Crown took over the colony from the Company of One Hundred Associates. Near the end of the century a huge glut of beaver fur completely disrupted the market in Europe and caused Louis Phélypeaux de Pontchartrain, the minister of marine responsible for the colonies, to try to force the Canadian fur traders to withdraw from the West completely. For political reasons this could not be done. Despite its economic unviability, the French, in order to maintain good relations with the Indian nations, were forced to continue the trade in furs. Then, in 1700, on the eve of a new war in Europe, Louis XIV embarked on an expansionist policy in North America to hem in the English colonies on the Atlantic seaboard. From that point forward, the fur trade was used mainly as a political instrument to further the imperial aims of France.

In the 1650s, after the Iroquois had virtually destroyed the Huron nation and scattered the Algonkian nations allied with it far to the west, French traders began to push into the interior of the continent, where they established direct trade relations with the hunting nations that had previously supplied furs to the Huron middlemen. These traders, a mere handful at first, voyaged through the Great Lakes and beyond, then down into the Mississippi Valley. This French thrust into the West occurred just as the Five Nations Iroquois Confederacy, having subdued the tribes surrounding them and being well supplied with firearms by the Dutch and English merchants of Albany, embarked on an imperialistic drive to conquer and control the Ohio Valley, a region almost as vast as the kingdom of France.[3] Their first incursion into the region in 1678 was repelled by the Illinois nation. The following year Robert Cavelier de La Salle began establishing fur-trade posts on the Illinois River and thereby claimed suzerainty for the French Crown over the lands of both the Illinois and the Miami nations.[4]

In 1680 the inevitable clash came between these rival imperial powers. La Salle's lieutenant, Henri de Tonty, attempted to mediate when an Iroquois army invaded the Illinois country. He received a nasty wound for his pains but managed to escape to Michilimackinac with his men.[5] The French presence in the West was now seriously threatened. An attempt to cow the Iroquois by military force failed miserably. Instead, the Iroquois dictated humiliating peace terms to the governor-general of New France, Le Febvre de La Barre, and stated their determination to destroy the Illinois, whom the French claimed to be under the protection of Louis XIV. When La Barre protested this arrogant Iroquois declaration, the great Onondaga chief and orator, Hotreouati, brusquely retorted, 'They deserve to die, they have shed our blood.'[6] To that La Barre could make no response. When Louis XIV was informed of what had transpired, La Barre was summarily dismissed from his post and recalled to France in disgrace.[7]

The long-range aim of the Confederacy appears to have been to bring under subjection all the Indian nations south of the Great Lakes as far as the Mississippi, and at the same time to divert the western fur trade from Montreal to Albany, with the Confederacy controlling it. Because the Iroquois failed to provide a written record of their aims, their motives cannot be determined with certainty, yet their actions and the policies they pursued during the ensuing decades indicate clearly enough that what they sought was power—dominance over this vast region—rather than mere commercial advantage.

A few years after this Franco-Iroquois struggle in the interior of North America was joined, events occurred in Europe that were to affect it profoundly. The Revolution of 1689 ousted James II and brought William of Orange, bitter enemy of Louis XIV, to the throne of England. This ushered in hostilities between England and France that were to occupy nineteen of the ensuing twenty-four years. The Iroquois, now confident of English military aid, pressed their attacks against the French in the West and at their settlements in the St Lawrence Valley, inflicting heavy casualties. The settlers, aided by some 1,500 *Troupes de la Marine*, regular troops sent from France, managed to beat back these attacks and in the process became, of necessity, highly skilled at guerilla warfare. The alliance with the Indian nations who had long feared the Iroquois was strengthened and the war was carried to the enemy. Iroquois casualties mounted, and the frontier settlements of their ineffectual English allies were ravaged by Canadian war parties. Both the Iroquois and the English colonials were relieved when, in 1697, the war ended in Europe. The Iroquois, now bereft of English logistical support, their fighting strength reduced by casualties and disease to half what it had been, were forced to sue for peace.[8]

This proud people had not been brought so low, however, that they would accept any terms that the French cared to impose. Consequently the negotiations dragged on for four years. Moreover, the twenty-eight tribes allied with the French had to be party to the peace treaty that was eventually drawn up at Montreal in 1701. The principal factor that now made possible an enduring peace between the French and the Iroquois, thereby ending a war that had lasted for nearly a century, was that the French negotiators recognized the Iroquois presence to be an essential buffer between their Indian allies in the Northwest and the English colonies. Moreover, the Iroquois had learned to their cost that they could not rely on the English for military support. Rather they perceived that the English had always sought to make use of them merely to serve English ends. There was no longer any question of the French seeking to destroy the Iroquois; in fact just the reverse had become the case. The Iroquois had now to abandon all hope of ever driving the French out of Canada or from the posts in the West. The French presence had become essential to them to balance that of the English and to allow them to play one off against the other. Thus the French negotiators were able to insert a clause into the peace treaty declaring that in any future war between England and France, the Iroquois would remain neutral. At one stroke the greatest military threat to New France and the main defence of New York had been eliminated; and this occurred just as England and France were preparing for a renewal of hostilities that were to last for more than a decade.[9]

On the French side the preceding wars had been fought for a specific Canadian aim, control of the western fur trade, and France had provided the military aid needed to achieve that end. The ensuing wars were to be fought solely for French imperial aims. In 1701, with the War of the Spanish Succession about to erupt, Louis XIV declared that the English colonies must be hemmed in between the Atlantic and the Appalachians. On no account were the English to be allowed to flood over that mountain range to occupy the region between it and the Mississippi. Were they to do so, Louis feared, their numbers would swell immeasurably and England's wealth and power would increase proportionately. In all likelihood they would then push southwest to conquer Mexico with its silver mines. With Louis XIV's grandson now on the throne of Spain, France had to defend the Spanish colonies as though they were her own.[10] Louis XIV feared that English domination of North America would upset the balance of power in Europe. The French in America, with their Indian allies, were to be the means of containing the English colonies.[11] In the implementation of this imperial policy the fur trade had a vital role to play, of an importance far in excess of its economic value.

In 1701 Louis XIV gave orders for the creation of the new colony of Louisiana, in the Mississippi Valley, to forestall the English, who, it was reported, planned to establish a settlement at the mouth of that great river.[12] Another French settlement was ordered to be placed at the narrows between Lake Erie and Lake Huron. This new colony, to be named Detroit, was intended to bar English access to the Northwest and maintain French control of the western Great Lakes.[13] It is not without significance that the Canadian merchants and the royal officials at Quebec were bitterly opposed to both these settlements, declaring that they would be the ruin of Canada—Detroit, because it would bring the Indian nations allied with the French into close proximity to the Iroquois, who might grant them access to the Albany traders; Louisiana, because the fur traders who obtained their trade goods on credit from Montreal merchants would be tempted to defraud their creditors by shipping their furs to France from the port to be established on the Gulf of Mexico.[14]

French imperial policy now required that the Indian nations of the West and of Acadia be welded into a close commercial alliance and that all contact between them and the English colonists be prevented by one means or another. The main instruments of this policy, it was envisaged, would be missionaries and fur traders. The great age of French proselytization that had produced the Jesuit martyrs was, however, a thing of the past. The clergy were eager enough to serve, but some of them were ill suited for the task and too often their efforts were hampered by squabbling among rival groups—

secular priests with Jesuits, Capuchins with both. For several years the bishop of New France was an absentee, unable to restore order and discipline from his residence in Paris.[15] Thus the implementation of this new policy was left to two groups: the Canadian fur traders and the officers and men of the colonial regulars, the *Troupes de la Marine*, who garrisoned the re-established posts.

The fur trade was now definitely subordinated to a political end. It was required to pay a large share of the costs of maintaining a French presence in the interior to bar the English from it. The West was divided into regions, each with a central post commanded by an officer of the colonial regulars. For some years these officers were not permitted to engage in the trade, the sole right to which in each region was auctioned off to merchants on a three-year lease.[16] When it was found that this led to exploitation of the Indians by merchants whose only aim was to make as great a profit as possible during their lease, the trade was turned over to the commandants, who could, it was thought, be kept under tighter control by the senior officials at Quebec.[17] Complaints against them by the Indians could bring instant recall and might jeopardize promotion or the granting of commissions to sons.

The post commandants usually formed companies in partnership with Montreal merchants who provided the trade goods, hired the *voyageurs*, and marketed the furs, and with professional traders who took charge of the actual trading with the Indians. The *modus operandi* was thus very simple: the companies usually comprised three men for a three-year term, at the end of which the merchant who had supplied the goods withdrew their cost, and whatever profit or loss remained was shared by the partners.[18] At the main bases of Michilimackinac and Detroit the trade was open to all who obtained a permit from the governor-general and paid the base commandant his 500-*livre* fee. From these fees the commandants had to pay the costs of maintaining the posts, thereby sparing the Crown the expense.[19]

Louis XIV, in order to end the war that was reducing his government to bankruptcy, agreed to make sweeping concessions on the Atlantic frontier of New France to avoid having to make them in Europe. He therefore agreed to cede Newfoundland and Acadia, the latter 'within its ancient limits', to England. A joint commission was appointed to determine those limits; but, predictably, no agreement could be reached and France retained Cape Breton, where it proceeded to construct the fortress of Louisbourg as a naval base for the protection of French maritime interests in the North Atlantic. The British continued to claim title to all the land up to the St Lawrence River, and it was upon the Indian nations of the region—the Abenaki, Micmacs, and Malecites—that the French relied to hold the English back from the vital St Lawrence waterway.[20] The governor-general at Quebec made sure that those nations were well supplied with all the European goods they needed, and that a continual state of hostility existed between them and the expanding population of New England.[21]

In the implementation of this policy the French received unwitting aid from the New England settlers. What the latter coveted most was land for settlement, the very lands that the Indians required to maintain their hunting economy and that they believed had been granted them by God for that very purpose. The Indians denied that they were or ever had been subjects of either the French or the English Crown. They asserted vehemently that the French could not have ceded their land by treaty as the Massachusetts authorities claimed, since no one could cede what had never been his.[22] Although the French, with their meagre population, did not covet any of that land, they were determined to deny it to the English. In 1727 the king stated in a *mémoire* to the governor-general and intendant at Quebec that he had learned with pleasure that the Abenaki of Saint-François and Bécancourt intended to continue the war against the English and not entertain proposals for peace until the English had razed the forts they had built on Abenaki lands. 'This is so important for Canada', the *mémoire* went on, 'that the Sieur de Beauharnois could not take measures more just than such as would foment that war and prevent any accommodation.'[23]

To the north, where France had relinquished its claims to Hudson Bay, a dispute arose over the interpretation of the covering clause in the Treaty of Utrecht. The British claimed that they had thereby gained title to all the lands whose waters drained into Hudson Bay—almost a quarter of the continent. They themselves, however, negated their claim by insisting that the operative clause in the treaty state that France *restored* rather than *ceded* to Great Britain the lands claimed by the latter—this in order to establish that Britain had always had the prior claim. France agreed but riposted by declaring that only the lands that Britain had formerly occupied could be restored to her: by definition, restoration could not be made of lands that had never been conquered, purchased, or occupied.[24] In fact, merely an infinitesimal fraction of that vast territory had ever been seen by a British subject. The argument was really an academic one, since the Hudson's Bay Company made no attempt to challenge French control of the interior. As long as enough furs reached its posts to produce a dividend for its shareholders, the company's servants were content to remain in a 'sleep by the frozen sea'.[25]

The French now established fur-trade posts on the rivers that ran down to the Bay and thereby controlled the flow of furs to the English. They kept the choicest furs for themselves and allowed the Indians to trade only their poorer quality pelts at the Bay Company's posts.[26] Had it not been that the Indians were astute enough to maintain trade relations with both the English and the

Canadians in order to reap the advantages of competition, Britain's hold on Hudson Bay would early have been severed.[27]

From the signing of the Treaty of Utrecht in 1713 to the conquest of New France, the French maintained their presence among the nations of the West, penetrating steadily farther into the interior until they eventually reached the barrier of the Rocky Mountains.[28] Only at Detroit, Kaskaskia, and Cahokia in the Illinois country, and on the lower Mississippi, were they able to establish small agricultural settlements.[29] Elsewhere they merely maintained fur-trade posts consisting of three or four log buildings surrounded by a palisade. Always these posts were placed in an area that no Indian nation claimed as its own—Detroit, for example—or were established with the express permission of the dominant nation of the region. Some of the posts had been maintained during the Iroquois war, ostensibly as bases and places of refuge for the nations allied with the French against the Iroquois Confederacy. Experience had proven that posts on the fringe of Iroquois-controlled territory were more prisons than forts. Their garrisons did not dare venture beyond musket range of the palisades, and too many of the men—deprived of fresh meat or fish, reduced to hard rations of stale salt pork and sea biscuit—succumbed to scurvy.[30]

After the Iroquois wars of the seventeenth century, and with the proclamation of Louis XIV's containment policy in North America, fur-trade posts had to be sustained among all the nations that could conceivably have contact, direct or indirect, with the English colonials or the Hudson's Bay Company. With the exception of the Sioux nation, who always kept the French at arm's length, most of the nations were glad to have these posts on their territory. Although the French maintained that the posts gave them title to the land, their claims were made to exclude the English, not to deny the Indians' title, something they did not dare do. The French were certainly not sovereign in the West, for sovereignty implies the right to impose and collect taxes, and to enforce laws—and they were never able to do either. The Indians never considered themselves to be French subjects, and the French were never able to treat them as such.[31] Moreover, the Canadian *voyageurs* who transported trade goods and supplies to the western posts and took the furs back to Montreal always had to travel in convoy for protection against the Indians through whose lands they passed. One or two canoes alone were an invitation to extortionate demands or outright pillage.[32] The Indians allowed the French only the right of passage to the posts, since this assured them a ready supply of European goods close at hand. The land on which the trading posts stood they considered still to be theirs, the French occupants being mere tenants during the Indians' pleasure.

Another significant factor in this imperial rivalry was the superiority of most French trade goods. In only one item, woollen cloth, did the English have an advantage, and even this is open to question. The factors at the Hudson's Bay Company's posts were continually pleading with their superiors in London to provide them with goods of the same quality as those traded by the French.[33] In one of the more important trade items, liquor, the French had a distinct advantage. Showing commendable good taste, the Indians greatly preferred French brandy to the rot-gut rum and gin supplied by the British and Americans. The Hudson's Bay Company produced imitation brandy made from cheap gin, adulterated to give it the colour and something resembling the taste of cognac, but it never replaced the real thing in the Indians' opinion.[34] Alcohol was crucial in the fur trade for two reasons. First, the Indians craved it more than anything else; even though they knew that it could destroy them, they could not resist it, and they would go to any lengths to obtain all that was available.[35] Second, from the purely economic aspect of the trade, alcohol was the ideal exchange item. Of other goods—cloth, wearing apparel, pots, knives, axes, muskets—the Indians had a limited need. It is now coming to be recognized that they were by no means as dependent on European goods as has been claimed.[36] A musket would last many years, as would other metal goods. A few items of clothing each year per family did not result in large entries in the Montreal merchants' ledgers. An Indian hunter could garner enough pelts in a couple of months' good hunting to provide for his family's needs, but the appetite for *eau de vie* was virtually insatiable, driving the Indians to produce furs in ever larger quantities. In the 1790s a Nor'wester, Duncan McGillivray, remarked, 'When a nation becomes addicted to drinking it affords a strong presumption that they will soon become excellent hunters.'[37]

The French traders who lived among the Indians were only too well aware of the terrible effects that liquor had on their customers. Frequently they paid for it with their lives when Indians, in their cups, went berserk and set about them with knife or *casse tête*.[38] Some of the senior French officials who were involved in the fur trade for personal gain tried to make light of these dread effects. Governor-General Louis de Buade, comte de Frontenac, for example, contended vociferously that the Indians did not get any more drunk, or behave any worse when in their cups, than did the average Englishman or Netherlander.[39] The French missionaries, in particular the Jesuits who resided in the Indian villages, knew better. They fought to have liquor barred completely from the trade and threatened excommunication for any traders who persisted in its use.[40] Governor-General Philippe de Rigaud de Vaudreuil and his successor, Charles de la Boische, marquis de Beauharnois, both recognized the horrors caused by the liquor trade, but for political reasons they had to condone it, while at the same time striving to restrict its use to prevent the worst abuses. As they and others pointed out to Jean-Fréderic Phélypeaux, comte de Maurepas, appointed minister of marine in 1723, were they to refuse to trade alcohol the Indians would go to the Anglo-American traders, who had no scruples whatsoever, despite frequent pleas from tribal chieftains to keep the rum pedlars out of their villages.[41] Thus in the imperial contest liquor was a powerful but pernicious weapon.

Throughout the eighteenth century the Montreal fur traders took the lion's share of the North American fur trade. The customs figures for fur imports at London, La Rochelle, and Rouen make this plain.[42] Moreover, the Albany merchants who dominated the Anglo-American fur trade admitted that they obtained the bulk of their furs clandestinely from the Canadians.[43] It could hardly have been otherwise, since they did not have access to the Northwest, which produced the fine-quality furs. The minister of marine, Maurepas, and after 1749 his successor, Antoine-Louis Rouillé, comte de Jouy, continually demanded that the smuggling of Canadian furs to Albany be stopped, but to no avail.[44] They simple-mindedly believed that if the English desired something, then France must strive to deny it to them. The senior officials at Quebec well understood the complexity of the situation. They declared vociferously that they were doing everything possible to curb this clandestine trade, but the evidence indicates that their unenthusiastic efforts were less than efficacious. They tolerated the existence of an agent of the Albany traders at Montreal and frequent visits of the merchants themselves. Similarly, Montreal traders called at Albany from time to time, and credit arrangements between the merchants of the two centres were extensive.[45] One suspects that the governor-general and the intendant despaired of bringing first Maurepas, then Rouillé, ministers of marine, to grasp how closely intertwined were the economics and politics of the situation. Certainly they did not make a determined attempt to explain the subtleties of the issue.

The main agents of this clandestine trade were the Christian Indians of Sault St Louis and Lake of Two Mountains missions, both close by Montreal.[46] The Canadian officials claimed that they dared not forbid these Indians to trade at Albany whenever they pleased lest they become disaffected and quit Canada. Since their services were vital in time of war, and in peacetime as intelligence agents, they had to be indulged. Thus they quite openly transported Canadian furs to Albany, along with fine French cloth, wines, and spirits, on behalf of Canadian merchants.[47] In fact Governor-General Beauharnois declared that the Mission Iroquois of Sault St Louis constituted virtually an independent republic over which he had no authority.[48]

Although the Canadian fur traders undoubtedly reaped considerable benefits from this clandestine trade, a far more significant consequence was that it removed any incentive the Albany merchants might have had to contest the hold of the French over the western nations.[49] This issue was of great concern to the Crown officials of New York, who took an imperial view of the situation, but the Albany merchants were interested only in preserving their well-established Canadian trade. When furs were shipped to their doors by the Canadians at prices that afforded them a good profit, they saw no reason to incur the great risks, capital outlay, and trouble that would be involved in trying to compete with the Canadians on their ground, the Indian country of the Northwest. Moreover, they lacked the birch-bark canoes, the *voyageurs* to man them, and the prime requisite, the willingness to accept the Indians on their own terms—in short, all the special skills needed for this particular trade.[50] In November 1765 Sir William Johnson commented sadly on this phenomenon to the Lords of Trade:

> I have frequently observed to Your Lordships, that His Majesty's subjects in this Country seem very ill calculated to Cultivate a good understanding with the Indians; and this is a notorious proof of it, for notwithstanding the Expence of transporting Goods from New Orleans to the Illinois is greater than by the Lakes and Consequently French goods are in general Dearer than Ours, yet such is the Conduct of all persons under the Crown of France, whether Officers, Agents, Traders, that the Indians will go much farther to buy their Goods, and pay a much higher price for them. This all persons acquainted with the nature of the Commerce to the Westward can fully evidence.[51]

Nor was the trade all one way. The Iroquois made annual trips to Canada to confer with the French authorities. The Crown officials of New York were deeply worried by the influence that the French gained over the Iroquois during these visits. The French entertained the Iroquois delegates lavishly, after a fashion that the British officials could not or would not match.[52] In October 1715 the Albany Indian commissioners stated: 'Trade between Albany & Canada is of fatal Consequence to the Indian Interest of this Colony, that of our Indians who are employed in it many stay at Canada & others return so Attached to the French Interest & so Debauched from ours that it puzzels them how to preserve amongst them that Respect & Regard to this Gov't so necessary to the Public Good and Transquillity.'[53]

By 1720 the French had gained a secure hold on the Great Lakes basin by ringing it with garrisoned fur-trade posts. Although the mercantile interests of New York were not perturbed by this development, the Crown officials were, and they sought to counter it. In 1719 the governor general of New France, Vaudreuil, heard reports that New York intended to establish a fort at Niagara, which would have given the English access to the West, including the Mississippi Valley. Vaudreuil very adroitly forestalled them by obtaining the permission of the Senecas to establish a post on their land at the mouth of the Niagara River. Ostensibly the post was to serve their needs; in reality it barred the West to the English.[54] The following year another post was established at the Toronto portage, barring that route from Lake Ontario to Lake Huron.[55]

Although the Iroquois had given the French permission to establish the post at Niagara and bluntly told the protesting Albany authorities that they had 'given the French liberty of free Passage thru Lake Ontario',[56] they had no desire to see the French become overpowerful in the region. To balance their position they therefore granted New York permission to build a trading post at Oswego on the south shore of Lake Ontario across from Fort Frontenac. At the same time deputies from the Iroquois Confederacy met with the Albany Indian commissioners, who reported that the Indians 'exhort us to live in Peace and Quiet with the French and carry on our Trade without Molesting each other'.[57] The Quebec authorities responded by claiming that the south shore of the Great Lakes belonged to France by right of prior discovery and conquest.[58] Governor-General Beauharnois began making preparations for a campaign to take and destroy Oswego, but he was restrained by the government in France, which at the time enjoyed good relations with Great Britain, this being the era of the *entente cordiale* established by Cardinal André-Hercule de Fleury and Robert Walpole.[59] Nevertheless the Canadian authorities replaced the trading post at Niagara with a solid stone edifice that would have required heavy canon to demolish, greatly to the dismay of the Albany authorities.[60]

Events were to demonstrate that Oswego posed no serious threat to French control of the Great Lakes. The fear was that it would seduce the western nations out of the French alliance by undercutting the French prices for furs and, more particularly, by the unrestricted sale of liquor. But here again, as at Albany, the New York traders were their own worst enemies. They did indeed supply all the cheap liquor the Indians desired, but the latter, when under its influence, were unmercifully cheated and their womenfolk debauched.[61] This bred bitter resentment.

Oswego posed an additional problem for the authorities at Quebec. Some of the less-scrupulous Canadian traders found it convenient to obtain large supplies of cheap rum there, as well as English woollens, which they traded at the distant Indian villages.[62] In an attempt to keep both the allied Indians and the renegade Canadians away from the English post, the French government retained the trade at forts Frontenac, Niagara, and Toronto as Crown monopolies so that prices could be kept competitive with those at Oswego by selling at a reduced profit or even a loss if necessary. The commandants at these posts had to see to it that nothing transpired that could upset the Indians and endanger their alliance with the French.[63]

The French thus managed to maintain a tenuous hold over the interior of North America west of the Appalachians, and in the vast region north and west of the Great Lakes as far as the Rocky Mountains. This tremendous feat was, moreover, accomplished at very little cost to the French Crown and by a mere handful of men. In 1754, when this military fur-trade empire was nearing its greatest extent, the cost to the Crown for maintaining the garrisoned posts was but 183,427 *livres*.[64] The number of officers and enlisted men in these garrisons in 1750 was only 261,[65] but in addition there were the men engaged directly in the trade with the Indians—the *voyageurs*, traders, clerks, and merchants—whose number cannot be calculated with any great degree of accuracy. All that can be offered here is an educated guess that the number directly employed in the western fur trade for the period 1719 to 1750 would have ranged from about 200 for the earlier years to some 600 at most by mid-century.[66] This means that with fewer than 1,000 men France maintained its claim to more than half the continent.

Had the French been content to confine their activities to the fur trade they might well have retained their control, in alliance with the Indian nations, over the northern half of the continent—that is, over the area that today forms the Dominion of Canada. However, the interests of the Canadian fur traders and French imperial policy began to diverge at mid-century, immediately after the War of the Austrian Succession. Fur traders from Pennsylvania and Virginia, serving as advance agents of land-speculation companies, had begun to penetrate the Ohio Valley by way of the Cumberland Gap with pack-horse trains.[67] To win the allegiance of the Indian nations they flooded the region with cheap trade goods, liquor, and expensive presents for the chiefs. A Canadian officer later declared, 'The presents that they receive are so considerable that one sees nothing but the most magnificent gold, silver, and scarlet braid.'[68] The Canadian fur traders had no interest in the furs of that region, which were of poor quality.[69] They preferred to confine their activities to the Northwest, where the furs were the best obtainable, river communications far easier than they were south of the Great Lakes, and the Cree tongue was a lingua franca in the entire region.

Marquis Roland-Michel Barrin de la Gallissonière, governor-general of New France, in opposition to the prevailing and strongly held Canadian sentiment, advocated that the Ohio Valley be occupied by the French and that forts be built and garrisoned, merely to deny the region to the English. He freely admitted that it would be of no economic benefit to France in the foreseeable future, but he feared that were the English to succeed in occupying and settling the valley they would become extremely powerful and dangerous. They would eventually sever communications along the Mississippi between Canada and Louisiana and then go on to conquer Mexico with its silver mines.[70]

The minister of marine, Rouillé, newly appointed to the post and without previous experience in colonial affairs, accepted this policy. Despite the strong opposition of the senior Canadian officials in the colonial administration,[71] and at immense cost in funds and Canadian lives,[72] the French drove the American traders out of the region. They established a chain of forts and supply depots from Lake Erie to the forks of the Ohio, thereby overawing the local tribes, who quickly abandoned their commercial alliance with the Anglo-Americans and pledged their support to the French.[73] This was accomplished by *force majeure* pure and simple, and the Indian nations remained in this uneasy alliance only as long as it appeared to them to suit their interests and, as events were to show, not a day longer.

Previously when the French had extended their fur-trade empire into new territory they had always done so at the invitation, or at least with the tacit consent, of the Indians. In the Ohio Valley, however, Gallissonière's successor, Ange de Menneville, marquis Duquesne, made it plain to the Iroquois, who claimed sovereignty over the region, that he would brook no interference, that he regarded the valley as belonging to the French Crown, and that if they chose to oppose him he would crush them.[74] Some of his Canadian officers, long accustomed to dealing with the Iroquois, were more diplomatic. They pointed out that the French did not covet the land but merely wished to prevent the English from seizing it, and that the Indians could hunt right up to the walls of the French forts, whereas wherever the English went the forest was destroyed and the animals driven out, the Indians with them.[75]

Here also the Anglo-Americans were the agents of their own defeat. They had treated two nations on the frontiers of Pennsylvania and Virginia, the Shawnee and the Delaware, so ruthlessly, seizing their land by dint of fraudulent title deeds, debauching them with liquor, murdering them with impunity, that it did not require a great deal of persuasion by the French to bring these Indians into a close military alliance once hostilities broke out.[76] This rejection of the Anglo-Americans was immeasurably strengthened by the initial French victories, first over Major George Washington's motley provincial force at Fort Necessity, where Washington accepted humiliating terms and fled back over the mountains; then, a year later when Major-General Edward Braddock's army of 2,200 British regulars and American provincials was destroyed near Fort Duquesne by 250-odd Canadian regulars and militia and some 600 Indians.[77]

The French were now able to arm and send out Indian war parties, accompanied by a few Canadian regulars or militia, to ravage the frontiers of the English colonies from New York to Georgia, thereby retaining the initiative and tying down large British and provincial forces. Successful though it was, this strategy posed massive problems in logistics that the minister of marine, Jean-Baptiste de Machault d'Arnouville, and his staff at Versailles were never able to comprehend. Appalled by the Canadian accounts for 1753, he warned Governor-General Duquesne that unless the excessive costs of the western posts were reduced, the king would abandon the colony.[78] He thereby blandly overlooked the fact that the expenditures had been incurred in consequence of his ministry's policy and direct orders. To implement this policy all the needs of the Indian allies had to be supplied.[79] This required the transport of vast amounts of goods from Montreal to Forts Niagara and Duquesne by canoe, barque, horse, and pirogue. The wastage at the Niagara portage alone was appalling. In 1753 Duquesne complained to Captain Paul Marin de la Malgue, commander of the Ohio expedition, that he had learned that forty-eight canoe loads of supplies had been stolen or spoiled by being left uncovered in the rain. He voiced the suspicion that the Canadians, who were bitterly opposed to the Ohio adventure, were destroying the supplies deliberately to force its abandonment.[80]

For many years the western Iroquois had demanded and received the right to carry all fur-trade and military supplies over the portage, which they regarded as their territory. This was a cost that the Crown officials at Quebec had been quite willing to see imposed on the fur traders in order to maintain good relations with the Iroquois Confederacy. Governor-General Duquesne, however, considered excessive the 40,000 *livres* a year that it was now costing the Crown to have military supplies transported around Niagara Falls by the Senecas. At the grave risk of alienating them and the other Iroquois nations, he had horses shipped from Montreal and dispensed with the Senecas' services. Many of the horses then mysteriously vanished.[81]

For the Canadian officers charged with the implementation of these orders, the task at times seemed insuperable. A lack of rain meant low water in the shallow rivers that linked Lake Erie, with a fifteen-mile portage, to the Ohio. The supply boats and pirogues then had to be manhandled along the river beds, driving both officers and men to despair.[82] To make matters worse, the Indian allies were extremely demanding and wasteful. Their loyalty could be counted on only as long as their demands for goods and services were met, and frequently not even then. In 1756 Vaudreuil ruefully explained to the minister of marine:

I am not in the least surprised that expenses have risen so high, the Indians are the cause of immense expenditures, forming the largest part of those charged to the Crown in the colony. One has to see to believe what they consume and how troublesome they are. I deny and reduce their demands as much as I can at Montreal, but despite it they succeed in having themselves equipped several times in the same campaign. They continually come and go between the army or the posts and Montreal, and one is forced to supply them with food for every trip which they justify by claiming that they have been refused things by the army, or that having been on a raid they must now return home, or they dreamt that they ought to do so. Every time that one wants to send them to support the army one cannot avoid supplying them. When they go on a war party they are given 10, 12, or 15 days rations . . . at the end of two days they return without food or equipment and say they have lost it all, so they have to be provided afresh. They consume an astonishing quantity of brandy and a Commandant would be in grave difficulties were he to refuse them, and so it is with all their requests.[83]

One important factor, all to often overlooked, was that these Indian nations fought alongside the French purely to serve their own needs. They were allies, not mercenaries. In fact they regarded the French as little more than an auxiliary force aiding them in their struggle to preserve their hunting grounds from further encroachment by the Anglo-Americans and to oblige the latter to treat them with respect.[84] this was compellingly illustrated when, in May 1757, the American colonial authorities entered into negotiations with Iroquois, Shawnee, and Delaware tribes to end the fighting that had destroyed their frontier settlements to a depth of over a hundred miles. For once the Indian negotiators refused to be put off with vague promises; in the past they had been hoodwinked all too often. Eventually a Moravian missionary, Frederick Post, who sympathized deeply with the Indians, went to the villages of the Shawnee and Delaware. There, within sight of Fort Duquesne, with frustrated French officers in attendance, the proposed terms of the Easton Treaty were promulgated.[85]

The Indian nations south of the Great Lakes then ceased to support the French. When Brigadier-General John Forbes, marching on Fort Duquesne with an army of some 7,000 British regulars and American provincial troops, suffered heavy and humiliating losses at the hands of the Canadians and Indians in one brisk battle, he deliberately slowed his advance until he received word that the Indians had signed a separate peace, the Easton Treaty. That defection left the French no choice but to abandon Fort Duquesne and, with it, control of the Ohio Valley. Colonel Henry Bouquet commented: 'After God the success of this Expedition is intirely due to the General, who by bringing about the Treaty of Easton, has struck the blow which has knocked the French in the head . . . in securing all his posts, and giving nothing to chance.'[86]

The following year, 1759, Quebec and Niagara fell. Despite a valiant last attempt by the French and Canadians under François de Lévis to retake Quebec in the spring of 1760, six months later they were compelled to surrender to the armies of Major-General Jeffery Amherst at Montreal. This spelled the end of French power on the mainland of North America.

The fate of that empire had been decided by the incompetence of its government at home and that of the headquarters staff—with the exception of the Chevalier de Lévis—of the army sent to defend Canada. During the course of the war there had been four controllers-general of finance, four of foreign affairs, four of war, and five of the marine.[87] In the fateful year, 1759, the minister of marine was Nicolas-René Berryer. Before his appointment to that post in November 1758 he had been *lieutenant de police* for

Paris.[88] As for the army sent to Canada, its morale and efficiency steadily deteriorated under the command of the incompetent, defeatist Louis-Joseph, marquis de Montcalm. It was not a shortage of supplies or overwhelming enemy superiority or corruption that brought on the British conquest of Canada. The West was lost when the Indian allies defected. Louisbourg fell because it lacked a fleet to protect it. Canada fell after the loss of Quebec in a battle that should have been won crushingly by the French but was lost owing to the stupidity and panic of Montcalm.[89] Even then Quebec might well have been retaken by Lévis had the minister of marine dispatched in time the reinforcements that Lévis had requested.[90] Etienne-François, duc de Choiseul, who was given charge of the ministries of war, foreign affairs, and marine, then decided that it would serve the interests of France better were England to acquire Canada since, with the menace of French power removed from mainland America, England's colonies could be counted on to strike for independence in the not-too-distant future. France's loss of Canada, Choiseul decided, would be as nothing compared to England's loss of her American colonies.[91]

If the Canadians had had control of French policy in North America, neither the decisive battle at Quebec nor, for that matter, the war itself would likely have taken place, for the Canadians had no real quarrel with the English colonies. In war the Anglo-Americans had demonstrated time and again that they were no match for the Canadians and their Indian allies. Their record in the Seven Years' War indicated clearly enough their lack of enthusiasm for the conflict.[92] The Canadians knew that they had little to fear from that quarter, nor did they have any illusions that they could conquer the English colonies. In commerce there was no real conflict between them. The fur trade was of vital economic importance to the Canadians but certainly not to France, and of little, and that declining, importance to the Anglo-Americans. Among the latter, a group of well-placed rapacious land speculators and a barbarian horde of would-be settlers coveted the lands of the Indian nations on their frontier, a region that the Canadians had made plain was of no interest to them. The Albany merchants who dominated the Anglo-American fur trade chose not to compete with the Canadians; instead they entered into a cosy commercial partnership. They had not exhibited any eagerness to dispute the French hold on the West. As for the Hudson's Bay Company, its steadily declining returns indicated its inability to compete with the Canadians; moreover, it no longer had the same influence that it once had wielded in government circles. It was a monopoly, and all trade monopolies were then being looked at askance in Britain.[93] Only the shareholders would have wept had the Hudson's Bay Company been driven to the wall by the Canadians.

For over half a century the fur trade was used by France as an instrument of its foreign policy and, owing to the peculiar skills of the Canadians, with considerable success. By means of it, most of the Indian nations supported the French cause in the colonial wars, but they did so only as long as it appeared to them to serve their immediate interests. The French were acutely aware of the Indians' true feeling towards them. Governor-General Beauharnois remarked that they had their policies just as had the French. 'In general', he stated, 'they greatly fear us, they have no affection for us whatsoever, and the attitudes they manifest are never sincere.'[94] A certain Monsieur Le Maire put the French position very succinctly, explaining that there was no middle course: one had to have the Indians either as friends or as foes, and whoever desired them as friends had to furnish them with their necessities, on terms they could afford.[95] The policy of the Indian nations was always to play the French off against the English, using the fur trade as an instrument of their own foreign policy.[96] Their tragedy was not to have foreseen the consequences were the French to be eliminated from the equation.

La Mer de l'Ouest:
Outpost of Empire

When one receives an invitation to give a paper at a conference to be held at a place that holds some interest, not necessarily academic—expenses paid and an honorarium to boot—it is not easy to resist. The roles of Grand Portage and Fort William in the fur trade were important enough to make a visit to these places worthwhile. Thus I accepted to give a paper at the Fourth North American Fur Trade Conference, 1981. My paper was to be given after the customary banquet, thus the main aim had to be to make sure the audience stayed awake. That is not always an easy task at such affairs, hence the paper had to be kept short. I was also requested to bear in mind that it was the 250th anniversary of La Vérendrye's arrival at the site. What follows is what the participants heard.

Two hundred and fifty years ago Pierre Gaultier, sieur de la Vérendrye, wintered at Grand Portage at the outset of his attempt to discover a route to the western ocean. Since the days of Verrazano and Jacques Cartier the French had dreamed of one day finding a way to the China sea. Samuel de Champlain, in appealing to the Crown in 1617 for support of his commercial venture at Quebec, declared that, 'one may hope to find a short route to China by way of the river St. Lawrence; and that being the case, it is certain that we shall succeed by the grace of God in finding it without much difficulty; and the voyage could be made in six months.' In carefully assessing what revenues could be derived from New France, he estimated that the customs duties to be levied on goods passing from Asia to Europe by this short route would be at least ten times greater than all those levied in France. The revenue from the trade in furs, it might be noted in passing, ranked very low in his prospectus.[1]

In 1634 he dispatched Jean Nicollet de Belleborne to the Baie des Puants to pacify the warring tribes of the region and to make inquiries about the Western Sea, which he believed could not be far distant from the Baie. With a commendable respect for mandarin protocol, Nicollet took with him a colourful flowered robe of Chinese damask in order to be properly attired when he met the eastern emperor's representatives. When his canoe landed at La Baie and he stood up in this apparel, he succeeded in frightening the wits out of the local tribesmen, if nothing else.[2]

The eventual discovery that the Mississippi River did not flow into the Pacific came as a disappointment;[3] but, as the maps of La Haye and Franquelin indicate, French knowledge of the extent and shape of the continent was, before the end of the seventeenth century, quite remarkable. Yet one peculiar myth persisted: that somewhere between the 40th and 50th parallels of latitude there was a vast inland sea, La Mer de l'Ouest, connected by a navigable strait to the Pacific Ocean. It was believed that this sea of the West stretched to within a few days' journey of Lake Superior. Royal Geographer Guillaume de l'Isle so described it in a memoir of 1706, and on his map of 1717 it is depicted as reaching more than half way to the Mississippi.[4] It may well be that de l'Isle and those many others who accepted this notion were influenced by the seventeenth century's love of symmetry. Since there was a huge bay, the Gulf of Mexico, in the southeast corner of the continent, Hudson Bay in the Northeast, and the Gulf of California in the southwest, then there had to be a similar gulf in the Northwest to balance them.

Before the end of the seventeenth century, Canadian *coureurs de bois* had voyaged hundreds of miles west of Lake Superior and were reputed to have reached Lake Winnipeg, or the Lac des Assinibouels as it was then called.[5] The glutting of the beaver market in France in the 1690s temporarily curbed westward expansion, but the decision, on the eve of the War of the Spanish Succession, to establish a base at Detroit and a new colony at the mouth of the Mississippi in order to prevent English expansion into the West, thrust the French into the interior.[6] It thereby pitted some 15,000 Canadians against the burgeoning population of the English colonies, estimated to be over a quarter million at the turn of the century.[7]

Prior to the Seven Years' War the French never had more than a few hundred men in the West, certainly fewer than a thousand. In 1750, when French expansion in the West had reached its limits, the troops garrisoning the posts from Fort Frontenac to La Mer de l'Ouest numbered only 261 officers and man.[8] In addition there were those engaged in the fur trade, *voyageurs*, clerks, tradesmen, and a few missionaries. It is unlikely that they exceeded, at the most, 600 at any one time.[9] As for the *coureurs de bois*, their numbers can only be guessed at—probably fewer than 200—and the role they played in extending French influence was, to say the least, equivocal. It is almost incredible that with this mere handful of men the French were able to lay claim to most of the continent for over half a century.

The seventeenth-century wars fought by Canada against the Iroquois, and later against the English colonies, had been fought for purely Canadian ends: security of the colony and control of the fur trade. In those wars France had unstintingly provided the military aid needed to achieve those ends. The ensuing wars of the eighteenth century were to be fought for the achievement of purely French imperial aims. From 1700 on New France was a mere instrument of French imperial policy, to contain the English colonies on the seaboard and tie down as large a part of the British army and navy as possible. This had to be done by enlisting the support of the Indian nations. If their active support was not to be obtained, then at least they had to be prevented from aiding the Anglo-Americans.[10] In this Anglo-French contest the fur trade became all important; it became a means to a political end rather than an economic end in itself. The French had to provide goods and services to the Indians in exchange for furs and military aid, at prices that were competitive with those of the English traders. In this they proved to be eminently successful.[11] They garnered the lion's share of the fur trade, and in the wars they had the support of almost all the Indian nations except the eastern Iroquois who, for the most part, remained neutral.[12]

The Indians were willing to allow the French to place trading posts on their lands and to travel through their territories; in fact they sometimes requested the establishment of such posts, but always these posts were maintained on their terms.[13] The French had to court them assiduously, bestow lavish presents on them,[14] entertain them extravagantly when they visited Montreal or Quebec,[15] send some of their chiefs to France to view the splendours of Paris and Versailles,[16] and overlook their frequent excesses. Many Canadians were killed in the Indian country, and the French but rarely were able to obtain redress.[17]

The French claimed title to all these lands through which they voyaged, but these claims had about as much substance as the claim of the kings of England to the crown of France. In reality these claims were made merely to exclude the English, and sometimes they were made without the Indians' having any notion that the French thereby maintained that they had taken possession of the land. The Chevalier de La Vérendrye, for example, laid claim to the lands of the *Gens de la Petite Cérise*, in what was later to be South Dakota, by surreptitiously burying an inscribed lead plaque, brought from Quebec for the purpose, beside a stone cairn. When questioned by the Indians as to its significance, the Chevalier told them that it was just to mark the occasion of his visit.[18]

The Indians regarded the land as theirs and themselves as subject to no one.[19] They tolerated the presence of the French because it suited them; when it ceased to do so, they quickly made their feelings known. Thus the post established among the Sioux had to be abandoned during the Fox wars; it was later re-established, but in 1731 it had to be abandoned once again.[20] Similarly the uprising of the nations at Detroit in 1747 made plain how tenuous was the French hold on the West.[21]

In fact French sovereignty in the West existed only within French posts, beyond no farther than the range of French muskets. En route between Montreal and the West the *voyageurs* had to travel in armed convoys. Every man had to carry a musket and return with it on pain of four months' imprisonment.

When Father Aulneau was about to leave with La Vérendrye, his friend and fellow Jesuit, Father Nau, remarked, with greater prescience than he knew: 'He has a good enough escort, but if these unknown peoples whom he seeks are ill-intentioned what could twenty French do against an entire nation?'[22] The French were not sovereign in the West; the Indian nations were.

In Europe, meanwhile, the Treaty of Utrecht of 1713 had ushered in thirty years of peace between England and France. In North America, however, the political climate was more akin to a cold war. French policy here was dictated by the expectation of future hostilities. How best to prepare for them? In 1716 the Minister of Marine instructed the governor-general and intendant at Quebec that attempts by the English to extend their influence into areas that incontestably belonged to France had to be opposed gently but firmly.[23]

That was the political climate when the French government decided that a determined effort should be made to discover a land route to the western ocean. Politics were not the only motive for the quest. Scientific curiosity and the desire of the Regent, the duc d'Orléans, and his entourage to have France gain the glory of first making this great discovery, were major factors in the decision. It was rather akin to President John Kennedy's determination that the first man to set foot on the moon should be an American. The thirst for knowledge of the continent's interior had previously contributed to Louis XIV's decision to establish the colony of Louisiana. La Salle's explorations had failed to determine the precise geographic location of the mouth of the Mississippi. As the historian Marcel Giraud put it: 'The topic held the attention of the erudite and the men of science, members of the *Académie française*, of the *Académie de Science*, of the *Académie des Inscriptions*. Some were interested essentially out of a spirit of scientific curiosity. . . . But national ambitions were, in general, combined with purely scientific pre-occupations.'[24]

In 1692 Louis Phélypeaux de Pontchartrain, minister of marine, was given charge of the *Académie de Science*. He gave it a new constitution, strengthened it immeasurably, and made it the chief instrument of French scientific leadership. Science was now accepted as a department of the modern state.[25] Scientific expeditions were sent to Peru, near the equator, and to the polar regions, in order to measure degrees of latitude and check Newton's theory that the earth is flattened at the poles.[26]

Canada was by no means excluded from this scientific inquiry. At Quebec, Michel Sarrazin, king's physician and corresponding member of the *Académie*, was sending plants to the *Jardin des Plantes* in Paris and reporting on Canadian animals that he had dissected as early as 1706. His devotion to science was indeed commendable; but then he, like many of us today, had to justify his annual grant in aid of research.[27] The intendant Claude Thomas

Dupuy brought with him a sizeable collection of astronomical instruments.[28] His successor, Gilles Hocquart, kept Father Gosselin and the Sieur Hubert Joseph de la Croix, surgeon and botanist, busy shipping plants to Georges-Louis Leclerc de Ruffon, *intendant du Jardin du Roi*,[29] thereby most likely unwittingly providing the ship's officers with mid-ocean salads. This interest in science permeated the upper levels of Quebec society among those who dined at the tables of the governor and intendant and who felt obliged to keep abreast of what interested those exalted dispensers of coveted patronage. This was something upon which Peter Kalm, professor of botany at the Abo Academy in Finland and member of the Swedish Academy of Science, who visited Canada in 1749, commented on at some length in his journal.[30]

As early as 1717 the Crown had given its official blessing to the search for the elusive Mer de l'Ouest. This support could well be described as all aid short of help. In July of that year Governor-General Vaudreuil had sent Lieutenant Zacharie Robutel de la Noue with eight canoes to establish three posts that would serve as bases for the discovery of the western sea. These posts were to be at Kaministiquia, Lac de la Pluie, and the Lac des Assinibouels, which would at that time have been either the Lake of the Woods or Lake Winnipeg.[31] The *Conseil de Marine* approved the project but insisted that it not cost the crown a *sou*. The proceeds from trade at the posts had to bear the costs. The council and the regent who made the final decision did agree that the Crown must underwrite the expenses of the voyage of discovery beyond the advance posts because the men chosen for it should not be concerned with trade, only with exploration. It was estimated that it would take two years and cost as much as 50,000 *livres*. The regent agreed that the funds should be provided, requiring only that the cost be kept as low as possible.[32] Three years later no advance had been made beyond Kaministiquia, and when a request was made to the Crown for 47,000 *livres* for another two-year venture, the regent decreed that it would have to be deferred.[33]

The Crown did, however, send Father Pierre-François-Xavier de Charlevoix, who had taught at the Collège de Québec for some years, on a fact-finding mission to discover the most practicable route to the western sea. After voyaging to Michilimackinac, to La Baie des Puants, and then to New Orleans he opined that the Missouri would be the best route since the elusive sea must be between 40 and 50 degrees of latitude.[34]

During these years all manner of strange tales were brought out of the West by the *voyageurs*, likely enlivening the long winter evenings in the Montreal taverns. These tales were of a people in the Far West who lived in French-style houses. Father Nau, the Jesuit missionary at Sault St Louis near Montreal, concluded that these people must be, not Spaniards, but Tartars who had fled the Japanese. This, to him, opened up the possibility of a rich new missionary field. He cautioned, however, that one had to view everything that the Canadians related with the deepest suspicion. 'For,' he declared, 'there is not a country in the world where they lie more than they do in Canada.'[35]

In 1730 Lieutenant Pierre Gaultier de Varennes et de La Vérendrye, commandant of the *poste du nord* at Kaministiquia, offered to establish a post on Lake Winnipeg as a base for a thrust to the western sea, and this at no cost to the Crown apart from some 2,000 *livres* worth of presents for the Indians. The proposition was accepted by the minister of marine, and so his oft-recounted odyssey began. There is no need here to discuss his career, his exploits, disappointments, or his failure to come anywhere close to his objective. For an officer who had served in both Europe and Canada, he appears to have been neither a good disciplinarian nor a competent administrator. He was manifestly a poor businessman and his finances were always in disarray.[36] Yet he has captured the imaginations of later generations of historians whose accounts of his career tend to be more panegyrics than critical studies. One thing about him cannot be disputed: his main concern in life, like that of most of his class, was *la gloire*, recognition, renown—to bequeath to his children not so much wealth, although that would certainly have been desirable, as a great name. In his case it was to be attained by his being the first Frenchman to reach the Western Sea.

Although in the commissions of all the *commandants* at the western posts—La Baie, Poste du Nord, Mer de l'Ouest—appeared the injunction that they send their men west to the legendary sea, few of them appear to have made any great effort to do so. The minister of marine complained that the Canadians sought not the sea of the west but the sea of beaver.[37] In a lengthy letter to Le Gardeur de St Pierre, dated May 15, 1752, business associate Meuvret made it plain that their sole concerns were the volume of furs and slaves being shipped to Montreal and the prices received.[38] Paul Marin de la Malgue, *commandant* at La Baie in 1750, was exhorted by the governor-general and the intendant to press on with the exploration required by the terms of his commission.[39] His successor and son Joseph's journal makes plain that Joseph was too fully occupied striving to keep the peace among the constantly warring tribes in his region to risk his men's lives in a war zone.[40]

Yet the criticism of these men who served in the West by officials comfortably ensconced at Versailles or Quebec was somewhat gratuitous. Just to survive in such a hostile environment was no mean feat. There they were, completely isolated, hundreds of miles and weeks in travel time removed from Montreal,[41] a score or two of men amidst a horde of Indians who might, at any time, decide that these foreigners had outlived their welcome. The extreme cold of the long, bitter winters in that bleak part of the world, with the men cooped up in drafty, hastily constructed log and clay huts, must have created morale problems. Isolation and confinement can make men who normally get on well together become irritable and barely able to endure each other's company. Under such circumstances men can do strange things. When they begin talking to the trees, one need not worry unduly. It is when the trees begin talking back that those in charge should become concerned.

Those who commanded at these western posts—men like La Vérendrye, St Pierre, Paul and Joseph Marin de Malgue, de Villiers, and others—had to be soldiers, obeyed by the Canadians and overawing the Indians by sheer force of character. They had to be astute diplomats, adept courtiers in their dealings with their superiors at Quebec, careful financiers and entrepreneurs in trade. The hardships they had to endure, the risks they ran, were enough to make most men quail, yet these postings were avidly sought by the colony's leading families. As Madame Bégon commented, when the postings were announced, the families that had been denied were livid with rage at those who had received western appointments.[42] They were, in peacetime, the best route to advancement in the service, offering financial rewards far in excess of a lieutenant's or captain's meagre pay. A captain, after all, received only 90 *livres* a month,[43] and a gentleman's life required an income of some 3,000 a year.[44]

The logistics of transporting food supplies, trade goods, tools, arms, and ammunition from Montreal to Michilimackinac to the far western posts by canoe was a constant nightmare for La Vérendrye and his successors, as their journals make plain. Father Nau, in October 1735, wrote to the mother of Father Aulneau: 'Nothing could be more heroic than the new sacrifice that our dear Father Aulneau has just made in leaving for the Mer de l'Ouest. I am not afraid to tell you that it is the longest, most arduous and most dangerous voyage that a missionary has ever made in Canada.'[45]

The *voyageurs*' rations en route were meagre, as valuable cargo space could not be wasted on food, and the less to carry over the portages the better. Leached corn and bear grease, with venison when available, was the staple fare. One bushel of leached corn and two pounds of bear grease were considered sufficient to last a man a month.[46] In addition each voyageur was allowed to take four *pots* (equivalent to eight litres) of brandy for his own use.[47] It was considered essential for the digestion. On the other hand, the officers in this hierarchical society were not stinted. Their official rations at the posts included generous quantities of butter, olive oil, vinegar, a large variety of spices, sugar, molasses, wine, and a litre of cognac per week.[48] Both officers and men were expected to live off the land to the greatest extent possible. Vegetable gardens were planted, but since corn, meat, and fish were the staples, scurvy was a constant menace. During the long winter months starvation was rarely far removed.

Sickness was another danger. Although the main posts had a surgeon on staff, given the state of medical knowledge and the predeliction for bleeding and purges a sick man's chances were likely better without those ministrations. La Vérendrye's nephew, La Jemerais, died on the banks of the Red River of some unknown lingering disease.[49] Years later both Le Gardeur de St Pierre and his lieutenant, Joseph-Claude Boucher, Chevalier de Niverville, were long delayed in their thrust up the Saskatchewan by a fever of some sort.[50] Just how serious disease could be when the entire garrison of a post was stricken was demonstrated at Toronto in 1751. The *commandant*, the Chevalier de Portneuf, sent an almost frantic appeal for aid. He blamed the disease that had struck him and his men on the bad air of the place and noted that 'the most robust of men were in a desperate condition from the onset. . . .'[51] It may have been malaria; but whatever, the incident will likely confirm many latter-day suspicions about the place.

The most important and most difficult task that the officers commanding the posts in the West had to face was putting an end to inter-tribal warfare. From time immemorial nation had warred with nation as extensions of blood feuds, for revenge, and in many instances merely because young braves wished to demonstrate their courage and martial prowess. The French— themselves not the most docile of peoples—sought to prevent these constant skirmishing wars from flaring up, and when they did, to negotiate a swift end to them.[52] In the instructions issued to Le Gardeur de St Pierre, when he was appointed to command at the Mer de l'Ouest, it was stated that his principal task would be to keep the nations there at peace and to do everything possible to keep the Cree from attacking the Sioux. Similar instructions were issued to all the post commanders. From the French point of view these wars were extremely costly, and frequently instigated by the English. Indeed, everything that caused trouble for the French in the West, or anywhere else for that matter, could be blamed on the English. The same paranoia dominated men's minds to as great a degree on the other side of the hill.

These inter-tribal wars frequently resulted in the loss of Canadian lives,[53] and for the French to offer comfort to one side meant incurring the enmity of the other. This was particularly the case in the two regions where bases for the thrust to the western sea were located: la Baie des Puants and the Mer de l'Ouest. This vast area was the frontier of Sioux territory and that of the Cree and the Assiniboine. La Vérendrye paid a heavy price for lending support to the northern tribes in a campaign against the Sioux. His son Jean-Baptiste and twenty of his men were subsequently massacred by the Sioux in retaliation.[54]

In 1753 Joseph Marin de la Malgue, *commandant* at La Baie, intervened after the Illinois had launched a surprise attack on the Puants and Sakis, killing three Sakis and a Canadian blacksmith.[55] Those two tribes appealed for aid to their allies: the Sioux, Folles Avoines, and Iowa. Several hundred of the warriors informed Marin that they were sure he would be glad of their aid to seek revenge for the killing of the Canadian whom the Illinois had hacked to pieces. It was only with the greatest difficulty, and the expenditure of over 10,000 *livres* worth of trade goods as presents, that he persuaded them to desist, reminding them that they had destroyed an entire Illinois village a year previous and that they had got off lightly with only three of their people killed.[56]

Two other major tasks were imposed on these officers: to prevent the Indian nations from having any dealings with the English at either Hudson Bay or the seaboard colonies, and to keep the Canadian traders in order. On the whole, the French were successful in both tasks. For the first purpose, posts were established when necessary, such as the one in 1751 at Lac de la Carpe,[57] northeast of Lake Nipigon, or that in the country of the Ouyatanons and Miamis.[58] It is true that the English, both at Hudson Bay and in the Thirteen Colonies, garnered sizeable quantities of furs; but virtually all that was exported from New York was obtained not from the Indians but clandestinely from Canadian traders by way of Albany and Oswego.[59] Since the French paid higher prices for such small furs as marten and otter and the English more for beaver, a lively exchange flourished between the Canadians and traders from New York, Pennsylvania, Virginia, and the Carolinas.[60] There is even cause to suspect that a proportion of the furs shipped from the Hudson Bay ports on the Albany River were provided by Canadians who found it more convenient to send a canoe a day's paddle to a Bay post when they needed supplies than all the way back to Montreal.[61] Both parties benefited, and what officials at Quebec and directors in London did not know would not hurt them.

Maintaining order among the Canadians in the West does not appear to have created any insuperable problems. The *voyageurs* who signed on with a notarized contract thereby agreed to obey all honest, legal, orders, and they did not receive their pay until the completion of their contract on their return to Montreal.[62] Those who frequently caused trouble were sent back under armed guard to face trial.[63] In the notarized engagement of one *voyageur*, the company hiring him inserted a clause stating that the *engagé* accepted that if he were to seek any inopportune quarrels while going up country or returning, his wages would be forfeit. The *engagé* insisted on a qualifying clause that the forfeiture would transpire only if any such fracas as might occur were, as the notary phrased it, *mal à propos*—uncalled for.[64]

From the posts established by La Vérendrye, furs were not the only item shipped down to Montreal. Indian slaves taken by the Cree and Assiniboine in their interminable war with the Sioux were purchased by the French and sold at a high profit in Canada. One, for example, was sold at auction in 1733 for 351 *livres*.[65] With beaver prices at four *livres* the pound at Quebec, a robust slave was the equal of a pack of prime beaver.[66] La Vérendrye boasted of the large number of slaves that he had shipped to Montreal over the years.[67]

Sometime between 1734 and 1737 Governor-General Beauharnois issued strict orders that no more slaves were to be purchased from the Assiniboine, 'it being', he declared, 'of the greatest consequence for the colony to put a stop to this trade.'[68] The prohibition does not appear to have endured long. In 1757 Colonel Bougainville reported that the Cree and Assiniboine sold from 50 to 60 Panis slaves a year to the French, along with three to four hundred packs of fur at the Fort des Prairies alone.[69]

These Indian slaves do not appear to have been too badly treated by their Canadian owners. Several of them were allowed to hire on as *voyageurs* at the same wages and conditions as Canadians. For the years from 1719 to 1726 six such engagements were registered in the notarial *greffes* at Montreal.[70] How many others served as *voyageurs* without such contracts but with a mere private written or oral commitment can never be known. Obviously their masters were confident they would return.

Some of these slaves were used for a humanitarian purpose. In 1748, when England and France were at war, Governor-General Galissonière wrote to Le Gardeur de St Pierre, commandant at Michilimackinac, asking him to purchase seven or eight slaves on the king's account. Galissonière had promised to provide them to the mission Indians, most likely the Abenaki of Bécancourt or St François, in exchange for English prisoners they had taken. This, he stated, would satisfy the most stubborn of these tribesmen and was the only way to get them to release their English prisoners.[71]

Canadian historians, for the most part, have not been kind in their judgements of St Pierre, whereas there has been almost universal praise for La Vérendrye. Yet St Pierre had a far more distinguished military career than did La Vérendrye. He put George Washington courteously but firmly in his place at Fort Le Boeuf in 1753,[72] he maintained control over his men, and he was far more adept in his negotiations with the Indians. This was made manifest when he caused a band of hostile Assiniboine who had invaded Fort La Reine, with the obvious intention of knocking the traders on the head and pillaging the stores, to flee precipitately. He merely picked up a keg of gunpowder, knocked off the lid, snatched a brand from the fire, and strode into their midst. He then told them that before they could execute their obvious design he would have the glory of taking them to the next world with him. They took the fort's gate off its hinges in their haste to depart.[73] There was nothing that the Indians admired more than such actions as St Pierre's.

St Pierre does appear also to have made one determined effort to reach the western sea. Some of his latter-day critics deny that Fort La Jonquière, which the précis of his journal states was established at the Rocky Mountains, was anywhere within hundreds of miles of those mountains, some placing it far to the east of the forks of the Saskatchewan.[74] Yet in the abstract of his journal it is stated that his lieutenant, de Niverville, sent ten of his men in two canoes 300 leagues beyond Fort Pascoya to the Rocky Mountains where, in May 1751, they built a good fort. A fresh outbreak of hostilities, following on a treacherous attack by some Assiniboine on a nation called Ihatche8ilini [*sic*], forced St Pierre to abandon all notion of maintaining that post, let alone pushing beyond it. He therefore concurred with Governor-General la Jonquière, who believed that the Missouri was the best route to the western ocean, since the Saskatchewan was manifestly too far north.[75] As long as the Assiniboine and the Cree persisted in their wars with neighbouring tribes it would, he asserted, be impossible to maintain a secure route across the northern plains.[76]

It would have been utter stupidity for him to fabricate this tale of a post at the Rocky Mountains in the journal that he was required to submit to the governor-general, who would merely have had to question de Niverville or any of his men to expose it. Therefore, unless convincing evidence can be produced that St Pierre's men did not reach the Rocky Mountains, his statement has to be accepted. It cannot be dismissed out of hand. That, surely, is one of the acknowledged rules of evidence.

If one accepts that for a brief few months Fort La Jonquière existed, where was it? Some day previously unknown documents may give us the answer; St Pierre's actual journal, or letters of de Niverville, could, for example. Such documents do surface from time to time, but until they do one can only conjecture. A.S. Morton claimed that if the French had gone beyond the forks of the Saskatchewan, which he denied, then they would have taken the south branch.[77] J.B. Tyrell argued, much more cogently, that they most certainly would not have taken the south fork.[78] On the face of it the mere fact that the South Saskatchewan ran through country that swarmed with buffalo, elk, and gophers, rather than the prime light furs that the French sought, would have caused them to take the north branch, which runs close to the fur-bearing parkland. Moreover the north branch was in Cree country, whose language was the lingua franca of the fur trade. To the south lay their mortal foes, the Blackfeet, who wanted nothing from Europeans since, as they told Anthony Hendry, the buffalo sufficed for all their needs. Bows and arrows were all that they required to kill them.[79] Since fur traders had a tendency to build their posts on the site of earlier existing ones, Fort La Jonquière may well have been built where Rocky Mountain House later stood. All that is needed to prove the hypothesis is sound evidence.

Finally we must ask why the French did not achieve their goal of being the first to cross the continent. If those bumbling American army officers,

Lewis and Clark, could eventually do it, why could not the far more experienced Canadians? St Pierre blamed his failure on the constant wars being waged by the Indian nations at the instigation of the English. To put an end to those wars the English would, he claimed, have to be driven out of Hudson Bay, and he asked that when the opportunity arose he be given the command.[80] There was some truth in what St Pierre stated, although the English at Hudson Bay were certainly not responsible for the Indian wars. He, his predecessor La Vérendrye, and Paul and Joseph Marin at La Baie went to great lengths to end the Sioux, Cree, and Assiniboine wars. Frequently they believed they were on the verge of success, only to have hostilities suddenly flare up again.

Seen, however, from the Indian point of view, why should they have ceased warring with each other at the behest of the French? For centuries it had been part of their way of life. How else could their young men distinguish themselves, display their valour, gain renown?

When the Sioux now suffered heavy casualties at the hands of enemies armed and supplied by the French, and when many of their women and children were sold into slavery at Montreal, it did not induce them to pay more than lip service to the demands of the French who patronizingly addressed them as children of Onontio, the governor-general far away at Quebec.[81] Similarly the Cree and Assiniboine, who when suddenly attacked while hunting had called out 'Who kills us?', must have taken it amiss when the answer came, 'The French Sioux.'[82] These were the woodlands Sioux who were supplied by the French traders at the headwaters of the Mississippi.

The Indians tolerated the French on their lands only because they provided useful services, a readily available source of goods, and a blacksmith to repair their tools, cooking pots, and weapons. They certainly did not regard them as a superior race. Physically the French were an inferior lot, much smaller than the Indians, their faces and bodies covered with hideous matted hair.[83] Without the Indians to show them the canoe routes and to hunt for them, they would have starved to death. Admittedly they fought well when they had to, and their *eau de vie* set a man up wonderfully, transporting him ever so swiftly to the spirit world. As for the vexing black-robed medicine men who sought to change the Indians' habits, they were easily ignored. Moreover, these French could not be trusted. They did not always live up to their commitments, as the Cree and Assiniboine pointed out when they demanded to know when La Vérendrye was going to establish a post at the foot of Lake Winnipeg as he had promised.[84] Sometimes they failed to have an adequate supply of goods on hand in the spring when the Indians brought in their winter's catch, and they sometimes altered the prices of their goods for no discernible reason. The goods were the same as ever, the furs of as good quality; therefore the price should not change. Sometimes, too, they were stingy with what they called their presents, but what the Indians regarded as tribute for being granted permission to travel through Indian territory and establish their posts. The best that could be said of them was that they were easier to deal with than the English. They could be tolerated because it had become difficult to get along without their goods; moreover, there were so few of them that they could not possibly constitute a threat to the Indian nations. As for their constant queries about, and search for, a vast body of salt water off to the west, the Indians had heard of it and some claimed to have been there, but they could hardly be expected to help the French find it.[85] Were the French to establish posts among those far Indians, the Cree and Assiniboine of the Lake Winnipeg region would be eliminated as traders.[86]

Despite all the problems that the French had to face in the Far West, there is no question that they could have reached the Pacific had they really been determined. It would have required a chain of garrisoned posts as supply bases across the Prairies and into the mountains and a separate 50-man military expedition to press on to the ocean. For the officers the prospect of promotion and the Croix de St Louis would have been incentive enough. For the men the promise of an immediate discharge and a half-pay pension upon their return would have found most of the troops in the colony rushing to volunteer.

There is just one nagging *caveat* to this hypothesis. When the continent was eventually crossed—first by Alexander Mackenzie in 1793, then in 1805 by Lewis and Clark—conditions in the West were far different than in La Vérendrye's and Le Gardeur de St Pierre's day. The Indians in the earlier period, their nations numbering thousands of warriors, were truly sovereign and independent, answerable to no one, and skilled at playing the English and French off against each other. By the end of the century their power was broken and a great flood of liquor and the smallpox epidemics (1780–1, 1786) had decimated and demoralized them.[87] They could then offer little opposition to encroachments on their lands. They were already bowing to the seeming inevitable.

The final question can still fairly be asked. Why did the French government of the day not make the effort? Why did it insist that the fur trade must bear the cost and the travail of the search for the route to the western ocean? Why did it will the end but not the means? One obvious reason is that its finances were always in disarray, and the department of marine was always at the end of the line when funds were doled out. Another reason may well have been that the authorities in Canada had begun to doubt the existence of the legendary Mer de l'Ouest. By 1750 they had accepted that if it did exist it was beyond a massive barrier, the Rocky Mountains.[88]

The underlying reason for failure, however, appears to be that the niggardly attitude of the French government in this particular instance was part and parcel of a more general attitude towards New France. The colonies of Canada and Louisiana cost the Crown considerable sums each year. They, unlike the Antilles, were not a paying proposition. They were maintained for a purely political purpose, the containment of England's American colonies,[89] and this had to be done at the lowest possible cost to the Crown. The ministry of marine firmly believed that colonies existed for the benefit of the mother country; it was not the other way around. As late as 1754 the then minister of marine, Jean-Baptiste de Machault d'Arnouville, informed the governor-general at Quebec that if the expenses recently incurred in pursuance of his predecessor in office's orders to occupy the Ohio Valley were not curbed, then His Majesty would surely abandon the colony altogether.[90] It was this attitude that prevented the French from reaching the western sea. In the longer term it also resulted in the loss of the French empire in North America. Given the meagre means at their disposal, the wonder of it is not that the French did not reach the Mer de l'Ouest, but that they accomplished as much as they did.

The Social, Economic, and Political Significance of the Military Establishment in New France

Little needs to be said about this article. For some time I had been impressed by the important role played by the military in New France. I finally decided to muster all the material on the topic that I had garnered over the years to see if a pattern, or patterns, emerged. The end result quite surprised me. Since writing the article more evidence has emerged but none of it contradicts—it merely strengthens—the arguments put forward sixteen years ago.

Mirabeau remarked that the primary industry of Prussia was war. The same could as aptly be said of New France. If it were possible to have an accurate accounting—unfortunately, it is not—it likely would be found that the military establishment ran the fur trade a close second as the economic mainstay of the colony. But it was not only the economy that was affected by this establishment. The whole fabric of Canadian society was imbued with the military ethos. This in itself was in remarkable contrast to the Anglo-American colonies. Moreover, the role selected for New France in eighteenth-century French imperial policy was that of the military fortress: a small garrison tied down a much larger enemy force and so prevented it from interfering with more important military operations elsewhere.

Attempts to establish colonies in both North and South America began with Francis I in order to offset the growing power of Spain and the Hapsburgs. They were a distinct failure. French interest in North America was maintained by the fishermen of the Atlantic and Channel ports until the fur trade proved profitable enough to warrant the establishment of permanent settlements in Acadia and at Quebec to protect and nourish the commercial bases. The religious revival in France in the early seventeenth century provided a futher incentive for colonization: to aid the missionary drive as the Roman Catholic orders took up the challenge offered by the pagan Indian nations.

Within a few months of the establishment of the commercial base at Quebec, the French were thrust into military action to aid their Indian commercial partners in their perpetual war with the Iroquois. As the fury of the Iroquois attacks on the struggling French settlements mounted, the peasant-stock colonists were obliged to become soldiers. Every male capable of bearing arms, and many of the women, had to be ready to fight for their lives at a moment's notice. In 1651 Pierre Boucher, captain of Trois-Rivières, formed the beleaguered settlers into militia units. Twelve years later the governor of Montreal, Paul de Chomedey, Sieur de Maisonneuve, formed the hard-pressed settlers at this frontier bastion into what he piously called the Militia of the Holy Virgin. The squads of this formation had the distinction of electing their officers, an innovation happily without consequence.[1] The commercial companies exploiting the fur trade were loath to provide troops because of the expense. They desired the maximum profit with the minimum over-head. Thus it was the Crown and the Society of Jesus that provided most of the funds to pay the handful of soldiers who were sent to the colony. In 1647 there were one hundred regular troops in garrison at the three centres of settlement; the following year their complement was reduced to sixty-eight.[2]

Eventually, to avert the destruction of the colony by the mass assaults of the Iroquois, the crown had to intervene. In 1662 Louis XIV dispatched one hundred regulars to the colony. Three years later Lieutenant-General de Tracy[3] arrived at Quebec with four companies of regular troops. Four companies of the Carignan-Salières regiment had already arrived and twenty more landed at Quebec two months later. In all, there were now approximately 1,300 regular troops in the colony, at a time when the civilian population was estimated to be 2,500. In other words the military now comprised almost thirty-five per cent of the total European population. This military force, in a rather blundering manner, succeeded in bringing the Iroquois to terms, and the colony enjoyed a twenty-year surcease from their devastating attacks.[4]

In addition to gaining security for the settlers, these regular troops brought economic prosperity to the tune of 150,000 *livres* a year for their subsistence alone.[5] The significance of this can be gauged by the fact that Colbert had decreed that the civil budget must not exceed 36,000 *livres* a year.[6] In 1665 Marie de l'Incarnation of the Ursulines commented in a letter to her son: 'Money, which was rare in this country is now very common, these gentlemen having brought a great deal with them. They pay for everything they buy with money, both their food and their other necessities, which suits our *habitants* very well.'[7]

When the regiment was recalled to France in 1668 several of the officers and 400 of the men chose to remain. Each man received a discharge grant of 100 *livres*, the sergeants 150 *livres*.[8] The following year fresh military blood was added to the population when six army captains, twenty-four junior officers, and 333 soldiers arrived as a unit to take up land and settle. They too received a subsistence grant amounting to over 52,000 *livres*.[9] Thus the colony retained, all told, nearly 800 regular officers and men. This figure must have exceeded the number of adult males who were resident in the colony in 1665.[10]

At the same time as these military forces swelled the population a new administrative system was imposed on the colony by the Crown, an administration organized on distinctly military lines. Throughout the regime the governors-general and local governors were career officers in either the *troupes de terre* or the *Troupes de la Marine*. The office of intendant was part military in origin and still retained a great many purely military functions.[11] The civil population was not subject to military law, but with this notable exception the government of New France was, in essence, military government.

In 1669 the entire male population between the ages of sixteen and sixty was, on orders of the King, organized into militia units. In every parish a company was formed. In the more populous parishes the companies had a captain, a lieutenant, and an ensign; in those more sparsely populated a captain sufficed. In the three governmental districts a commandant of militia, a major, and an aide-major had overall command under the local governors.[12] These officers, almost all of them *habitants* rather than seigneurs,[13] had to muster the men periodically and ensure that they had serviceable muskets and acquired a rudimentary acquaintance with discipline. Neither officers nor men were paid. The intendant Raudot appealed to the minister to grant the *capitaines* an honorarium of 100 *livres* a year and the rank of sergeant in the colonial regular troops,[14] but the Crown, always financially hard pressed, saw no reason why it should pay for what it customarily received for nothing. The captains of militia enjoyed an elevated social status; the men accepted militia service as a proper obligation, if not always cheerfully, at least willingly.[15] In addition to their purely military function the *captaines de milice*, although appointed by the governor-general, served as agents of the intendant throughout the countryside to see to it that his *ordonnances* were carried out and law and order maintained.[16] What is particularly significant, however, is that the entire male population was armed, and could be swiftly mobilized by its *habitant* captains. This gave Canada a tremendous advantage in time of war over the adjacent English colonies.

In 1683, when the Iroquois reopened hostilities against the French in the west, the Minister of Marine was reluctantly persuaded to send 150 *Troupes de la Marine* to Quebec. These were regular troops, raised to guard the French naval bases and to serve in the colonies. They were under the authority, not of the minister of war, but of the minister of marine who guarded his prerogative very jealously.[17] The manner in which these troops were organized was a radical departure from seventeenth-century practice, reflecting Colbert's reforming zeal. They were grouped not in regiments but in independent companies of fifty men, *les compagnies franches de la Marine*, each commanded by a captain. Thus one of the more serious abuses attendant on the European regimental system was obviated. On both the continent and in England most regiments were the private property of their colonels, bought and sold at very high prices, and expected to bring a reasonable return on the initial investment. In the better French infantry regiments in the eighteenth century the colonelcy cost some 75,000 *livres*, and cavalry regiments more. Companies also had to be purchased, and although commissions below the rank of captain were not strictly venal, a few thousand *livres* frequently had to be forthcoming before a colonel could find room in his regiment for a *lieutenant* or an *enseigne*.[18] No matter how able a junior officer might be, if he lacked money and influence there was little hope of advancement. In the *Troupes de la Marine*, in contrast, certainly in Canada, commissions were not purchased and promotion was based squarely on merit, as determined by the governor and the intendant who submitted a separate annual report on each officer to the minister.

As the Iroquois menace increased, more *Troupes de la Marine* were sent to Canada, until by 1685 they numbered over 1,600,[19] at a time when the civilian population was less than 11,000. These troops did not live in barracks but were billeted on the people, and all things considered there was, so far as we know, little trouble.[20] Moreover, the men provided a sorely needed pool of labour for the colony, working on the land for wages, or in the towns as tradesmen, while most if not all of the officers held seigneuries.[21] They were, in short, well integrated into the colony's social and economic life.

Peter Kalm, the Swedish professor of botany who toured Canada in 1749, was struck by the general prosperity of the regulars. He noted that they were very well fed and clothed, paid regularly, enjoyed good relations with their officers, and were particularly well treated on discharge.[22] These conditions were in marked contrast to those of the regular troops in the adjoining colony, New York. In 1700, on the eve of war, the Lords of Trade complained that the 400 troops supposedly on strength in that province had been reduced to fewer than 200 by death and desertion; that these survivors were in a miserable condition, almost naked and about to perish 'by reason of the great arrears that are due unto them'.[23] Lord Bellomont, governor of the colony, reported in July 1700:

> The soldiers there in Garrison [at Albany], are in that shameful and miserable condition for the want of cloaths that the like was never seen, in so much that those parts of 'em which modesty forbids me to name, are expos'd to view; the women forced to lay their hands on their eyes as often as they pass

by 'em. This sad condition of the Soldiers, does us great hurt with the Indians . . . they being a very observing people, measure the greatness of our King, and the conduct of affairs, by the shameful ill plight of the Soldiers . . . Some of the old crafty Sachems of the Five Nations, have ask'd . . . whether they thought 'em such fools as to believe our King could protect 'em from the French, when he was not able to keep his Soldiers in a condition, as those in Canada are kept; who by the way . . . are 1400 men, and duly paid every Saturday in the year.[24]

Society in New France, like virtually all societies in all places at all times, can be divided into two main segments: the mass of the people at the base, and the dominant class comprising perhaps 1 per cent of the population. In Canada the first group comprised the *habitants*, the artisans, and urban labourers. They, for the most part, did not aspire to rise in the social scale. Satisfied with their status, they were concerned with maintaining their family security, their creature comforts, and simple pleasures. They made up the body of the militia and saw active service in all the colony's wars. As Ruette d'Auteuil remarked in 1715, from infancy the Canadians were accustomed to hunt and fish, to undertake long voyages by canoe, and this had made them tough. Moreover, the wars with the Iroquois—who more often than not subjected their prisoners to unspeakable torture, burning them to death by inches, '*au petit feu*'—had conditioned the Canadians to fight with the utmost ferocity and desperation, with little regard for their own lives.[25] A swift end was merciful, infinitely preferable to being taken alive.

Between 1608 and 1760 there were barely fifty years of peace all told in Canada. The longest uninterrupted stretch without the militia's being engaged in fighting somewhere was the twenty-two years from 1666 to 1684. It is therefore likely that nearly all the able-bodied men served on at least one campaign during their lifetime. In short, with the exception of that one tranquil period, war was the norm in New France. A British observer commented in the mid-eighteenth century on the significant difference between the Canadians and the English colonials as martial men:

Our men are nothing but a set of farmers and planters, used only to the axe and hoe. Theirs are not only well trained and disciplined, but they are used to arms from their infancy among the Indians; and are reckoned equal, if not superior in that part of the world to veteran troops. These [Canadians] are troops that fight without pay—maintain themselves in the woods without charges—march without baggage—and support themselves without stores, and magazines—we are at immense charges for those purposes.[26]

It was, however, among the dominant class, the colonial 'establishment,' or élite, that militarism and the military ethos took the firmest hold. Governor-General Denonville, shortly after his arrival in the colony, recommended that the sons of indigent Canadian nobles be sent to France for training as officers in the Guards. His motive was to keep what he regarded as a dangerous group of young hellions out of mischief. He subsequently succeeded in having the officer corps of the *Troupes de la Marine* opened to the sons of Canadian seigneurs.[27] By the end of the century, of one incomplete list of eighty-seven officers, thirty-five were Canadian born. Of the fifty-two officers born in France, several had married in the colony, acquired seigneuries, and could be regarded as colonials.[28] In addition, several Canadians served as officers in the *Troupes de la Marine* in France and other of the colonies.[29] By 1753 the officer corps in Canada had become a caste. Commissions were reserved for the sons of Canadian serving officers.[30] In 1733 the Baron de Longueuil, in asking for a commission for one of his sons, plaintively stated that he was the only captain who did not have a son serving as an officer.[31]

Contrary to eighteenth-century custom, Canadian officers had to undergo long and arduous training in the ranks before they were commissioned. This was enough to discourage all but those who were really determined on an active military career. Before being commissioned as junior officers they served as cadets. In this capacity they were supposed to be treated as merely the senior soldiers in their respective companies, receiving the same pay and rations, the same uniforms and equipment as ordinary soldiers. They did, however, show a tendency to take advantage of their social station and their prospects to obtain better treatment than the rank and file. Governor-General Duquesne considered this a sign that the Canadians were becoming 'effeminate' and he likely made himself unpopular with the cadets by ordering their officers to curb these pretentions.[32]

Each of the thirty companies was allowed two cadets and they served as such until vacancies occurred among the ensigns. They could, therefore, expect to serve in the ranks as cadets for eight to ten years.[33] In 1719 one cadet, the Sieur de Grandpré, had served for twenty-two years.[34] Moreover, in time of war they saw more than their share of the fighting. They were sent out on small war parties to raid the English settlements, and with Indian scouting parties to take prisoners for intelligence purposes. To cite but one case, in 1746 the Intendant Hocquart wrote in his annual dispatch to the Minister: 'I must not forget to tell you of the eldest son of the sieur Sabrevois de Bleury, a senior cadet, he is a young man 17 to 18 years of age who for the past year has taken part in all the sorties against the enemy.'

Despite the hazards, the very low pay,[36] and the extreme hardships on military campaigns in the North American wilderness, the members of the Canadian dominant class were avid for commissions for their sons as soon as they were big enough to handle a musket. In 1707 the Minister rebuked Governor-General Vaudreuil for appointing mere children as cadets. He ordered that in future they must be at least seventeen.[37] Vaudreuil's wife, who although Canadian born had considerable influence at Versailles,[38] pleaded with the Minister to reduce the requisite age to fifteen. The Minister remained adamant;[39] but Madame de Vaudreuil was possessed of remarkable persuasive powers and she argued her case well. 'I have no ulterior motive, My Lord, in telling you that it was an excellent thing for the country to accept sons of our families as cadets in the Marines at the age of 15 to 16. That early training makes them capable, after having undertaken light duties, to cope with greater responsibilities and thus to become very good officers.'[40] By 1729 the age limit had been reduced to fifteen. The Governor and Intendant assured the Minister they would hold the line there.[41]

Given this demand for commissions, with an officer corps totalling around 130, and with the population doubling every generation, the competition among the leading families was extremely keen; in fact, bitter. Thus in the eighteenth century a new 'shadow rank' was created, called the *expectative*.[42] Seniority lists were drawn up by the governor-general and intendant for every rank in each company, from cadet to lieutenant. Families pleaded to have their fourteen-year-old sons placed on the *expectative* list for cadetships. Junior cadets given the *expectative* listing acceded to the first vacancies as *cadets à l'éguillettes*; *expectatives* of the latter rank were next in line to be commissioned *enseignes en second*, and so on up the ranks. In 1745, however, with war raging, the Ministry of Marine ordered the abandonment of the *expectative* lists. Vacancies now had to be filled by those who had distinguished themselves in action, without regard for seniority.[43] This was an excellent means to stimulate an aggressive spirit in the officer corps—not to mention casualties, and hence accelerated promotions.

Much research must be done before definite conclusions can be drawn on the social consequences of this military caste system. Research already carried out depicts the progress of some families up the social scale. The path is clearly marked: the original settler comes from France as a humble soldier or indentured worker. Four generations later his great-grandson returns to France after the Conquest as an officer and a member of the nobility, holding the Croix de St Louis for distinguished service. In between is likely a *voyageur*, a captain of militia, a merchant trader, a local official, a seigneur.[44] There were some 200 lay seigneuries in 1760[45] and it would seem a logical assumption that they comprised the leading colonial families—that is, the dominant class. There were 112 officers in the twenty-eight companies of *Troupes de la Marine* after 1700, plus several supernumerary officers, and a few Canadians commissioned in the navy proper or serving in France. In addition there were fifty-six cadetships, two per company, making a total of nearly 200 officers or potential officers. It would therefore seem likely that most of the seigneurial families had at least one member in the officer corps, or aspired to gain entry into it.[46] Thus the military ethos, with its aristocratic values, must have dominated the colonial establishment by sheer weight of numbers. The first British governor of Quebec, James Murray, who had good reason to know, commented in 1764, 'the Canadians are to a man Soldiers.'[47]

This absorption into the military of a goodly proportion of the available supply of brains, initiative, and ability—assuming these qualities to have been required of the officer corps to some degree—may well help to explain why the colony's economic development was not more flourishing. In this connection a brief glance at the population figures is revealing. In 1716 the population of Canada was 20,890 and in 1718, 23,325.[48] In 1717 Governor-General Vaudreuil informed the Minister that there were 4,484 Canadians between the ages of fourteen and sixty fit to bear arms;[49] that is, approximately one quarter of the population. If that ratio is taken as the norm, the labour force can be assumed to have numbered one quarter of the total population at a given time. In 1726, therefore, the labour force would have been approximately 8,000 of the total population of 31,169.

The next question is: of that number, how many could be expected to have had the requisite education, entrepreneurial talent, drive, and adequate supply of capital required to undertake the establishment of large-scale commecial and industrial capitalist enterprise? If the arbitrary figure of 1 per cent of the total population is assumed, then the group numbered some 300. Even if that figure is doubled, then the officer corps of the *Troupes de la Marine* absorbed one third of the available pool of possible industrialists.[50] Perhaps this helps explain why what little heavy industry there was in New France was capitalized and directed by the state—the wholesale trade largely in the hands of French merchants, and only the retail trade in Canadian hands.[51] The military presence was by no means the only factor affecting this situation. Nor is it at all certain that had military careers not been available and so attractive to the seigneurial class, its members would then have devoted their energies to developing the colonial economy on capitalist lines. But that the military option was a significant factor can hardly be doubted, much less ignored.

Another reason frequently advanced for the frailty of the Canadian economy was the dominance of the fur trade, and there is a good deal of evidence to support this thesis. Yet it requires qualification. Until 1696 the trade prospered, providing large profits for the merchant traders and some favoured officers in the *Troupes de la Marine* who were given command of posts in the West during King William's War, as well as relatively high wages for a few hundred salaried employees—*voyageurs*, blacksmiths, and *commis*. By that year, 1696, the French beaver market was bankrupt owing to over-production during the preceding years that had completely glutted the market.[52] In desperation the King and his Minister of Marine sought to restrict the beaver trade by abandoning the western posts and withdrawing from the West. For military and political reasons, however, this decision was rescinded. The Indian nations had to be retained in the French alliance, and the garrisoned fur-trade posts were essential for this purpose.

In 1700, on the eve of the War of the Spanish Succession, Louis XIV embarked on his imperialist policy in North America to occupy the West from the Great Lakes to the Gulf of Mexico in order to contain the English colonies.[53] The fur trade was now not merely a means to derive commercial profit, but primarily an instrument of French imperial policy. The northern and western Indian nations had to be retained in the French alliance, and this could only be done by making it worth their while to obey French political and military directives. At all costs these allied tribes had to be kept away from the English in peacetime and induced to oppose the enemy in time of war. This required that the French provide the Indians with the goods and services they demanded in both peace and war. All that the Indians could offer in return was furs in peacetime and military aid, or at least benevolent neutrality, in war. The French had to prevent the establishment by the English of trade relations with these Indian nations. This forced the French Crown to subsidize the fur trade, directly and indirectly.

When in 1705 the *Compagnie de la Colonie*, which had taken over the beaver marketing monopoly, was bankrupt, the Crown had to step in and place it in the hands of the *Domaine d'Occident*.[54] At the end of the war, when the Treaty of Utrecht gave the English the right to trade in the West, the Canadian authorities had to employ every possible device to prevent them from taking advantage of this clause.[55] At the posts closest to the English traders the Crown acted as merchant-trader to keep the price of goods lower than private traders could profitably do. For a time the other, more distant, posts were leased to Canadian merchants, but this was not a political success. In 1729 Governor Beauharnais had warned that it would be dangerous to lease the posts to merchants since '*ces sortes de personnes*' had nothing in view but profits.[56] To maintain the Indian alliances, the trade was given over to the military commandants at the posts who were expected to subordinate their private pecuniary interests to the political aims of the crown.[57] By 1729 ten served in this capacity,[58] and the competition for the appointments was very bitter.[59]

Whether or not this militarization of the fur trade effected the desired improvement in Indian relations is a moot point. The post commandants doled out 20,000 *livres* worth of presents to the Indians, furnished by the Crown; recommended chiefs for the coveted silver and enamel medals presented by the governor-general; provided the services of a blacksmith; and acted as mediator in intertribal disputes.[60] All this cost money; in fact it cost a lot of money. In 1717 the Council of Marine accepted Governor-General Vaudreuil's estimate of costs amounting to 50,000 *livres* to establish three new posts in the far west.[61] In 1754 the total cost borne by the Crown for the maintenance of the western posts was put at 183,427 *livres* a year.[62] Other costs were incurred in wartime when the governor-general and intendant found themselves obliged to raise the prices paid to the Indians for beaver by as much as fifty per cent to keep them from entering into negotiations with the English.[63] The picture was the same in Louisiana. Governor Vaudreuil-Cavagnial declared that only the Choctas post was worth leasing; that at the other posts the price of trade goods had to be subsidized by the Crown. The post at Tombocbé, he stated, had to be maintained to retain the alliance of the Choctas and eliminate English influence. Were it to be abandoned the English would flood into the region.[64] This may help explain why the Louisiana budget climbed from 322,629 *livres* in 1742 to 930,767 in 1752.[65]

Some of these post commandants were reputed to have made vast fortunes out of the fur trade. Even though the reports of the profits they realized were likely greatly exaggerated, the competition among the leading Canadian families for these appointments indicates that there were compensations for an arduous, and hazardous, existence in the distant wilderness. But whatever profits were made, there is no evidence that they were invested in the economic development of the colony; rather they appear to have been spent on conspicuous consumption, after the fashion of the nobility. Although the conomic climate for capitalist exploitation and development of the colony's resources was not thereby enhanced, the social ambiance of the military ruling class was rendered very civilized.

When Peter Kalm visited North America in 1749 he was struck by the wealth of the Albany merchants, and also by their 'avarice, selfishness and immeasureable love of money . . . their sparing manner of living', and their boorishness.[66] In contrast, continuing on his way to Canada he arrived at Crown Point where he formed a highly favourable opinion of Canadian society. The commandant of this frontier fort, Captain Paul-Louis Lusignan, is described as 'a man of learning and of great politeness [who] heaped kindness upon us, and treated us with as much civility as if we had been his relations . . . In short he did us more favors than we could have expected from our own countrymen, and the officers were likewise particularly obliging to us.'[67] Twenty years later Captain John Knox, with Amherst's army, entered Montreal immediately after the capitulation and he was taken aback by the apparent affluence of its citizens. In his journal he noted: 'The inhabitants are gay and sprightly . . . and from the number of silk robes, laced coats, and powdered heads of both sexes, and almost of all ages, that are perambulating the streets from morning to night, a stranger would be induced to believe Montreal is intirely [*sic*] inhabited by people of independent and plentiful fortune.'[68]

How may we explain that Canadians apparently enjoyed a higher standard of living than their social counterparts in France?[69] The fact that they paid no taxes, except the occasional one for local improvements, and were tithed at half the rate usual in France was one factor. A *habitant* could have as much land as he could till free for the clearing of it, and paid seigneurial dues—when he paid any at all—amounting to only ten per cent of his income from the land; but obversely these low seigneurial dues meant that the seigneurs' revenue from their *censitaires* was not great.[70] Moreover, the seigneurial land-holding system precluded the concentration of capital through speculation in land.[71] These negative factors militated against the existence of a poverty-ridden proletariat, hence of concentration of capital and cheap labour; but they did not create affluence.

The colony's main exports consisted of wheat and other foodstuffs in good years, some timber, a few ships, ginseng for a time, and furs. The latter commodity was, of course, the major item. In 1715 Ruette d'Auteuil, one time attorney-general, estimated the beaver trade to be worth 500,000 to 600,000 *livres* a year. In addition, there were hides for leather and small furs. Of the latter, 250,000 to 300,000 *livres* worth of martin pelts alone were exported. All told, the total was upwards of a million *livres* a year.[72] But from these sums the cost of trade goods, salaries, wages, commissions, freight, insurance, and storage had to be deducted. It has been asserted that between 1675 and 1760 seventy-two per cent of the fur-trade revenue went to France, fourteen per cent went to Canadian merchant traders, nine per cent was spread about the colony, and five per cent went to the state.[73] In other words, if these figures are accepted, then roughly 200,000 *livres* a year, at most, remained in the colony—about 140,000 *livres* of that amount being divided among perhaps twenty or thirty families.[74]

There was, however, another major source of revenue: the military establishment. Every year the Crown spent large sums for the maintenance of the regular troops in the colony, and in wartime the amounts spent on fortifications and campaigns, for goods and services, were astronomical. With money flowing into the colony to maintain the military machine, there was no great need, hence little incentive, to be frugal in order to amass capital to develop the colony's resources.

Unfortunately French government accounting practice in the eighteenth century was utterly chaotic and usually a few years in arrears.[75] In 1712, before military expenditures really soared, Ruette d'Auteuil stated that the cost of maintaining the troops in the colony amounted to 150,000 *livres*, with another 150,000 *livres* going to the civil administration and a modest 25,000 to fortifications.[76] Prior to 1730, expenditures by the Crown amounted to about 500,000 *livres* a year, about 600,000 down to 1743, and in the millions from then on. A large share of these amounts was spent on fortifications, and in providing profits and employment for merchants, *habitants*, and artisans. In 1710, for example, 150,000 *livres* were spent on fortifications when an English assault was expected.[77] In 1745 the extraordinary defence expenditures for Quebec and Louisiana, but mostly for Quebec, amounted—according to the Minister of Marine—to 681,408 *livres* 14 *sols*.[78] The following year the bill for military construction at Quebec alone was 186,102 *livres* 14 *sols*.[79] In 1736 the amount spent for supplies to maintain a garrison strength of seventy-two men at Crown Point for one year was 13,537 *livres* 14 *sols* 10 *deniers*;[80] and in 1745 the cost of maintaining Fort St Frédéric for the year amounted to 76,000 *livres*.[81] Colonel Bougainville commented in 1757: 'La guerre enrichit le Canada.' He also noted that the *habitants* were well provided with silver platters, bowls, and goblets, manufactured from melted-down *écus*.[82]

Not only were the economy and the social ethos of the colony dominated by the military, the political effects were also very significant. The fact that commissions in the colonial regular troops were reserved for Canadians, for the sons of serving officers in fact,[83] ensured the maintenance of close ties between the Canadian dominant class and the metropolitan government. This in turn ensured stability for the colonial administration. Entry into the officer corps and promotion were dependent on the recommendations of the governor-general and the intendant to the Minister of Marine. The annual report of the intendant on the state of the troops contained terse comments on the character, ability, and economic circumstances of each officer. Petitions from Canadians for commissions for their sons were forwarded with critical comments.[84] Without the recommendation of these two officials, appointment and promotion stood little chance. But in the final analysis the commission and promotion came from the king through the minister. This meant that the Canadian leading families looked first to the senior officials, who were the creatures of the metropolitan government, then to the senior officials in the Ministry of Marine for the realization of their hopes and ambitions. This condition was in marked contrast to the situation in the English colonies where only the governors, a handful of royal officials, and, to a lesser degree, the appointed members of the provincial councils—usually twelve in number—had ties with the metropolitan government.[85]

In Canada colonial society came to be divided into two main groups, which can be labelled Metropolitans and Provincials. The Metropolitans were the dominant force in colonial society; to use a modern colloquial term, the Establishment. Because they looked to France for the advancement of their careers, and the careers of their children, the development of anything akin to Canadian nationalism, or even particularism, was out of the question.[86]

They regarded themselves primarily as citizens of France—resident overseas. The bitter resentment in the Spanish colonies of the *creoles* against the *peninsulares* was conspicuously absent in Canada. Only during the final years of the Seven Years' War did anything resembling it begin to develop, and even then it was mainly a clash of personalities at the top level; specifically, between Montcalm and Vaudreuil.[87] Lower down the scale it was manifested more by the French officers of the *Troupes de Terre* than by the Canadian officers and officials.

The mass of the Canadians, the Provincials—*habitants*, artisans, town workers, and shopkeepers—had few ties with France. Their economic existence, their peculiar mores, virtually everything in their lives was firmly rooted in Canada where, by the eighteenth century, the overwhelming majority had been born. Although they regarded themselves as Canadians and were readily distinguishable as such, without grievances—either real or imagined—social friction, propaganda, and direction from above, the virus of nationalism could not take hold among these Provincials. Between the Canadian *habitants* and the French regular soldiers recently come from France relations were not good. Too many of the *Troupes de Terre* behaved as they were accustomed to do when on enemy soil, and treated the Canadians accordingly.[88] Yet some of them married Canadian girls, and at the capitulation in 1760 some 2,000 of them chose to 'filer à l'Anglais'. They stayed in Canada, with the connivance of the Canadians.[89] They thus helped to compensate for the heavy losses suffered by the Canadian militia during the six years of hostilities.

Finally the military role played by Canada in French imperial policy explained much that is otherwise baffling. One of the main motives for the attempts to establish a French colony in North America in the sixteenth century was to counter the growing power of Spain. In this it failed and Spanish power was eventually contained by other means. In the first half of the seventeenth century commercial colonies and missionary bases were established in Acadia and the St Lawrence valley. The one was temporarily crippled by the English and Scots, the other almost destroyed by the Iroquois. In 1663 the Crown took over and consolidated both colonies; but neither lived up to the expectations of Colbert, who desired commercial and industrial expansion comparable to that of the English colonies. Here again a main aim was to counter the growing economic power of European rivals, the Netherlands and England.

At the end of the seventeenth century the Canadian beaver trade was bankrupt, the colony an economic liability, and fears were expressed that France would withdraw its support, abandoning the colonists to fend for themselves. Then, suddenly, almost overnight, New France became vitally important. During the winter of 1700–1, with the onset of the War of the Spanish Succession, Louis XIV adopted a policy of imperialism in North America to contain the English colonies and protect Mexico. From Acadia to Louisiana a fortified zone was to be established behind the English colonies.[90] The loss of part of Acadia necessitated the creation of the naval base at Louisbourg at immense cost. This line of fortifications, from the Atlantic to the Gulf of Mexico, was maintained and strengthened during the ensuing thirty years' peace.

In the 1740s this peace was threatened by the war hawks of England who were greatly alarmed by the rapid expansion of French overseas trade. They feared that unless French commerce were curbed it would overtake that of England and drive the English out of some of their more profitable markets, as had already happened in the Levant and had begun in the Spanish empire. The ensuing War of the Austrian Succession damaged French commerce considerably—not enough to cripple it, but enough to indicate that a better-conducted spoiling war would have the desired effect.[91] England, therefore, was determined to renew hostilities at the first opportunity, but this next time to reduce its continental commitment to the minimum and devote itself to gaining maritime supremacy in order to destroy French overseas trade.[92]

The French, fully aware of England's strategic aims, had to find some means to counter them. The policy they adopted was intended to force the English on the defensive by attacking Hanover, and by compelling them to disperse their powerful navy to protect their own colonies. This would have the desired effect of preventing the Royal Navy from blockading the continental ports and scouring the Atlantic shipping lanes. The French colonies in North America were to play a major role in the execution of this global strategy, and Canada was a key base.[93]

On the eve of the Seven Years' War, France made the first move by seizing the Ohio valley, driving out the Anglo-American fur traders and land speculators. The governor-general of Canada, Galissonière, had advocated this move to force the English to send large military and naval forces to America. He was confident that the Canadians, with some help from France, could contain them by exerting strong pressure on the frontiers of the English colonies.[94] Given the superior military organization of New France, their control of the communication routes along the continent's major waterways, and the contrasting military records of the Canadians and Anglo-Americans in the previous wars, he had good cause to be confident of the outcome. Thus relatively small forces in Canada would tie down a much larger enemy force in the forthcoming global struggle.

In the early years of the war this policy enjoyed considerable success; but eventually the French forces in Canada were obliged to surrender. England was then able to withdraw the bulk of its military forces for service in other theatres. In short, Canada had failed to fulfil successfully its intended role in French imperial strategy.

This failure likely weighed heavily in the Duc de Choiseul's decision to abandon Louisiana and relinquish all thought of regaining Canada. His main concern was to obtain a peace settlement on almost any terms. The longer the war lasted, the worse the French position became. Peace was imperative in order to recuperate, rebuild, then renew the conflict five years hence. France and the other European powers were convinced that England was bent on world dominance and had already gone a long way towards achieving it. The whole aim of French foreign policy now centred on the need to strengthen the Family Compact, then rebuild the naval forces of France and Spain sufficiently to protect their own maritime trade, and cripple that of England. In this strategy it was intended that Canada would, once more, play its old 'fortress' role—but in a markedly different fashion. The Duc de Choiseul now believed that his policy of revenge, of restoring the balance of power in Europe, would be better served were Canada retained by England and Louisiana ceded to Spain.[95] In December 1759 he had consoled himself for the inevitable loss of Canada, following on the fall of Quebec, with the thought that this would increase the strength of the Anglo-Americans and foster their latent urge to strike out for independence.[96]

As had others before him, Choiseul clearly foresaw the removal of French power in North America as leading to the revolt of England's American colonies and the disruption of her commercial empire.[97] This is, of course, exactly what happened. Canada in the hands of the British finally fulfilled the purpose that France had long before assigned to it. Ironically, it did this at no cost to France but at immense cost to Britain. With the benefit of hindsight it would appear that England, in 1763, would have been wiser for both political and economic reasons to insist that France retain Canada.

After the Conquest the military establishment again became a major factor in the colonial economy. It was also a heavy drain on the imperial exchequer. In 1765 the merchants of Quebec and Montreal pleaded with the British government to maintain a large garrison in the province and to embark on a naval construction program to avert economic collapse. They pointed out that military expenditures had always been the mainstay of the colony.[98] In 1800 Britain's annual expenditure for the military in Upper and Lower Canada alone was estimated at £260,000, and it increased steadily.[99] The War of 1812 poured money into British North America, and the flow did not stop with the Treaty of Ghent. In 1828 the estimates for Kingston and Halifax amounted to £330,644 and by 1843 the military establishment of 9,000 men was costing the British taxpayer £698,000 plus £34,000 for civil departments, including the clergy and Indians affairs.[100] In short, for the better part of two centuries war, and the threat of war, was one of the great staples of the Canadian economy. As for the influence of the military on post-Conquest Canadian society, that topic is long overdue for thorough investigation.

The Battle of Quebec:
A Reappraisal

More nonsense has been written over the years about this momentous battle—
the battle that changed the course of North American and European history—
than about any other event in Canadian history. One has only to imagine
what would likely have been the ultimate course of events had the French
destroyed Wolfe's army on that day in mid-September 1959 to appreciate
how significant an event it was.

The paper here reprinted was written to be read at a meeting of the French
Colonial Historical Society. Having only twenty minutes allotted time, I had
to make it brief. Nothing that further research has uncovered since it was
written, however, has caused me to alter my interpretation of the event one
iota. A considerably extended study of the battle will appear in a forthcoming
work. This paper contains the gist of it.

The battle that took place on the Plains of Abraham on 13 September 1759
continues to exercise fascination for historians and romantics alike. Hardly
a year goes by without another work appearing on some aspect of the epic
struggle. Field Marshall Viscount Montgomery described it as 'one of the
great battles of the world'.[1] He was right about that, but about little else
concerning this particular event. General Douglas MacArthur is reputed to
have stated that his famous 'end run' in Korea, effecting a landing far in the
enemy's rear, was modelled on Wolfe's tactics. He obviously had not studied the terrain at Quebec or Wolfe's actual disposition of his army.

A common feature of most of the works on the battle is the bland acceptance of the stated, or unstated, premise that the outcome was a foregone
conclusion. Yet with one notable exception the main actors in the 1759 drama,
on both sides, did not regard an eventual British victory as assured; quite
the contrary. In May, when an English assault on Quebec was anticipated,
Captain Montgay of the Béarn regiment, the comte de Malartic, and the
chevaliers de Lévis and de Montreuil, all expressed optimism that it would
be beaten off.[2] In the second week of September the French were confident
that the campaign was over, and that they had ended it with glory. The recent
movements in the English camp were interpreted as preparations for their
departure,[3] as indeed to some extent they were.[4]

After the event James Murray remarked in a letter to Amherst, 'the Fact is we were surprised into a victory which cost the Conquered very little indeed'.[5] And at Louisbourg, Thomas Ainslie wrote to his friend and mentor, Murray, 'I now congratulate you on your success at Quebec, a thing little expected by any here, and posterity will hardly give credit to it that such a handful of Men should carry so great a point against such numbers, and with such advantages, thank God you have escaped, it is a miracle that you have.'[6]

Wolfe himself admitted in a dispatch dated 2 September that he was not at all sanguine of success.[7] The defences of Quebec were far more formidable than he had anticipated. His attempts to take the city had failed, his assaults on the French lines had been beaten back with heavy losses. Much has been made of the desperate conditions in Quebec, then in ruins, and the shortage of supplies. On the English side, however, conditions were far worse. Their supply line extended down the treacherous St Lawrence to Halifax and then across the Atlantic to Portsmouth. By the end of August over a thousand men were in hospital, suffering from wounds, dysentery, and scurvy. In the hot weather the camps—plagued with flies, mosquitoes, and inadequate latrines—stank to high heaven.[8] Wolfe was not the only one to be taken ill.

Of the 8,500 troops who had left Louisbourg, nearly half were unfit for duty by the end of August. On the opposing side Montcalm had some fifteen to sixteen thousand men, less than four thousand of them regulars,[9] but the Canadian militia had shown that they were a fearsome adversary when properly used. In addition there were a thousand to twelve hundred Indian warriors in the French camp.[10] They were a psychological weapon of no small account. Desertion increased in the British ranks as the campaign dragged on. The reports of these deserters to their interrogators kept the French well informed of conditions in the enemy's camp. They also raised their confidence. The intendant Bigot remarked after one such interrogation, 'those types make everything look rosy.'[11] And Montcalm informed Lévis that several of these deserters had stated that the British now despaired of taking Quebec unless Amherst's army arrived to support them.[12]

The French, however, knew that Amherst would not appear before Quebec during the present campaign. The Abenaki of Saint-François had captured two British officers, with their Mohawk guides, bearing dispatches from Amherst to Wolfe informing him that he was waiting for word of the taking of Quebec before advancing, with his habitual speed of a glacier, farther north than Fort Saint-Frédéric on Lake Champlain.[13] In fact Amherst was manifestly convinced that Quebec would not fall. He devoted the entire summer to the construction, at enormous expense, of a massive fortification at Crown Point. That structure could patently serve no useful purpose were

Quebec to be taken. Its function could only be to bar the Lake Champlain route to an army ascending the lake from Canada for an invasion of New York.

It was, therefore, in desperation that Wolfe ordered the devastation of the countryside around Quebec, some four thousand farms being put to the torch.[14] The bombardment of the city continued until only a handful of buildings were habitable.[15] Wolfe had decided that if Quebec could not be taken, then the usefulness of the colony to the enemy would be reduced to the minimum.[16] It made no sense whatsoever to destroy what it was intended to occupy and subsequently put to one's own use, particularly with winter fast approaching. This too gave the French rueful cause to be confident of the final outcome of the campaign.

The one person in the French camp who was convinced that the city would eventually fall to the British was, ironically, the commander in chief, the Marquis de Montcalm. All through the war he had been a chronic defeatist. Before the opening of each campaign he had declared vociferously that it would end badly and he sought to ensure that the blame would fall elsewhere than on him. On 24 February 1759 he wrote to Lévis. 'The colony is lost unless peace comes. I can see nothing that can save it.'[17] And on 9 August he wrote to the Chevalier Bourlamaque, 'I maintain that the colony is lost.'[18] He made his plans accordingly and what ensued was a self-fulfilling prophecy.

Montcalm's tactics stipulated that what remained of the French and Canadian regular troops after the inevitable debacle, but before the ensuing capitulation of the colony, would withdraw to Louisiana in a fleet of canoes by way of the Ottawa River, the Great Lakes, and the Mississippi. This move, he assured the minister in a *mémoire* sent to the court with Bougainville in 1758, would prevent the loss of a sizeable body of men and preserve the honour of French arms by a feat rivalling the retreat of the Ten Thousand that had immortalized the Greeks.[19] It was likely for this reason, later seen to have been a disastrous mistake, that he established his main supply base at Batiscan, 50 miles above Quebec.[20] On strategic grounds this made no sense, since it left Quebec vulnerable to an enemy landing across that vital supply line. On the other hand were the town to fall, as Montcalm anticipated, then the supplies would be there ready for a withdrawal to Montreal and the epic retreat to Louisiana.

When the British were known to be ascending the river, Montcalm drafted the terms to be submitted to them for the capitulation of Quebec and gave a copy to the town commandment, the Sieur de Ramezay.[21] He made careful preparations for defeat, but he conspicuously failed to prepare the town's outer defences. Relying on the opinion of his self-serving engineering officer, Major Pontleroy, who informed him that an enemy landing above Quebec could not hope to succeed and that the range across the river from Pointe

Lévis was too far for cannon fire to be effective,[22] he did not fortify that vital point and made only the feeblest of attempts to dislodge the British when they landed and began constructing their batteries.

The British objective all through the campaign was to take Quebec, it being rightly assumed that once Quebec fell the French would be forced to surrender the entire colony. Attempts to take the town by manoeuvre on the left flank of the French lines had conspicuously failed, with heavy losses. Massive bombardment of the town had accomplished nothing except destruction of eighty per cent of the buildings. Attempts to cut the French supply line upriver had been beaten off. The only way the objective could be gained was somehow to force Montcalm to come out from behind his fortified lines to give battle in the open and then destroy his army. Wolfe admitted that he could not stay in the river beyond the end of September.[23] Vice-Admiral Saunders dared not risk a quarter of the Royal Navy's being caught in such dangerous waters by the onset of winter. On 5 September, Saunders wrote in a dispatch to the Admiralty, 'I shall very soon send home the great ships.'[24] By early September a protracted siege was out of the question. All that the French had to do was hold the enemy off for a matter of days.

Wolfe, frustrated at every turn, felt that he had to make one last desperate attempt to take Quebec before admitting defeat, abandoning the campaign, and sailing ignominiously back to England. He proposed another assault on the Beauport lines, but when he submitted his plans to his brigadiers they curtly rejected them. They pointed out that even were Montcalm to be defeated in an action there, he could still withdraw his army either into Quebec, or upriver to his supply depot then westward to Montreal, thereby necessitating another campaign the following year.[25] They proposed instead a landing well above Quebec, between the town and Montcalm's supply base at Batiscan. This, they pointed out, would force him to come out and give battle, and if defeated, then not only Quebec but the entire colony would have to capitulate.

Wolfe accepted the brigadiers' plan in principal, but made a change that nullified its main strategic aim and placed the British army in grave jeopardy. The road from Batiscan to Quebec forked some fifteen miles above the town. The northern branch road went through Ancienne-Lorette, five miles north of the Saint Lawrence, then proceeded across the Saint Charles river to join the Quebec-Charlesbourg road. Instead of landing above the fork, thereby severing all communication between Quebec and Batiscan, which was the essential feature of the brigadiers' plan, Wolfe chose to land at the Anse au Foulon, thereby leaving the vital northern road open. It was this road that the French army was to use, after the debacle, to make good its withdrawal to Saint Augustin and later to Montreal.

Much ink has been spilled over Montcalm's failure to strengthen his right flank, and the colossal good luck that allowed the British to scale the heights, virtually unopposed, and assemble their army on the Plains of Abraham. Blame for the event has been duly apportioned to certain individuals with varying degrees of regard for the evidence,[26] it being assumed that once Wolfe had gained that position what ensued was inevitable. C.P. Stacey has stated that since Wolfe was astride Quebec's supply line, which he clearly was not,[27] 'Nothing was left but for Montcalm to take the chance of a desperate stroke against an army far better than his own.'[28] Stacey also opines that no matter how Montcalm had reacted to Wolfe's surprise landing, the French were doomed to defeat, 'so serious was the difference in military quality between the opposing forces'.[29] This assertion begs the question why it was that 3,500 troops of that same French army had been able to inflict such a crushing defeat on 15,000 British and American troops at Carillon the preceding year. Or why the chevalier de Lévis, again with that selfsame army, was able to defeat resoundingly the British under Murray on those same Plains of Abraham just seven months later.

What we have here is a classic case of the argument that because some-thing happened, it *ipso facto* had to happen, was in fact virtually preordained. As the American novelist Mary McCarthy remarked about other battles in another war, 'a successful action is never examined in terms of what caused it, the result is seen as the cause.'[30] Anglophone historians are particularly prone to take this view since what the consequences of a French victory would have been are too mind-boggling to contemplate. Toronto, for example, might then today be a French-speaking city; and the Americans would have had to postpone their bid for independence.

If we strip ourselves of hindsight and examine closely the position of the British and French forces on the morning of 13 September, what do we actually find? Wolfe's army, numbering at most 4,500 men, extended in two lines from the edge of the cliff overlooking the Saint Lawrence to the wooded escarpment overlooking the Saint Charles river. To cover that front of some 1,300 yards the ranks had to be stretched thin. The files were over three feet apart, with a forty-yard interval between each of the battalions.[31] The sol-diers had spent the previous day on the ships manoeuvring upriver or preparing to embark. At nine o'clock at night they had begun embarking in the landing craft. Five hours later the first of the three waves began slipping downstream with the tide towards the Anse au Foulon. They made their first landing in the final hours of darkness. The boats then returned to embark the next wave. By eight the entire force was on the heights, having had little or no sleep for the past twenty-four hours. They carried the usual hard rations and the only water they had was in their canteens. They had no tents or blankets, their only ammunition was that in their pouches. Two light field guns were brought up, but for one of them they had the wrong ammunition.

They apparently had no doctors or surgeons with them.* This small army was ready for battle, provided it were to be fought within a few hours. Manoeuvre in that confined area, or a protracted assault on the town's fortifications, was out of the question. Time was not on their side.

One vital element that Wolfe had achieved, however, was surprise. Everything therefore depended on how Montcalm would react. Although he had been informed at dawn that the British had effected a landing, he refused to believe it. It was not until six-thirty, after receiving further frantic reports that the British were massed on the Plains, that he rode off to see for himself, then gave orders for the troops in the Beauport lines to be brought up at the double.[32]

The significance of this three-hour interval between Wolfe's arrival on the heights and Montcalm's appearance is that Wolfe was thereby afforded ample time, undisturbed, to survey the terrain and make his dispositions accordingly. The position that he chose and its relation to his objective, the destruction of the French army and the occupation of Quebec, therefore deserves critical examination.

It was axiomatic that an army, in the presence of an enemy, should seek to occupy the high ground. In this particular instance one would have expected Wolfe to occupy the heights of the Plains of Abraham, the broken ridge known as the Buttes à Neveu, which would have given him a clear view of the town. Provided he could hold that commanding site, he could have brought up his heavy guns to batter a breach in Quebec's fortifications prior to an assault. Montcalm would not necessarily have brought his army out to give battle. He would still have had the option of keeping his main forces behind the town walls, relying on his own guns to disrupt the enemy's artillery emplacements[33] and using the Canadians—in conjunction with Bougainville's élite force ten miles upriver—to harass the British rear, with its precarious supply line. The obvious move for Wolfe to make under the circumstances was to occupy the commanding heights no matter how Montcalm reacted.

The astonishing thing is that Wolfe did *not* occupy those heights, despite the fact that nothing stood in his way. Inexplicably he drew up his little army on the low reverse slope, some six hundred paces from the crest of the ridge. From that position he could not see the walls of Quebec, or any part of the town.[34] Had he managed to bring up every gun in his massive armoury, not one of them could have ranged in on the walls of Quebec. If the French *quartier général* had racked their brains to devise a disposition of the enemy's

---

* When Vaudreuil learned that Wolfe had been wounded he wrote to Bougainville that he believed M. de Ramezay, commander of the Quebec garrison, had already sent two surgeons to the English general. Arthur G. Doughty and G.W. Parmalee, eds, *The Siege of Quebec and the Battle of the Plains of Abraham*, 6 vols. Quebec, 1901, vol. IV, 127; Vaudreuil à Bougainville, 13 sept. 1759.

forces best suited to their own purpose, they would have been hard pressed to come up with anything better than that position. If they had lured Wolfe into it, they could have expected plaudits from the shade of the Maréchal de Saxe. There Wolfe waited for Montcalm to come to him, while the Canadian militia spread along the brush-covered slopes on both his flanks and began inflicting casualties. In front of him, but out of sight, was the fortified town and the main French force. Ten miles to his rear was Bougainville with an élite force of 3,000 regulars and militia with some light cannon.[35] They could be expected to arrive on the scene at any moment. They would then have been across the British communication route and line of retreat to the Anse au Foulon. Wolfe had no reserves. Were he to fail to gain a crushing victory, retreat would have been extremely difficult, if not impossible. His army would have had to fight its way through Bougainville's force, then withdraw down the steep path to the beach and there wait for the tide to allow the boats to come in from the fleet to take them off. This would have been a lengthy operation, since it would have required three trips. It could hardly have been expected that the French would allow this withdrawal to go unharassed. Even if the first wave of boats managed to get away un-scathed, the troops remaining on the beach would have been rendered all the more vulnerable. It is difficult to see how such a hastily improvised operation could have resulted in anything but surrender or slaughter. Wolfe and his men must have been aware of this as they stood there, waiting. Montcalm had that British army at his mercy.

All through the summer Montcalm had fought a defensive campaign, forcing Wolfe to come to him only to be beaten back with heavy losses. He had passed up obvious opportunities to launch limited attacks on the enemy's vulnerable position at Montmorency, and both officers and men had been sharply critical of his timidity.[36] He is reputed, on one occasion, to have rejected Lévis's urging to attack with the sage comment, 'Drive them thence and they will give us more trouble. So long as they stay there they cannot hurt us. Let them amuse themselves.'[37] All that Montcalm now had to do was to continue to employ that same Fabian strategy: seize the vacant high ground, bring up his guns, and wait for Wolfe to make a move. The longer he could delay an action the stronger became his position.

His contemporary defenders, and some historians, have sought to excuse his fatal decision to attack precipitately on the grounds that to have waited would have allowed the British to entrench themselves, thereby rendering an attack on their lines hopeless. Yet the British could have built the most formidable of entrenchments with the material available, logs and earth, and it would have availed them nothing. They would have dominated nothing more than the six hundred paces of terrain facing them. Guns on the commanding ridge would quickly have rent any such entrenchments asunder. Moreover, the British could sustain themselves on that site only for a matter of days, and only provided that they kept their supply line open. Water would have been a major problem. The Canadians and Indians, not to mention the French gunners, could have seen to it that they got precious little sleep. Moreover, the logs of the British ships state that on the 16th the weather broke. For the ensuing three days there were gale-force winds and heavy rain.[38]

There is just one point that needs to be made concerning the actual battle. Everyone remarks on Wolfe's thin red line of two ranks. What was really significant was that Montcalm chose not to advance in line but to attack in column. Captain John Knox, in his journal, states that the French attacked in three columns, two inclining to the right, opening fire obliquely as they advanced, at the extremities of the British line from 130 yards' distance.[39] Major Patrick MacKellar stated that when the French were within a hundred yards of the British line, 'it mov'd up regularly with a steady fire, and when within 20 or 30 yards of closing gave a General One,' which caused the French to turn and flee.[40] The British centre had not come under fire and it was its volleys, according to Knox, that broke the French charge.

In French military circles at this time a debate raged over the relative effectiveness of attack in column and attack in line. Eventually the proponents of attack in line gained the ascendancy. It came to be accepted that the column should be used to bring the army as close as possible to the the enemy without coming under serious fire, then deploy into line by a variety of complex parade-ground manoeuvres ready for the attack. This allowed every man in the ranks to bring his musket to bear on the opposing force. To attack in column meant that only the front ranks could fire; those in the rear could merely take the places of those before them who fell, or else the columns had to change direction oblique to the enemy line, but even then only the outside file of one side of the column could use their muskets effectively. This is what occurred in Montcalm's attack, and with predictable results.

Some military thinkers in France, however, maintained that the shock effect of a charging column would break the line. It was also held that training and discipline were so poor in the French army that the line formation was too difficult to execute on the battlefield and maintain under fire. Moreover, it was believed that the French temperament, with its reckless but mercurial bravery, made attack in column something that only exceptionally well-trained and disciplined troops could withstand.[41]

The battle at Quebec on 13 September 1759 proved all the above points. The battle fought on the same ground the following year, between the same two armies, and again of equal numbers,[42] added further proof. This time it was the British commander, Brigadier-General James Murray, who obliged the enemy and marched out of the fortified town to give battle in the open.

He massed his troops on the Buttes à Neveu, the same ground that Wolfe had allowed Montcalm to occupy undisputed. As C.P. Stacey succinctly puts it, 'This rise was an admirable position for a defensive battle, and with his numerous guns disposed in the intervals between his battalions Murray could expect to inflict a severe reverse on Lévis if the latter had the temerity to attack him.'[43] Exactly the same, of course, had held true for Montcalm. Murray, however, repeated Montcalm's mistake. Fearing that Lévis would construct redoubts and be difficult to dislodge, he abandoned the high ground and launched an assault, hoping to strike them before they could form to receive the charge. In this he failed. Lévis got his battalions into line, repelled the British attack, then counter-attacked their flanks. The left flank was turned. A bayonet charge then broke the British line. They turned and fled, abandoning their guns. Murray came dangerously close to having his army destroyed.[44]

There was one signal difference between this battle and the previous one. This time both generals survived, which was perfectly normal for eighteenth-century warfare. The odd fact that in the 1759 battle both Wolfe and Montcalm received mortal wounds is a sure indication that there was something seriously wrong with the tactics they employed on that day. Yet regardless of how haphazard it all was, the outcome caused the history of North America to take a drastic turn with consequences that still plague us today. It gives one to think that perhaps the most overlooked determining factor in history has been stupidity.

New France
and the French Impact
on North America

This paper was read at a meeting of The Association for Canadian Studies in the United States, held at Washington in the spring of 1973. When I wrote it I had no idea that the papers read at the conference were to be published. When a copy of the published transactions of the conference arrived on my desk I was surprised and somewhat disconcerted. This explains the absence of footnotes and some repetition of topics discussed in other of my articles. There are, however, some new ideas in the paper, which was intended primarily for an American audience—who, I assumed, and rightly as it turned out, would know little or nothing about New France and French imperial policy in the seventeenth and eighteenth centuries. Regretfully, the same has to be said of most of the Canadian participants.

In the mid-eighteenth century France was the dominant power in North America. It held sway from Louisbourg on the North Atlantic coast to New Orleans on the Gulf of Mexico, and westward to the Rocky Mountains. In the West Indies, France held the more lucrative islands, supplied continental Europe with sugar, coffee, and other tropical produce, and had begun to overhaul Britain in foreign trade. Britain's response to this challenge was to commence hostilities without the formality of a declaration of war—hoping, like the Japanese at Pearl Harbor, to gain the upper hand by a pre-emptive strike. During the ensuing two years 70,000 Canadians brought over a million and a half Anglo-Americans almost to their knees. By 1757 their leaders were pleading for peace.

Three years later this French colonial empire had been all but swept away. Nothing remained except two tiny islands in the Gulf of St Lawrence, fishing rights on the North Shore of Newfoundland, and the sugar islands in the Antilles. Yet the role of France in North America was by no means played out. In fact its impact on events and the course of history in the western hemisphere had greater consequence after the loss of its American empire than before. The explanation of this initial French success, its sudden reversal, and the apparent paradox that resulted, lies in the role the French colonies were called on to play in the furtherance of French imperial policy, and in the peculiar nature of one of these colonies, Canada.

At the beginning of the seventeenth century the French established commercial bases in Acadia, Canada, and the West Indies. Their colonizing efforts in Acadia were not a success and that colony languished until, in 1713, it was ceded to England, whereupon it continued to languish down to the present day. The French fishing settlements in Newfoundland suffered a similar fate. In the West Indies the French had more success, beginning with the seizure of Spanish-claimed islands by French buccaneers. The introduction of sugar cane by the Dutch early provided a secure economic base, but these French islands were more a part of the Dutch economic orbit than of the French. Not until the 1670s were they brought back into the French commercial empire. Despite early vicissitudes they eventually flourished and by 1740 the value of their exports to France was one hundred million *livres* a year—over four million pounds sterling at the then current rate of exchange—and their imports, mainly slaves, were valued at seventy-five million. Six hundred ships were employed in this island commerce, which represented sixty per cent of French external trade. The French Antilles were an extremely important item on the mother country's economic balance sheet.

The same could not be said for Canada. It began as a commercial outpost, meagrely maintained by private enterprise, with minimal assistance from the Crown. Only when the French branch of the Roman Church established, first missionary bases, then settlements, did the colony sink firm roots and begin to expand. The troika arrangement of Crown, Church, and private enterprise endured for less than fifty years. At the end of that period the population was barely 2,500. Internal strife and the Iroquois onslaughts made it impossible for the hard-pressed settlers to take advantage of the colony's economic resources.

Only when the Crown took over the direction of the colonies, under the rule of Louis XIV and Jean-Baptiste Colbert, did they begin to realize their promise. During the ensuing thirty-five years expansion was rapid. By 1687 the population of Canada was approximately 10,000; that of the French West Indies 47,312, nearly 19,000 being whites, 27,000 slaves, the rest freed Negroes and mulattoes. Acadia, however, had less than a thousand settlers.

It was during this period, from 1663 to the end of the century, that the institutional and social framework of the colonies was firmly established. Naturally enough it mirrored that of France. Briefly, it was hierarchical, status ordered, paternalistic, aristocratic, and in the case of Canada, militaristic, rather than bourgeois and democratic. As for the economic organization of these colonies, that of the West Indies was essentially capitalist, based on the large-scale production of tropical staples by slave labour: that is, plantation-owner capitalists and a slave proletariat—little different from the English plantation colonies. Canada, however, was a Marxist's nightmare. It had no proletariat, hence, no capitalists, and its major industry was war or the threat of war.

To begin with, the seigneurial land-tenure system prevented the emergence of a class of large landholders, such as occurred in the West Indies and subsequently in Louisiana. The size of seigneuries was kept relatively small by the Crown, and the seigneurs had to grant sections of their land, without charge, to any bona fide settlers who applied. The seigneurial dues they could charge for services rendered were very low, thus they could not hope to become rich by exploiting their *censitaires*; they were not landlords, and their *censitaires* were not tenants. Moreover, the availability of free land and the provisions of the *Coutume de Paris*, which decreed that the land of a *habitant* had to pass in equal shares to his children, made land speculation an exercise in futility. Capital could not be accumulated by that dubious device as it was in the English colonies. This abundance of free land made labour very scarce, hence expensive; no man had to work for wages unless he chose to, and this in turn kept the land holdings down to a practicable size, usually about 150 acres. There was then no proletariat worth mentioning, that is, men and women with no means of support other than their labour for wages. This resulted in another phenomenon, the absence of villages, the traditional abode of the landless labourer. Given this lack of a proletariat, there could be no capitalist bourgeoisie. Without these two essential ingredients the development of the colony's economy along the usual European capitalist lines, despite Colbert's efforts, was virtually impossible.

In the seventeenth century the fur trade was the mainstay of the economy, and it would appear possible to cast the Indian suppliers in the role of proletariat, but on closer examination it becomes obvious that they would be miscast. In any event little of the fur-trade profits garnered by the Canadians were used as capital for industrial development in the approved bourgeois manner; instead the money was spent on conspicuous consumption after the fashion of the nobility. For such industrial development as there was—ship building, the iron forges of St-Maurice—most of the capital and managerial talent was provided by the Crown. Yet a singular feature of Canada was its relative economic self-sufficiency. By the mid-eighteenth century, when the population had reached 50,000, it required only two dozen ships, not more than 4,000 tons in all, to supply the colony with the things it could not provide for itself. Significantly by far the largest item in the cargoes of these ships was wine and spirits. Canada imported one per cent of the Bordeaux region's production. The paucity of the colony's external trade has usually been viewed by historians as evidence of economic weakness. A good case can be made for the opposite conclusion.

Another unique feature of this colony was the absence of direct taxation. In France the peasantry paid between one-third and one-half of its income in taxes of one sort or another. The Canadian *habitants* paid modest seigneurial dues, when they paid any at all, of not more than ten per cent of their revenue from the land, plus a tithe to the Church of one twenty-sixth of their grain—half the usual rate of northern France. There was an export tax of twenty-five per cent on beaver pelts, ten per cent on moose hides, but these taxes were removed in 1717. The only other tax was an import duty of ten per cent on wines, spirits, and tobacco.

The absence of direct taxation greatly simplified the task of administration and made government by appointed officials much more tolerable than it otherwise might have been. James Murray, the first British governor of Quebec, expressed surprise that under the French the colony had been administered by so few officials and at such low cost. From the tone of his remarks one might surmise that he thought they had set an awkward precedent. Moreover, the French officials appointed by the Crown were, with a few notable exceptions, far more competent than any the colonists could have provided from among their own ranks. When Colbert took charge of the colonies he instituted several notable reforms. One of the more significant was the ban on venality of office. The administrative and judicial posts in the colonies could not be purchased as they could in France; they were awarded on merit and held during the King's pleasure. After a few senior officials had been summarily dismissed, the notion took firm hold that abuse of power, or gross incompetence, would not be tolerated. Although the senior posts of governor-general and intendant were invariably held by metropolitan Frenchmen, within a few years of the beginning of royal rule the subordinate ranks of the administration and judiciary were staffed by colonists. As the eighteenth century wore on a few Canadians rose to senior posts in the Imperial administration outside Canada. Thus it was possible for the colonists to regard themselves as part of a wider world where careers were open to talent.

Anglo-Saxon historians, such as Francis Parkman—not to mention his many paraphrasers—have condemned this authoritarian system of government. It did not conform to the English model; more specifically, it made no provision for an elected assembly. Government was from above, not from below, hence the Imperial struggle between England and France in North America was depicted as a struggle between the forces of light and the forces of darkness, the ultimate outcome of which could not be in doubt. This interpretation of the past begs a great many questions, and distorts or ignores a great deal of evidence. It ignores, for example, the fact that this authoritarian government was responsible and humane; in several significant ways it was more solicitous of the well-being of the colonists than were the elected assemblies in the English colonies. It also ignores the fact that the French colonial administration was far more efficient, particularly in wartime, and less corrupt, than that of the English colonies. Most serious of all, it fails to comprehend that every system of government depends, ultimately, on agreement between the governors and the governed. This last condition demands that the governors remain constantly aware of the needs, hopes, and grievances of the governed and respond to them. One device to achieve this end is the elected assembly, but it is not the only such device, nor is it necessarily the best in all circumstances. In the French colonies a variety of institutions were utilized: local *ad hoc* assemblies to discuss specific issues, *bureaux de commerce*, the *capitaines de milice* who served as civil agents of the intendants, and the right of the individual to petition the Crown. That this system worked, and worked well, is made evident by the lack of civil disturbances, the absence of any indication that the colonists desired changes, and the tenacity with which they all fought to defend their homeland and its institutions. In these respects the institutions of New France compare very favourably with those of the English colonies, and with the British regime in Canada after the Conquest.

One remarkable thing about New France is the absence of anything remotely resembling nationalism prior to the Conquest. There is evidence of an awareness that the Canadian way of life, Canadian social values, manners, and attitudes, differed from those of France, just as they varied from region to region in France itself; but one searches in vain for evidence that the Canadians wished to be free of control by the mother country, to establish themselves as an independent, sovereign people. Although some historians do maintain that this national spirit had come into existence prior to the Conquest, they conspicuously fail to produce any viable evidence to support the contention. This negative condition is in marked contrast to the spirit of independence in the English colonies, the resentment frequently expressed there against royal control. In 1710 the comte de Ponchartrain, Minister of Marine, sought to foment a rebellion in New York and New England. He stated, 'the people of these provinces [have] always maintained themselves in a sort of republic, governed by their Council and unwilling to accept the abolute governors of the kings of England.'

There was never any fear, or hope, of such a movement in New France, and the reasons why have to be sought. Several explanations could be advanced, and they all boil down to the fact that the Canadians knew when they were well off. They enjoyed far too many benefits from their dependent condition to wish to change it. These benefits derived from two main sources, the Crown and the Church. Here, unity of religion and the close alliance between Church and State were important factors. There were some disputes between the clergy and the Crown officials in the early years of the royal regime, but the mass of the people were not involved. Too much has been made of these disputes by historians. What is deserving of study is not so much the disputes themselves, but the fact that there were so few of them. In the eighteenth century Church-state relations were marked by harmony and close co-operation, not by friction. At the same time, despite the growing secular spirit, and even libertinism, noted by contemporary observers, the people remained deeply religious, deeply committed to their Church. This is demonstrated by Jacques Henripin's very perceptive demographic study, *La population canadienne au début du XVIII siècle*. One of his graphs depicts the rate of conceptions month by month between 1700 and 1750. It shows a precipitous drop in March and April, followed by an equally sharp rise in May and June, then a drop to the January level, which endures for the rest of the year. How else can one account for that sharp decline in conceptions at that particular time of year other than by the fact that the Canadians abstained from more than the pleasures of the table during Lent? And how else account for that phenomenon except by their adherence to the precepts of the Church?

Another related factor was the social services provided by the Church. Hospitals, schools, almshouses, and a college were heavily subsidized by the Crown and endowed by donations from the private fortunes of the bishops, who were all metropolitan Frenchmen, and by donations from wealthy individuals in France. The Canadians were exceptionally well served by the Church, at minimal cost to themselves.

The administration of justice, a fertile field for controversy and resentment, was singularly lacking in both. Colbert had initiated several reforms, thereby eliminating the worst abuses that prevailed in France—one of which was to bar lawyers from practising in the colonies. Justice in Canada was, on the whole, cheap, swift, and equitable. It compared very favourably with the system in vogue in the English colonies, and with that introduced by the British after the Conquest.

Although the social system was hierarchical and status-ordered, there was enough upward mobility to prevent the more enterprising and ambitious of the settlers from feeling frustrated. Similarly, the fur trade offered opportunities for the adventurous, and the socially maladjusted, to find a less restrictive ambiance among the anarchists of the wilderness, the Indian nations of the West.

To be effective, movements of protest have to enlist support and leadership among the upper ranks of society—from within the establishment. In Canada the dominant social group, the seigneurs, displayed no dissatisfaction with the institutional framework, no desire for change. There is nothing in New France that even remotely resembles the wranglings and power struggles that occurred between the elected assemblies and the royal officials in the

English colonies, or the disputes in the Spanish colonies between metropolitan officials, *peninsulares*, and the leading Creole families.

This significant silence resulted from the fact that the social status, the esteem in which a seigneur was held by his peers, was not dependent on wealth *per se*, but on the rank held in the royal service. Commerce and industry were regarded as demeaning occuptions, and wealth acquired in such pursuits was used to emulate the way of life of the nobility in order to be found worthy of a military or administrative appointment. What was most esteemed was commissioned rank in the colonial regulars, the *Troupes de la Marine*. During the course of the eighteenth century this officer corps, some two hundred strong, became a monopoly of the Canadian seigneurs—in fact a caste, commissions being reserved for the sons of serving Canadian officers. These commissions could not be purchased as they sometimes were in the French army; they were granted by the King upon the recommendation of the governor and intendant, and only after the aspirant had had several years' service in the ranks as a cadet.

The governor and intendant disposed of enough patronage in the form of these military commissions, and of civil appointments in the administration or judiciary, to render the leading Canadian families subservient to the Crown. Only by acquiring merit in the eyes of these senior officials could the Canadians hope to receive the coveted initial appointment, and subsequent promotion. All of them, therefore, looked first to the governor and intendant, then to the Minister of Marine at Versailles, and ultimately to the King, for the satisfaction of their ambitions. Moreover, the number of appointments available was quite adequate either to gratify the families seeking them, or to give them good cause to anticipate an appointment in the not-too-distant future. As the eighteenth century wore on some Canadians succeeded in obtaining commissions and civil appointments in the Ministry of Marine outside Canada. The leading Canadian families therefore had every reason to be loyal to the Crown, to resist change, and to be imperial rather than colonial in their outlook.

Given these conditions in the colony—free land for the working of it, absence of taxation, efficient and equitable civil administration, ample career opportunities for the ambitious and talented, the provision of social institutions by the parent organizations in France and by the Crown of much higher quality, and at minimal cost, than the Canadians could have provided for themselves, and with the Crown pouring money into the colony for the maintenance of a standing colonial army—life for the Canadians would appear to have been almost idyllic; so much so, in fact, that it appears to be too good to be true, and one begins searching for flaws. In looking for concealed rifts in the social fabric, however, it is all too easy to overlook the real, constant danger that finally brought about the destruction of this unique society. The

Canadians ultimately had to pay a very high price for the material benefits they had received from the mother country. They paid it because they were not their own masters and were eventually sacrificed on the altar of French imperial policy, just as had been the Acadians half a century earlier, and as were also to be the colonists of Louisiana.

All three of these colonies were liabilities on the French economic balance sheet. (The sugar islands of the West Indies, on the other hand, were a source of great profit. When late in the war all of France's overseas maritime trade seemed about to be lost, France adamantly refused to sacrifice them.) From 1700 on, the mainland colonies were maintained by France chiefly for political and military reasons. Louisbourg was constructed, at great expense, to protect the French fisheries on the Grand Banks, to serve as a naval base for the protection of the Atlantic shipping, and to guard the sea route to Quebec. Louisiana was established, also at heavy cost, purely and simply to give France control of the Mississippi. Canada was made into a garrison colony to control the Great Lakes and the western hinterland. From Quebec to New Orleans a chain of forts was constructed and garrisoned to hold the Indian nations in the French alliance, thereby curbing the expansion of the English colonies, hemming them in along the coastal strip between the Alleghenies and the Atlantic.

The effectiveness of this containment policy was demonstrated when Anglo-American land speculators laid claim to the Ohio valley. Had this issue been left to the Canadians there would have been no quarrel in the first instance; they had never evinced the slightest interest in that territory. They were, however, called upon to oust the Americans; and at heavy cost in life and limb to establish a sizeable military presence on the Ohio. This they were required to do in the interests of French imperial policy. The ensuing hostilities were the occasion, rather than the cause, of the Seven Years' War.

Had this conflict been left to the colonials, had no European troops been employed by either side, the Canadians would have won, hands down, despite their gross inferiority of numbers. Given the nature of the terrain, the size of the forces that could be effectively employed was severely limited. It was not quantity of troops but their quality, that mattered. The Canadians, in all their wars with the English colonies, had demonstrated their military superiority. New France was organized on military lines, its men trained from infancy in the arts of guerilla warfare. Moreover, they controlled the river line of communication. Consequently during the first two years of the war the Canadians, supported by six battalions of poorly officered troops from the French army, won a series of crushing victories. Only the ineptitude of the commander of these French troops, the Marquis de Montcalm, prevented the victories from being even more telling than they actually were. By the end of 1757 the leaders of the English colonies were pleading for peace on any terms, fearing that their situation would be even worse when campaigning began the following year. Britain was forced to bolster the totally inadequate American forces with 23,000 British regulars and to detach a quarter of the Royal Navy for their transport and supply. Canada thus fulfilled its appointed role in French imperial strategy: that of a fortress. With a small military force it tied down a much larger enemy force, thereby preventing its employment in other more vital theatres—the Caribbean for one.

Unfortunately for the Canadians, the French government and its military machine were at this time in a very dilapidated state. During the course of the conflict there were four ministers of foreign affairs, four controllers general of finance, four ministers of war, and five ministers of marine—all of them incompetent. As for the army, a contemporary critic, Jacques-Antoine-Hippolyte de Guibert, remarked: 'The machine is so worn out that even a man of genius could only touch it with trepidation. His genius would not suffice to guarantee his success.' Montcalm, who in 1759 assumed supreme command of all the armed forces in Canada, was the personification of all that was wrong with this army. It is, therefore hardly surprising that when Major-General James Wolfe committed one of the most grievous of military sins and presented the French with an opportunity to destroy the British army on the Plains of Abraham, Montcalm chose to adopt the one course of action that virtually guaranteed his own defeat.* Once Quebec was lost, the colony could not be defended. It had to capitulate the following year.

The Canadians, when they had recovered from the initial shock, could not bring themselves to believe that they would be abandoned by the imperial government. They hoped, and expected, that France would somehow restore them to French rule at the eventual peace negotiations. But the duc de Choiseul now had other plans for Canada. His foreign policy had just one simple theme: to obtain peace as soon as possible, rebuild the French armed forces, consolidate the treaty with Spain, then renew the conflict with England at the earliest opportunity in order to remove the menace of British world dominance, and to restore the balance of power both in Europe and in the Americas. Canada and Louisiana were intended to play vital roles in this scheme, but they were not roles that the colonists would have chosen. They, however, were not consulted; their interests received no more consideration than had those of the Acadians in 1713. To consolidate the Family Compact Louisiana was ceded to Spain. As for Canada, Choiseul preferred to let England retain that conquest. He was confident, as were some in Britain, that with French power removed from North America, England's old colonies would soon strike out for independence. Were they to gain it, Britain's

---

* See pp. 128–33.

commerce, the source of her strength, would likely be crippled and France might well be the gainer thereby. Moreover, Britain would be forced to devote much of her military might and wealth to the protection of her remaining colonies, Canada and Nova Scotia.

That is, of course, exactly what happened. It took somewhat longer than the five years that Choiseul had hoped, and he was out of office when the Americans obligingly carried out their appointed role in French foreign policy, but his successor, the comte de Vergennes, was equal to the occasion. Without the military supplies and financial aid provided by France, Washington's forces could not have maintained themselves for long in the field. The rebellion would soon have been over. But what finally decided the issue, what forced the British government to grant the Americans their independence, was the defeat of Cornwallis at Yorktown. Prior to that engagement, Washington's war-weary forces were just about at the end of their tether. It was the combined action of the French fleet and a French army that forced Cornwallis to surrender. It is indeed ironic that it was the defeat of the French in Canada by a British army and navy that made it possible for the Americans to strike out for independence, and the defeat of the British in America by a French fleet and army that eventually gained it for them.

During the course of that war, and during the subsequent peace negotiations, the French declined to aid the Americans to acquire Canada. Although they were willing to foment trouble among the Canadians to distract the British, they made no attempt to reconquer their former colony. Vergennes preferred to see Britain retain Canada and thus be obliged to play the same role there that France had played prior to the Conquest. The result of this considered policy was that the division of North America north of Mexico was restored, and with it, temporarily, the balance of power in the New World. This time, however, it was Britain, not France, that had to foot the not-inconsiderable bill. To this extent French colonial policy proved to be both shrewd and successful.

As for the Canadians, they had enjoyed a great many privileges under the French regime, paid for by the overtaxed peasants of France. In return they had been required to serve their imperial masters in a struggle that was not of their making. Although they rendered valiant service, in the end they were regarded as expendable. Regardless of whether or not any other course of action had been open to them, they now had to pay a heavy price for their former dependence on forces over which they exerted no control.

The Role of the American Colonies in Eighteenth-Century French Foreign Policy

This paper was written to be read at an international conference on American history held at Genoa, Italy, in May 1976, in celebration of the bicentenary of the American Revolution. Professor Raimondo Luraghi, who holds the chair of North American history at the University of Genoa and who organized the conference, has always maintained that North American history was not that of the United States alone. Thus, in addition to the papers on aspects of the history of that republic given by American, Italian, Portuguese, English, French, and German scholars, Professor Marcel Trudel and I were invited to give papers on the Canadian connection with the Revolution.

Some of the American historians there were rather taken aback by my contribution, but they bore up manfully, were polite, and did not dispute it during the discussion period. The European scholars, particularly the Marxists, seemed quite impressed: their questions were stimulating.

The view taken by most Americans of their country's history can be described as teleological, if not apocalyptic. They regard the achievement of their political independence as preordained, in the natural order of things, and that their Revolutionary generation achieved this end virtually by its own unaided effort, by its own military prowess. If external aid is acknowledged it is not usually considered to have been decisive. The so-called 'patriot' forces would, in the long run it is believed, inevitably have defeated the British—not to mention the Loyalists, or Tories as they are usually labelled. Some scholars, however, admit that without French supplies, French gold, French military assistance on land and sea, both direct and indirect, the Americans would not likely have gained their independence when they did. It could also be argued that this last outcome might not necessarily have been a bad thing, that in fact the Loyalists had a good cause. By the same token a case can be made that Canada owes its independence from the United States, in no small degree, to decisions made by eighteenth-century ministers of the French Crown. Indeed, Canada too can celebrate a bicentary:

that of its liberation from the invading American forces that in 1776 were forced to abandon their attempt to conquer the colony and to retire, rather precipitately, whence they had come.

If events are viewed through eighteenth-century eyes, then it appears plain that the United States of America and the present political division of North America emerged as a direct consequence of the smouldering hostility between France and England that endured throughout the first half of that century. In fact, both the infant United States and the colony that was to become the Dominion of Canada were mere cat's-paws of the European powers. As early as 1710, during the War of the Spanish Succession, the notion first occurred to the French that England could be brought low were her American colonies to be induced to strike out for independence. On 10 May of that year the Comte de Pontchartrain, Louis XIV's minister of marine, sent an urgent dispatch to Philippe de Rigaud, Marquis de Vaudreuil, governor-general of New France at Quebec:

> Monsieur de Costebelle [who happened to be the lieutenant-governor at Plaisance in Newfoundland] has informed me that the main object of forces raised by the English last year was to establish their sovereignty at Boston and in the province of New York, the people of these provinces having always maintained themselves in a sort of Republic, governed by their Council and unwilling to accept the absolute governors of the Kings of England. It seemed to me that this was highly probable and it would be greatly to be desired that the Council of Boston be informed of the English Court's design, and of what consequence it is for it to maintain itself as a Republic and elude the administration intended to be imposed on it. The King would even approve joining with the Council to aid it in this undertaking. It would be necessary to sound out the leaders of this Council to discover their true feelings and induce them to it if possible. If you see any signs of succeeding in this every means must be utilized, for it is of the greatest importance.[1]

Pontchartrain was, of course, misinformed. That English expedition had been raised for an ill-fated assault on Canada. Yet it is rather astonishing to see the cool pragmatism of this minister of Louis XIV who was willing to aid and abet the establishment of a republic.

By mid-century several observers had remarked that the only thing that kept the Thirteen Colonies tied to the mother country was their chronic fear of the neighbouring French. In 1748 Peter Kalm, a Swedish professor of botany and a member of the Royal Swedish Academy of Science, commented during his travels in the English colonies and Canada that he had been told by several Englishmen:

> 'The English colonies in North America, in the space of thirty or fifty years, would be able to form a state by themselves entirely independent of Old England. But as the whole country which lies along the seashore is unguarded, and on the land side harassed by the French, these dangerous neighbours in

time of war are sufficient to prevent the connection of the colonies with their mother country from being quite broken off.[2]

Some observers on the French side were no less percipient.[3]

It thus appeared that were French power to remove itself from the mainland of North America, the old antagonist, Britain, would quickly suffer severely in consequence. France, however, was not yet willing to abandon its own American empire merely to cause England the loss of hers, even though her colonies imposed an increasingly heavy financial burden on her strained finances.[4] In fact, from 1700 on French imperial policy was designed to contain the English colonies, to curb their future expansion to the west and north. They were to be kept hemmed in between the Atlantic and the Appalachian Mountains.[5] Louisiana, Detroit, and the settlements along the Mississippi were established for the purpose. This policy was based on the fear that if the English colonies were allowed to expand westward to the Mississippi they could eventually overwhelm New France, go on to seize New Spain, and dominate the entire continent. If this were to occur and the allegiance of His Britannic Majesty's American subjects were to be retained, then England's economic and military power would become overwhelming. The role of New France in French imperial policy was to forfend this eventuality. Were it to fail to do this New France would no longer be worth retaining. In short, in the final analysis France regarded its colonies on the mainland of North America as expendable. England, however, did not so regard hers.

It was not until mid-century that the Anglo-Americans actually challenged French claims to the lands west of the Alleghenies. The French response was swift. The Americans were ignominiously driven back over the mountains by Canadian regular troops and their Indian allies. These events were the occasion, if not the main cause, of the Seven Years' War.

Ironically, had the Canadians had their way they would have let the Anglo-Americans take the Ohio Valley. Their only interest in the West was the fur trade, and that area produced only poor-grade furs. To them it was not worth a war to deny it to the English.[6] But French imperial policy took no account of the interests of the Canadians. In 1748 the Marquis de la Galissonière— soldier, scientist, man of letters, and recently appointed governor-general of New France—had instructed the minister of marine that the Mississippi valley was of little economic value to France, nor was it likely to be valuable in the foreseeable future. What was more, he declared, 'we should never delude ourselves that our colonies on the continent . . . could ever rival the neighbouring English colonies in wealth, nor even be commercially very lucrative.' For a long time to come, he explained, their only value would lie in the calibre of the martial men they nourished: before long their numbers would have increased to the point that, far from having to fear the encroachments of the Anglo-Americans, the Canadians would be able to lay down the law to them. Moreover, the English set such great store by their American colonies that they would think twice before embarking on adventures that would put them in hazard. Were they to do so they would be forced to divert a sizeable part of their navy to North American waters and transport an army to defend the colonies against the Canadians and Indians who, in three previous wars, had demonstrated that the Americans were no match for them. This would prevent England from using those forces in assaults on other and much more valuable French possessions, such as the sugar islands of the West Indies.[7]

This policy enjoyed a large measure of success in the early years of the Seven Year's War. Attacks by the Canadians and allied Indians on the Anglo-American frontier settlements brought some of those disunited colonies to their knees. Their leaders pleaded that peace be made at any price, fearing that future campaigns would bring worse disasters. England was obliged to transport 23,000 regular troops to America and employ a quarter of the Royal Navy to turn the tide, whereas France sent only eight of its 395 infantry battalions to Canada and four to Louisbourg.[8]

In 1760 Canada was finally conquered, but this was accomplished only as a result of the defeatist ineptitude of the French commander, the marquis de Montcalm, who, when offered the opportunity by his equally inept counterpart, Major-General James Wolfe, to destroy completely the British army before Quebec in September 1759, chose instead the course of action that resulted in defeat.[9] With the loss of Quebec the rest of the colony could not be successfully defended. The following year the shrunken French forces were obliged to capitulate at Montreal. If it be accepted that the conquest of Canada was a necessary prerequisite for the Americans to strike out for independence, then they have cause to be grateful to Montcalm. Certainly the Anglo-Americans could claim no credit for this British victory; they could never have conquered Canada on their own. Yet they were to be the chief beneficiaries.

The reaction in France to these events is revealing. The King's only concern was over the fact that his troops had been obliged to lay down their arms without receiving the honours of war. That concerned him greatly; the loss of half a continent and the fate of his Canadian subjects concerned him not at all.[10] Nor did his chief minister, the single-minded duc de Choiseul, appear dismayed at the unexpected turn of events. Even before Quebec fell a senior official in the ministry of marine, the marquis de Capellis, had advised the abandonment of Canada when the time came to negotiate for peace, since to do so would lead to the ruin of Britain by bringing on the defection of her American colonies. With the acquisition of Canada, he argued, those colonies would soon surpass old England in wealth, and indubitably they would then throw off the yoke of the metropolis.[11] A year later, upon receiving word that Quebec had fallen, Choiseul concurred with the view of Capellis.[12]

Choiseul also saw clearly that the longer the war endured the worse it would be for France. Peace was now essential, but not yet at any price. It had to be a negotiated, not an imposed peace. The main West Indies sugar islands had to be restored to France, along with a land base in the Gulf of St Lawrence to maintain the French fishing industry. The King, he instructed Monsieur de Bussy, the French plenipotentiary in London, would relinquish title to his economically profitable possessions only when France was no longer able to wage war.[13] Despite the unpopularity of the war in French Court and intellectual circles Choiseul encountered strong opposition in the King's Council to his proposed peace terms. At times, he complained, it became vituperative. But he persisted. He informed the marquis d'Ossun, French ambassador at Madrid, that he would insist on the abandonment of Canada in order to drive a rift between England and her colonies. The English yoke would have to be endured, he informed the ambassador, to obtain peace and thereby gain the respite needed to rebuild the navy. That done—hopefully in five years' time, before the enemy was prepared—hostilities could be reopened to humble England and restore the European balance of power.[14]

In England, too, controversy raged over the decision to treat for peace. The commercial element of the city of London, led by the Lord Mayor, was bitterly opposed to the terms being considered by the cabinet. This faction wanted to retain all the colonial conquests and seize more, to strip France of its overseas trade and deny its fishermen access to the North American fisheries.[15] The government successfully rode out that storm, despite the fear of the London mob, only to become embroiled in another controversy over which of the colonial conquests to retain, which to hand back in order to end hostilities before the feared collapse of England's strained finances ensued. Specifically, the dispute centred on Canada and the West Indies sugar Island, Guadeloupe. There is no need to go into details; the issue has been discussed at length elsewhere.[16] Suffice it to say that those in favour of retaining Guadeloupe claimed that were Canada to be retained, then the original Thirteen Colonies would soon strike out for independence. Canada would thus prove to have been acquired at far too high a price. In May 1761 Lord Bedford, the British plenipotentiary in Paris, cautioned Newcastle: 'I don't know whether the neighbourhood of the French to our North American colonies was not the greatest security for their dependence on the mother country, which I feel will be slighted by them when their apprehension of the French is removed'.[17] Choiseul was counting on it.

Among those opposing this stand, and the most vociferous in their demands that Canada be retained by Britain, were the Anglo-Americans. It was their view that carried the day. Their leading spokesman was Benjamin Franklin.

He vigorously denied that Canada, joined to the other British colonies, could ever enable them to pose a threat to the mother country. If, he pointed out, the Thirteen Colonies were unable to defend themselves against the Canadians, how could they possibly hope to defy successfully the mother country? Were Canada to be retained, he declared, the loyalty of the Anglo-Americans to Britain would be indissoluble. But, he warned, were Canada to be returned to France there could be no such guarantee, for it would check the Anglo-American drive for expansion, and they would know who to hold accountable for such a denial of their aspirations. Nothing, he added, could be better contrived to detach the colonies from the Empire, perhaps even drive them into the arms of France.[18] In that veiled threat there was a note of prophecy, made all the more ironic coming as it did from a future leader and beneficiary of the American Revolution. The debate, however, was purely academic. The British government had to retain Canada, regardless of the long-term consequences, for not to have done so would have strengthened to a dangerous degree the opposition in Parliament.

After the signing of the Treaty of Paris, French foreign policy was straightforward: to rebuild her navy, restore her overseas trade, keep England isolated, avoid continental entanglements, and above all to avoid war until French strength was fully restored—and when that had been achieved, at the first favourable opportunity to strike hard to reduce Britain's power and restore the prestige of France. Meanwhile preparations for the inevitable conflict had to be made. The ink was barely dry on the peace treaty when Louis XV ordered the duc de Broglie to have a careful survey made of the English coasts in order to revise the existing plans for an invasion of England.[19] Even before hostilities had ended Choiseul had set about rebuilding the navy. By 1763 there were forty good ships of the line in service, by 1770 sixty-four ships of the line and fifty frigates, and in 1778 there were eighty ships of the line in good condition. Naval arsenals and storehouses were replenished, an ample stock of masts and ship-timber laid by, and better and heavier-calibre guns were installed throughout the fleet. Reforms were effected in the training and discipline of the seagoing personnel: a body of ten thousand naval gunners was formed and drilled once a week during the ensuing decade.[20] Similar reforms were effected in the army: incompetent officers were weeded out, more rigorous training and discipline were imposed, the artillery was completely reorganized, and new battlefield tactics were adopted.[21] The old belief in the shock effect of attack by column, which had proven so disastrous at Quebec, was abandoned in favour of the fire power of attack in line.[22] These reforms were costly, but the economic resurgence of France in the years 1673–70 was little short of miraculous.[23]

On the diplomatic front France retained her allies after the war, with the exception of Russia, while Britain lost all of hers. The ruthless way in which

Britain had conducted the past war—the ambushing and murder of a French emissary by George Washington in peace time, the surprise attacks on French shipping before the declaration of war—had provided the French with the opportunity, quickly seized, to depict Britain in all the Courts of Europe as prefidious Albion.[24] The trampling on neutral shipping rights by the British navy, while at the same time British and American ships, for commercial gain, had kept the French West Indies, and possibly also Quebec, well supplied, had embittered the neutral maritime nations.[25] Frederick the Great was convinced that Prussian interests had been sacrificed whenever Britain had stood to gain. All of Europe was worried by the power acquired by Britain, and past actions caused them to fear how it would be used in the future. No state in Europe was willing to ally itself with Great Britain. Choiseul did not have to work to isolate Britain, it had isolated itself.

On the English side of the Channel, victory had created greater problems than had defeat for France. The government was wracked with internal strife and faction; the task of governing the newly acquired territories overseas, with their myriad alien peoples, seemed beyond the capacities of the shifting and shiftless men at Westminster. Financial retrenchment was the order of the day, and the armed forces suffered in consequence. The national debt had almost doubled and now stood at £137,000,000; the interest alone ran to £5,000,000, while the Crown's revenue did not exceed £8,000,000.[26] The costs involved in the administration of the new territories were not inconsiderable. The maintenance of twenty battalions, 10,000 men, just for the defence of the American frontiers cost £350,000 a year and the American colonial assemblies refused to share in that burden.[27] They clamoured for the right to despoil the Indians of the western lands; but when their actions resulted in a sudden, savage uprising by Pontiac's warriors that drove in the frontier settlements, it was the British army that had to suppress it, the British taxpayer who was faced with the bill. It is indeed ironic that this inability of the Americans to defend their frontiers and their refusal to pay for the security vouchsafed them by British soldiers induced the British government to introduce fiscal measures that provided the American dissidents with a justification for rebellion, and at the same time resulted in financial restraints in Britain that in turn hampered British military operations against the rebelling colonies at the onset of the ensuing war.[28]

Although France was not yet ready to become involved in another war if it could be avoided, no opportunity could be overlooked to fish in troubled waters. In 1765 Choiseul had informed Louis XV that only a revolution in America, which would surely come but likely not for some time, would weaken England sufficiently that she would no longer need to be feared in Europe.[29] Three years later a revolution in an unexpected quarter, that of the French Creoles of Louisiana against Spanish misrule, offered an opportunity to angle for a sizeable fish. Here again the French government sought to use an American colony, this time one that was no longer its own, as a cat's-paw to further its long-term policy of bringing Britain low.

After their ouster of the Spanish governor and his entourage, the leaders of the revolt, several of them Canadians, appealed to Louis XV to revoke the cession of the colony to Spain and restore them to French rule.[30] The comte d'Estaing, a naval commander of considerable renown, and the comte de Châtelet, French ambassador to the Court of St James's, separately urged that Louisiana be made a semi-autonomous republic, its independence to be guaranteed jointly by France and Spain. They claimed that, once established, this republic would continue to serve the purpose for which it had originally been founded, that of a barrier to an Anglo-American invasion of New Spain. Moreover, it would no longer be a financial burden to Spain. Over and above that, and what was of much greater significance, the establishment of such a republic, with New Orleans becoming a free port open to trade with all the maritime nations, would be sure to incite the Anglo-Americans—who were already chafing against the Stamp Act and the Townshend duties that had superseded it—to demand at least an equal degree of independence for themselves. This the British government would be sure to refuse. Nothing, d'Estaing and Châtelet concluded, would be more likely to result in an armed clash between the Americans and the British or to end with the disruption of the British Empire and the reduction of Britain's overweening power. The scheme was indeed ingenious, but when approached the Spanish government refused to co-operate, fearing that were it to be implemented and to succeed, its own colonies would demand equal treatment and this Spain could not contemplate. Instead, Spain aroused itself from its lethargy, despatched an army from the West Indies to New Orleans and with the aid of the firing squad firmly re-established its authority in Louisiana.[31]

Frustrated in that quarter, France continued to watch and wait as relations between Britain and her American colonies steadily deteriorated. When the comte de Vergennes was appointed foreign minister upon the accession of Louis XVI in 1774, he continued the policy of Choiseul, and every bit as adroitly. Then, when hostilities began in New England, arms and supplies were quickly provided the rebel forces by way of the West Indies. What was more, the American Congress was assured that it need have no fears whatsoever that France intended to take advantage of the situation to regain Canada. Fear of that eventuality might well have inhibited the American rebels in their drive for independence. At the same time, however, Vergennes had no desire to see the Americans conquer the old French colonies. An independent Thirteen Colonies could be counted on to disrupt and weaken England's economic power, but a too-powerful American republic would likely become, in the not-too-distant future, as great a menace to the tranquility of

Europe's maritime powers as Britain then was.[32] An independent American republic, by all means, but confined within its pre-Seven Years' War territorial limits and kept within bounds by Britain at Britain's great cost rather than, as in the past, by France: that was what Vergennes wanted.

The invasion of Quebec by an American army in 1775 and its precipitate retreat the following year suited the French admirably. The Americans had once again demonstrated their military ineptitude. They were no more able to conquer Canada now than they had been in their previous attempts. Their taking up of arms in this fashion ensured a strong riposte by Britain and they would have to depend on French aid to avoid the eventual crushing of their revolt. Upon learning of this American defeat at Quebec, Vergennes commented: 'Do not disturb them in their desperate eagerness to wage war with their fellow citizens. Let them wear themselves down in this civil strife while we reserve our strength to be used as best suits us.'[33]

All of the American cities along the Atlantic seaboard were at the mercy of the British navy, but the rebels could control the hinterland and deny its supplies to the British forces. The war thus became one dominated, to a large extent, by logistics.[34] The British had to transport from England most of the supplies required by the army of over 32,000 regulars that they had sent to America. At the same time France and Holland provided the rebels with everything they needed to keep their army in the field. In the final analysis two things determined the outcome of the struggle: geography and the French navy. In 1782 one of Général le comte de Rochambeau's aides-de-camp remarked to a friend of Charles Fox: 'No opinion was clearer than that though the people of America might be conquered by well disciplined European troops, the country of America was unconquerable.'[35]

It was, however, the French navy that finally decided the issue. The English historian, Piers Mackesey, in his history of the revolution, observed: 'Whatever the condition of the rebel colonies, whatever the grounds for believing that capitulation was near, a shadow hung over the British path of conquest: the shadow of the French fleet.'[36] For in this war, unlike the preceding one, Britain did not enjoy naval superiority. This time the French held the initiative. The British navy had to disperse its ships to parry the threatened invasion of England, and it had to fend off attacks on its Mediterranean possessions, and in India as well as on its West Indian islands. At the same time it had to maintain a fleet in North American waters spread between the Gulf of St Lawrence and Florida. A large part of the British army, close to 64,000 rank and file in 1781, had to be retained in England for home defence; the disease-ridden West Indies devoured men at a frightful rate, and close to 9,000 troops were tied down in Canada to guard against a threatened Franco-American invasion.[37] The war had become a global one. Yet despite the forces of France, Spain, and Holland arrayed against them, not to mention Washington's motley army of some 15,000 men, by 1781 the British had gained the upper hand in America. The collapse of the rebel forces appeared imminent and some of their leaders began making their dispositions accordingly to save their hides. Vergennes began to think it might be expedient to treat for peace on the basis of *uti possidetis*, which would have left Britain in control of the Carolinas, Georgia, East Florida, the port of New York, and most of Maine. The fear was that were the rebel cause to collapse, Britain would be able to concentrate her forces and sweep the French out of the West Indies.[38] The British government, however, had no intention yet of treating for peace. George III was determined to put an end to foreign intervention in England's own affairs. The war in America appeared to be virtually won and the expected collapse of French government finances would, it was expected, soon force France out of the war.[39] It was at this juncture of events that the French took a desperate gamble.

To make another attempt at an invasion of England was out of the question, since no reliance could be placed on the Spanish fleet. It was therefore decided to concentrate de Grasse's West Indies fleet on the American coast—ready, if the worst happened, to evacuate Rochambeau's troops in the event of an American collapse. De Grasse then stripped the West Indies garrisons of 3,000 men to reinforce Rochambeau's army against Cornwallis at Yorktown. The French thereby placed the sugar islands and the year's convoy in hazard, something that a British admiral would never have dared to do, hence never thought the French would. But it worked. Rochambeau, Washington, and de Grasse achieved strategic surprise and a concentration of overwhelming force at the crucial point. Cornwallis, with his 6,000 men (four of his regiments were American Loyalists), found himself contained in an indefensible position by 7,800 French regulars with a powerful siege train, 5,800 American regulars, and 3,000 Virginia militia. In the Bay was de Grasse's fleet, rendering escape or reinforcement impossible. When his ammunition was exhausted and the rank and file fit for duty reduced almost by half, Cornwallis had to surrender. French initiative, French tactics, French ships, French guns and men achieved that decisive and unexpected victory. The Americans could not have done it on their own.

Britain now found itself in much the same position as France had been in 1760. The national debt had taken on frightening proportions. The longer the war endured the worse the outcome would likely be. With the surrender at Yorktown the entire south was lost and the Loyalists now suffered savage reprisals. Britain also had had reverses in India, Ireland was on the verge of revolt, West Florida and Tobago were lost, Minorca had been invaded and the scurvy-ridden garrison was soon to succumb, Gibraltar was threatened, heavy shipping losses had been inflicted by the French corsairs, a French naval squadron captured then destroyed Fort Churchill in Hudson Bay, a

French fleet threatened Jamaica, and a combined French and Spanish fleet cruised in the English channel. Britain now had no recourse but to check France and Spain, at whatever cost, before its own powers of resistance crumbled. When, therefore, Benjamin Franklin approached the British government to begin discussions to end the American war, the independence of America had to be accepted as a pre-condition. The resolutions of the House of Commons of 28 February 1782, which repudiated the coercion of the American colonies, made certain of that.

Lord Shelburne, who had just acceded to the office of secretary of State for Home, Colonial, and Irish affairs, hoped that the granting of independence would lead to a reconciliation and the preservation of England's commercial ties with the erstwhile colonies. When, however, Franklin demanded that Canada and Nova Scotia be ceded to the infant republic, the British negotiators balked. The Americans had conspicuously failed to take these provinces by force of arms and their blandishments had been rejected by the peoples concerned. After Yorktown, Washington had sought to use the French army in an assault on Canada, but its commander, the comte de Rochambeau, on prior oral instructions from Vergennes, refused to consider it.[40] Vergennes was no more willing than Shelburne to allow the Americans to acquire this vast territory by devious means. He held to the original policy of Louis XIV and strove to have their territorial limits restricted to the lands east of the old Proclamation Line of 1763 that had run along the crest of the Appalachians.[41] The region between the mountains and the Mississippi he wanted held for the Indian nations, under British suzerainty. American land speculators, however, among them Franklin and Washington, had long coveted those lands and were determined to have them. In the hope of weaning the Americans out of the French alliance, Shelburne gave way. It is rather ironic that the British government here insisted on giving away what France had once sought to deny to Britain but now desperately wanted the British to retain. The cession of those lands spelled the doom of the Indian nations, whose country it really was. Within a very few years they were overrun, despoiled, and utterly destroyed by the land-hungry Americans, some of whose slave-holding political leaders wrote so glibly of the rights of man.

Having gained their main objectives, independence, and a huge acquisition of territory, the American negotiators, without informing the French of their intentions, signed the preliminary articles of peace. Vergennes was outraged when he learned of this, deeming it, at the least, as an act of bad faith. In a letter to the French minister at Philadelphia he commented: 'If we can judge the future by what passes presently before our eyes we shall be badly paid for what we have done for the United States of America, and for having assured them of that title.'[42] A few weeks later France and England signed a preliminary peace treaty.

And so this bitterly fought war came to an end. For Britain the granting of independence to the Americans was a humiliating defeat. George III tried to console himself with the thought that separation might after all be for the best. As he put it, 'knavery seems to be so much the striking feature of its Inhabitants that it may not in the end be an evil that they become Aliens to this Kingdom.'[43]

The grapes of peace were indeed sour. France had gained its main objective: the disruption of the British Empire and the restoration of its own national pride. It gained little else, except a few scraps of overseas territory and a further crippling load of debt that its creaking financial structure proved unable to support. The hope of replacing England as America's trading partner was not realized and its treaty of alliance with the United States was abrogated by the Americans the moment it was put to the test in the next Anglo-French war. Britain emerged from that conflict more powerful than ever, master of the greatest empire the world has seen, and was to remain the dominant power for the ensuing century.

The chief beneficiaries of the 1776–83 war, in the long term, were of course those Americans who were prossessed of white skins. Within a century they dominated the continent. Vergenne's fears of the threat that an independent America would pose for the European colonial powers, were it not to be restrained from the outset, proved to have been justified.

Sovereignty Association, 1500–1783

Some time after the Parti-Québecois came to power and it appeared that Quebec might actually secede from Canada, the late Professor W.L. Morton wrote a letter to the Globe and Mail *giving it as his opinion that were this to transpire then an independent Quebec should be restricted to the lands it had controlled prior to Confederation: the northern half of the province, he opined, had to revert to the federal government. That raised a question in my mind: by what right could the federal government, or the Quebec government for that matter, lay claim to the land in question? It seemed to me that title to that land rightfully rested with the aboriginal peoples who had occupied it from time immemorial, had never sold it or ceded it to anyone by treaty or any other conveyence, and had not had the lands taken from them by conquest: therefore, in logic and equity, if not in law, they still retained the title to their lands. That being the case, neither the federal government nor a provincial government could do anything to the lands without the sanction of the titleholders, the Indian and Inuit peoples. I made a mental note at the time that I really ought to investigate the issue.*

Some years later I found myself involved as an expert witness in an Indian land-claim case heard in the Supreme Court of Ontario: the Attorney-General of Ontario versus Bear Island Foundation, et al. This forced me to sort out my ideas on the sovereignty issue as it pertained to the French regime, and to devote several months to research. Question after question was raised and answers had to be sought. The result was a slightly flawed version (due to haste) of the article here reprinted that was entered as evidence by counsel for the defence. The judge, Mr D.R. Steele, was not impressed by this or any of the other historical evidence presented. He inadvertently revealed that he had no knowledge of the history of this country, frequently demanding of counsel for the defence why they had always to go back to consider the charter granted to Jacques Cartier by Henry VII. The historical background to the case he dismissed, in his reasons for judgement, as totally irrelevant. He also dismissed a decision of the Supreme Court of Canada, Guerin et al v The Queen et al, *released 1 November 1984, that contradicted his judgement, and gave judgement for the Crown. The judgement is presently before the appellate court of Ontario and most likely will have to be decided by the Supreme Court of Canada. It could even go further, to an international court.*

At the close of the sixteenth century all of present-day Canada was in the possession of the Indian and Inuit peoples. No Europeans resided anywhere in the land. Fishermen landed on the Atlantic coast and in the Gulf of St Lawrence to dry their cod, obtain wood, water, fresh meat, and to trade with the Indians for furs—but permanent settlements there were none.[1] Today the Indian peoples retain title to only a small fraction of their ancient lands. Sovereignty over the entire country is claimed by the federal and provincial governments of Canada; the rights of the indigenous peoples are either ignored or given short shrift. In recent years, some of these native peoples have resorted to the courts to assert their claims to their ancestral lands. It is, therefore, of some consequence that the history of how this situation came about should be investigated. It is also important that future legal judgements should not be based on ignorance or misconceptions of history, as has happened on occasion.[2]

The historical process of this centuries-long development in Canada has passed through three main stages: that of the French regime, that of the ensuing British colonial period, and, post-1867, that of the Dominion of Canada. The relations of the French with the Indians were markedly different from those of the British prior to 1760, and those of both the British and the later Dominion of Canada were different from the policies and attitudes of the United States authorities in this regard. Yet, after the cession of Canada to Great Britain in 1763, the end result for the Indians of Canada was roughly the same as for those caught within the confines of the burgeoning republic to the south.[3]

At the turn of the fifteenth century when the Americas were rediscovered by Europeans, rivalry, hostility, and warfare between the major European powers were the norm. The countries first making these discoveries, both in the Americas and the Orient, were determined to exclude all other nations from the benefits to be derived from the new-found lands. Although military force was the real determinant, various theories were promulgated on how title to these lands not occupied by Christian peoples could be acquired. Spain and Portugal claimed that prior discovery and conquest gave them title to pagan lands in Africa, Asia, and the Americas, to the exclusion of all others. Papal bulls granted by Alexander VI in 1493 were interpreted to represent the division, between themselves, of the world beyond the confines of Europe. The dividing line was at first drawn from pole to pole, 100 leagues west of the Azores, then hastily amended, at the behest of Jean II of Portugal by the Treaty of Tordesillas, to 370 leagues west of those islands. Portugal thereby retained Brazil, but the whole of North America fell under Spanish sovereignty.[4]

Although this was a much more civilized way to proceed than by force of arms, the other maritime powers could not accept being denied overseas ventures. Francis I of France, for one, rejected the notion out of hand. He asserted that title to pagan lands had to rest on three things: prior discovery, conquest, and occupation. Lands that might have been discovered first by the subjects of a Christian prince but were not subsequently occupied by them had, perforce, to be open to trade for all comers.[5] At that time the French were more interested in overseas commerce than in the establishment of colonies.

The English, when they came to settle Virginia, quickly resorted to force of arms to seize land from the resident Indians. As Governor Wyat put it in 1623–4: 'Our first work is Expulsion of the Salvages . . . for it is infinitely better to have no heathen among us, who at best were but as thornes in our sides, then to be at peace and league with them.'[6] Some 132 years later Hermon Husband of Orange County, North Carolina, reported to John Earl Granville, Viscount Carteret: 'Some here I find are so stupified as to secretly think & desire an occasion against those savages to have them destroyed in order to possess their lands with Negroes & have more room to employ their slaves upon.'[7]

In New England the Puritans occupied land left vacant when the great plague of 1616–17 killed a third or more of the Indians between Narraganset Bay and the Penobscot River. This the Puritans regarded as 'divine providence'.[8] When they began to expand inland the New Englanders were constrained to adopt the practice of the Dutch West India Company and to buy land from the Indians.[9] The ravages of disease had left the survivors with more land than they needed, and for the New Englanders acquisition of land title by purchase was cheaper than seizing it by force of arms. It required the drawing up of deeds to which Indian representatives affixed their symbols. The deeds were then registered and preserved for future reference.[10] No matter that too many of these deeds were fraudulent, the fact remained that a prior Indian title to the land was explicitly recognized.[11]

According to European custom, sovereignty carried with it four rights: that of the sovereign power to impose taxes on the people residing on the land over which sovereignty was claimed; to enact laws and enforce them; to demand military service from the adult males; and the right of eminent domain. It therefore follows that a European state could not be regarded as sovereign if it could not exercise those rights. Put another way, external sovereignty meant that the 'state was entirely free to regulate its relations with other states.' It also meant that a sovereign people 'did not yield habitual obedience to any other power.' If they were independent—that is, they were not subject to any legal superior power—then they were a sovereign people.[12] The Indian nations with whom the French had dealings could, and did, maintain that they satisfied all those requirements.

Some of the English colonies claimed, by virtue of their royal charters, that they held title to the land within lines of latitude westward to the Pacific

Ocean.[13] Virginia, under the royal charter of 1609, with only a handful of settlers clinging desperately to a foothold in the malarial swamps on the St James River, laid claim to all the land enclosed by the line of latitude at approximately 35°, and by a northwestern line from, roughly, the northern shore of Delaware Bay through Lake Ontario, Georgian Bay, and on across present-day Ontario, Manitoba, and the North West Territories.[14]

Claims were made by the interested European powers to vast areas in North America merely by virtue of a subject's having been the first to travel through them. Title was also claimed to lands by monarchs whose subjects had never seen, had only heard of, them. Thus France claimed the entire Ohio and Mississippi valleys by virtue of the voyages of Jolliet, Marquette, and La Salle. In fact, La Salle had not voyaged down the Ohio and he did not lay claim to having done so, yet France rested its claim to the region on his supposed voyage of discovery.[15] Needless to say, neither England nor Spain recognized these claims. Indeed, had they been deemed worthy of credence, then Venice, in the fourteenth century, could have claimed title to all of China as a consequence of Marco Polo's journey to the court of the Great Khan. In the final analysis sovereignty rested on two things: occupation and military force sufficient to impose the will of the occupying power on the people in the territory to which title was claimed.

The French Crown early adopted the practice of granting letters patent to certain of its subjects, giving them the right to seize land from the pagans by conquest or to obtain it by other means—this, it was piously stated, in order to bring them to a knowledge of God. It was hoped that the establishment of the King's authority in the new land would bring benefits to the commerce of his kingdom.[16] In this early period the French hoped to find sources of mineral wealth such as Spain had discovered in Mexico and Peru.[17] The disappointment occasioned by the discovery that Cartier's famous gold and diamonds were mere dross and worthless quartz did not end the search for minerals,[18] but by the end of the century a more tangible source of wealth had been found in the furs that the Indians were eager to exchange for European goods. This was enough to attract Europeans in large numbers to Acadia and the Gulf of St Lawrence. Companies were now formed and monopoly charters granted by the Crown in an attempt to exclude foreigners from this lucrative trade.[19]

From that point on the notion of seizing land from the aborigines by conquest had to be abandoned by the French. Good relations had to be maintained at all costs with the Indians who supplied the coveted furs. When permanent settlements were eventually established in the Bay of Fundy they were made on dyked tidewater land that was of no value to the Indians.[20] These settlements posed no threat to the indigenous peoples, who welcomed the French in their midst, since they provided a year-round supply of trade goods at their posts. Moreover, in Acadia the French were so few in number that they represented no tangible or imaginable threat to the Micmacs, Malecites, and Abenaki.[21]

Similarly, in the St Lawrence valley the French established a trading post at Tadoussac with the sanction of the local Indians, nomadic hunters who transported their surplus trade goods to nations far in the interior in exchange for furs. As for occupying any part of that inhospitable region, the French certainly had no such desire. The French Crown laid claim to the land, but it was really a claim intended to exclude all but French subjects from the Indian trade, the Gulf fishery, and the seal and whale hunt.[22] The French then had no interest in the land itself, only with what it and its adjacent waters produced. They brought no womenfolk with them and made no attempt to cultivate the soil. When settlement was eventually undertaken its purpose was solely to make the fur trade and the fishing stations secure from foreign attack. These tiny French settlements were a means to an end, and the end required that the Indians and their way of life be preserved.

In 1608 the French established a trading post at Quebec under the local command of Samuel de Champlain. The region from Quebec to the island of Montreal had, when Jacques Cartier visited it in the 1530s and 1540s, been occupied by the St Lawrence Iroquois. It was they who had forced Cartier and Roberval to abandon their attempt to establish a colony near Quebec, or Stadacona as it then was.[23] When Champlain arrived on the scene those Indians had disappeared. Their warriors, archaeological evidence indicates, were killed in battle, their womenfolk and children absorbed by their triumphant Huron foes, likely after being decimated by some disease contracted from European traders.[24] The entire St Lawrence valley was unoccupied. There was, therefore, no need for the French to seize the land by conquest or to obtain title by purchase. The Hurons and Algonquins welcomed them, since they provided a secure supply, close at hand, of European goods. Moreover, to consolidate this commercial alliance Champlain felt compelled to give them military aid in their war with the Iroqouis Confederacy. In 1611 the Algonquins requested that Champlain establish a settlement at the Lachine rapids to shorten their journey and remove the need to run the Iroquois gauntlet along the St Lawrence from the mouth of the Ottawa to Quebec. It was not until 1634 that Champlain was able to establish a second post, not at Montreal as requested, but at Trois-Rivières. He did so with the concurrence and at the behest of the Hurons and Algonquins, who wished to make use of the French as an auxiliary military force.[25]

In 1627 Cardinal Richelieu, who had had himself appointed Grand Master and Superintendant General of the Navigation and Commerce of France, organized the Company of One Hundred Associates, each associate providing 3,000 *livres* of working capital. All previous charters were thereby rendered null and void. The stated aims of the new company were, first and foremost, to convert the Indians to Christianity and cause them to adopt a civil mode of life; second, it was hoped that by establishing royal authority in the fledgeling colony with its pathetic population of 107, the King's subjects could reap economic benefits. Provision was made for the establishment of 4,000 French Catholic settlers in the colony within fifteen years, this to prevent the King's enemies seizing the lands now claimed by France. These lands were nothing if not extensive—from those previously claimed in Florida, along the Atlantic seaboard to the Arctic circle, and inland from Newfoundland to the *mer douce*, Lake Huron, including all the land drained by the St Lawrence River and all waters flowing into it, and then as far beyond as His Majesty's subjects would find it possible to go. There was, however, no mention of lands being seized by right of conquest. The officials in France who drafted the charter could have had only the vaguest notion of what was being claimed. Their obvious purpose was to forestall claims by other powers.

French attitudes and policy for the Indians were clearly revealed in Article 17 of the charter, wherein it was stated that descendants of the French who would inhabit the colony, along with those Indians who became practising Christians, would be treated as French subjects. As such they would have the right to reside in France whenever they desired and there acquire, bequeath, and succeed to property, and accept grants or legacies just as could the King's subjects in France, without the necessity to make any declaration of intent or obtain letters of naturalization. In short, Indians who were converted to Christianity were entitled to all the rights and privileges of French citizenship. The authors of the letters patent here manifested a lamentable ignorance of Indian predilections, but at least they had what they imagined to be the Indians' best intersts at heart.[26]

Subsequently, when on 17 December 1640 title to a large part of the island of Montreal was ceded to the 'Messieurs de Saint-Sulpice', the opening sentence of the patent stated: 'Our greatest desire being to establish a strong colony in New France in order to instruct the Indian peoples of those regions in the knowledge of God and to bring them to live in a civilized manner. . . .'[27] In 1644 the concession was ratified and again it was spelled out in great detail that the sole purpose of the settlement was to serve the Indians.[28]

In 1645 the Company ceded its monopoly on the fur trade to the colonists and once more it was stated that the King had no other purpose than 'the furthering of the glory of God and the honour of this Crown by the conversion of the uncivilized peoples, and to reduce them to civility under the authority of His Majesty.'[29] It was then believed that the only effective way to Christianize the Indians was, to persuade them by one means or another, to abandon their nomadic life and to settle at Montreal as sedentary farmers merged with the French settlers. That this would have destroyed the fur trade was either not considered or was regarded as inconsequential. The fact that this policy enjoyed virtually no success whatsoever does not detract from its altruistic intent.[30] It was implicit that since the Crown wished, and expected, the Indians to occupy and exploit the land, their title to it would have been recognized, as was that of the French settlers. When some of the Hurons who had survived the Iroquois holocaust of 1649 fled to Quebec they were granted land at Sillery under seigneurial tenure, with the Jesuits acting for them, in exactly the same manner as seigneurial concessions were made by the Crown to French settlers.[31]

In theory the King was the true proprietor of all property, movable and immovable, in his kingdom. In his memoirs Louis XIV declared: 'Kings are absolute rulers, hence naturally they have the full and free disposition of all property in their realms, that of the laity as well as of the clergy, hence they must make use of it as would a wise steward, that is to say, according to the needs of the State.'[32] He maintained that his subjects were merely allowed the use of whatever property they might have acquired, during his pleasure. In New France Louis XIII had granted title to the land under seigneurial tenure, in perpetuity, to the Company of One Hundred Associates. The Associates merely had to make obeisance, swear fealty, and present the King with a gold crown of eight marks' weight at each succession to the throne.[33]

The 'in perpetuity' clause availed the Company nothing when Louis XIV, in 1663, decided to take the colony out of its hands on the grounds that it had failed to live up to the terms of its charter.[34] Title to all lands claimed by France in Canada, Acadia, Newfoundland, the West Indies, and Africa was now vested in the newly created Compagnie des Indes Occidentales. The Company's charter stipulated that all these lands in America—as far as they extended by virtue of occupation by the French, or would extend in the future by right of conquest—were conceded to the company under seigneurial tenure, which meant that title ultimately rested with the Crown. This charter repeated in a modified form Article 17 of the charter of the defunct Company of One Hundred Associates. French subjects who immigrated to the colonies were guaranteed the same rights and privileges as were subjects residing in France. These rights were also extended to children born of marriages with Indians. It was the earnest desire of the minister responsible for the colonies, Jean-Baptiste Colbert, to have the French colonists and the Indians intermarry and form one race. This, he fondly believed, would serve two purposes: populate the colony without the need to ship a large number of emigrants from France at great expense, and bring the Indians to accept the French way of life by assimilation.[35]

Royal policy towards the Indians was succinctly stated by Louis XIV in a directive to the governor of New France, Daniel de Rémy de Courcelle:

The King has two main aims regarding the native Indians.

The first is to gain their conversion to the Christian and Catholic faith as quickly as possible, and to attain this end, apart from the instructions that they will receive from the missionaries whom His Majesty maintains for this purpose under the direction of Mgr de Petrée, his intention is that the officers, soldiers, and all his other subjects should treat the Indians gently, with justice and equity, without ever doing them any harm or violence; the lands they inhabit must never on any account be usurped under the pretext that the French find them more convenient and prefer them.

His Majesty's second aim is eventually to make these Indians his subjects, labouring usefully for the increase of trade, which will develop little by little in Canada once it becomes well cultivated; but his intention is that this should be done equitably and that the Indians should come to it of their own free will.[36]

The clergy, who had originally espoused the policy of 'Frenchification', became convinced that contacts between the Indians and lay Frenchmen had to be reduced to the minimum since, it seemed to them, each acquired the worst traits of the other.[37] They therefore sought to introduce what can be likened to latter-day South African 'apartheid', but with a difference. In New France it was espoused by the clergy purely for the benefit and protection of the Indians. The French were eventually constrained to abandon their attempts to make the Indians into Europeans and accept them as Indians.

Although Colbert strongly espoused the policy of assimilating the Indians and was very critical of the clergy for their rejection of it, at the same time he strongly opposed any territorial expansion of the settlements west of the island of Montreal.[38] He also ordered that the colonists were not to voyage to the Indian country to trade for furs. They had to remain in the settlements and let the Indians bring their furs to trade at Montreal or Trois-Rivières. He wanted the central colony strengthened rather than allow its meagre man-power resources to be scattered about in the wilderness.[39]

In the colony, however, certain of Colbert's officials disagreed with this policy. The Intendant Jean Talon had quickly come to realize the great wealth to be garnered from the fur trade. He also warned of the potential threat to French interests posed by the English in New York, recently seized from the Dutch, and their presence in Hudson Bay. Within a few weeks of his arrival at Quebec he wrote to Colbert advising him that there was nothing to prevent the French expanding their claims on the continent as far south as Mexico. He proposed the establishment of garrisoned forts on both sides of Lake Ontario, with a sailing barque to supply and maintain communications between them. By this means, he declared, the Iroquois would be cowed and French control of the fur trade assured.[40] Colbert would have none of it. He informed Talon that they had to concentrate their activities within an area that they could expect to hold securely, rather than grasp at too great an expanse and one day be forced to abandon part of it with a consequent loss of prestige.[41]

Undeterred, Talon sent what he called 'exploration parties' north to Hudson Bay, down the Mississippi, and west into Lake Superior.[42] He stated that their purpose was to search for mineral deposits and also to claim for France the lands traversed. In reality they were little more than a means to circumvent Colbert's restrictive fur-trade edict and garner large quantities of the choicer northern furs. One such party was sent out by Talon in October 1670 with orders to voyage as far west as possible to discover the copper deposits of Lake Superior, the route to the western ocean, and at the same time to lay claim to the Great Lakes for France. Led by Simon-François Daumont, sieur de Saint-Lusson, with Nicolas Perrot as interpreter and four Jesuits in attendance, an assembly was held near Sault Saint-Marie on 14 June 1671 with representatives of fourteen western tribes. According to Perrot's account written several years after the event, and the edited version of the Jesuits, a post bearing the arms of France was erected, an official act of possession drawn up and read to the tribesmen, who were thereby considered to have placed themselves under the protection of, and in submission to, the King of France.[43]

It is extremely doubtful that the Indians had any understanding of what the ceremony purported. The notion that these strangers could somehow claim to have taken possession of their lands would have seemed utterly ridiculous to them; they might as well have laid claim to the air. As for their now being under the protection of a king thousands of miles away, that too would have appeared nonsensical, since it was obviously the French who required the protection of the Indians in that part of the world. The episode is likely an early example of what might be termed the 'Janusian'—two-faced—attitude of the French towards the Indians at that time: tell Europeans—friends or foes—one thing, and the Indians something quite different, or nothing at all.[44]

A more likely version of the Saint-Lusson episode was related four generations later by a Métis descendant of one of Saint-Lusson's companions. (The memories of illiterate peoples are far more reliable than those of the literate, who do not have to rely on their memory and hence rarely do.) This Métis recalled that according to the collective memory of his mother's people, Saint-Lusson had requested free passage to the Indians' country at all times to trade in their villages. 'He asked that the fires of the French and the Ojibway nations might be made one, and everlasting. He promised the protection of the great French nation against all their enemies. . . .'[45] There is no mention in this recollection of any awareness that they had ceded their lands to the French, and something as significant as that, had it actually transpired, would not easily have been forgotten. That the Indians were uneasy over the ceremony is indicated by the fact that immediately afterward they removed the copy of the act of possession that Saint-Lusson had attached to the post behind the coat of arms and threw it in the fire, fearing that it was intended to cast a deadly spell on them.[46]

Talon, seemingly in some trepidation over Colbert's reception of his account of this expedition, assured the minister that it, and his other expeditions, had not cost the Crown a sou. He blandly stated that after taking possession of the Indians' lands Saint-Lusson had, in the King's name, granted them back to those who occupied them and in return had received several packs of beaver pelts.[47] Certainly on an occasion such as this there would have had to be an exchange of presents; Indian protocol insisted on it. It is difficult to escape the conclusion that this episode had been nothing more than a profitable trading venture to cement commercial ties with the northwest tribes. The asserted act of possession was, in reality, an empty gesture likely fabricated to assuage Colbert. The Indians remained in complete possession of their lands and in no way submissive to the French, who could travel through their territory only with their permission and establish trading posts only with their consent. The Indian nations were in the stronger position. The French dared do nothing that might offend them. They had to be provided with trade goods at favourable prices; trading practices that offended them had to be curbed swiftly.[48]

These proud nations refused to submit to French justice when, in their own country, they committed crimes against French subjects. All that the French authorities could do in cases where Canadians were murdered or pillaged by Indians was appeal to the chiefs of the offenders' nation and demand that those responsible be either punished or handed over to the French, but these appeals appear to have been consistently rejected.[49] In 1708 Governor-General Vaudreuil and the Intendant Jacques Raudot wrote to the Council of Marine, following one such incident, that 'these Indians pointed out to him that they were not sufficiently the masters, the ones of the others— and that is the truth—to be able to hand over one of their own men. . . .'[50] François Clairambault d'Aigremont, naval commissary, after his tour of inspection in the West, reported: 'One will never succeed in establishing subordination amongst them, they will have none of it, for they do not obey even their Chiefs who never order them about, do not even dare to try, but only to suggest to them that such and such should be done.'[51] The Indians had their own concept of justice and in their own country they meted it out as they saw fit.[52] When the presumptuous Jean-Louis, comte de Raymond, submitted a *mémoire* on colonial affairs wherein he recommended that *haute*, *moyenne*, and *basse* justice be imposed on the Indians of the North, Governor General Duquesne declared that the man was clearly out of his mind to have made such a preposterous suggestion.[53]

Even in the case of crimes committed inside the colony by Indians, either by those residing there or those coming from afar, the French authorities had great difficulty in bringing those responsible to justice. The crimes were, invariably, acts of violence against a person, committed while the perpetrator was intoxicated. The Indians claimed, with cause, that they could not be held accountable for their actions under those circumstances since it was the alcohol, and not they, that had been responsible.[54] In 1676 the Sovereign Council had decreed that all Indians would be subject to the penalties required by French law for the crimes of theft, murder, rape, drunkenness, and other misdemeanours.[55] The Indians refused to comply; they declared that they were not subject to French law and could not be imprisoned against their will.[56]

During the period 1712–48 three Indians were convicted of murder and two of them were swiftly executed.[57] Significantly, although all three were mission Indians, resident in the colony at Sault Saint-Louis and Lac des Deux Montagnes, they were not tried in the Royal Court at Montreal but by military tribunal, for, as Governor-General Vaudreuil and the Intendant Michel Bégon explained, to bring Indians into the courts risked 'raising up all the Indian nations against us, and that they would only take the side of the party whom we wished to punish.'[58]

The French authorities had to admit there was little they could do except to punish severely the Canadians who had provided the liquor to Indians when a crime ensued in consequence, as in the case of Jacques Detaillis in 1719. He was tried for selling liquor to a group of Sault Saint-Louis Iroquois who, while drunk, killed a Canadian child. They denied their culpability, blamed the incident, which they deeply regretted, on the liquor that they had drunk, and were not brought to trial.[59] The usual fine for anyone convicted of giving or selling liquor in excess to the Indians, in defiance of the Royal Ordonnance of 14 May 1679, was 50 *livres*; but in serious cases, where death had resulted from the offence, the fine could be 500 *livres*.[60] In some cases the penalties were more severe than that but still they proved to be no deterrent. In October 1735 Father Nau of the Sault Saint-Louis Mission reported that in the past two months one Frenchman had been sent to the galleys, two whipped in public by the hangman, and one put in the stocks to be reviled, yet the Indians of his mission were still obtaining supplies of liquor.[61] Clearly the King's writ was ineffective at Sault Saint-Louis. To all intents it was an independent republic, in no wise subordinate to French authority.

Where territorial rights were concerned the French had conflicting claims only with the Five Nations Iroquois Confederacy. The Iroquois claimed that all the land south and west of the Ottawa River and around the shores of Lakes Erie and Huron belonged to them, they having conquered it from the Hurons, Petuns, and Neutrals in the mid-sixteenth century.[62] They were bitterly resentful when Governor-General Louis de Buade de Frontenac established his trading post at Cataracoui in 1673. When, during the 1689–97 war between France and England, the French were constrained to abandon and destroy the fort, the Iroquois swore that they would never allow them to reoccupy the site.[63] However, during that war their manpower losses were so great that they were unable to enforce their mandamus and the French subsequently restored the fort.[64] Under pressure from their northern Algonquin foes they were also obliged to abandon all the villages that they had established on the north shore of Lake Ontario. Only a few families remained ensconced near Fort Frontenac.[65] Similarly the western Iroquois claimed sovereignty over the Ohio Valley by right of conquest. This vast area they maintained as their hunting territory and it was not until the 1720s that they allowed a few bands of Delawares and later, Shawnee, to settle there.[66] The British subsequently claimed that the region belonged to them, since the Iroquois were their subjects, hence the Iroquois title ultimately rested in the British Crown,[67] a pretension that both the Iroquois and the French refused to countenance.[68]

For their part the French, on occasion, claimed that the Iroquois had been their subjects since the initial French discovery of their lands.[69] They also claimed title to the Mohawks' land by right of conquest. When Alexandre de Prouville de Tracy marched a few hundred French troops and Canadian militia into their abandoned villages he had an official act proclaimed taking possession of the land for Louis XIV. The fact that he had not conquered the Mohawks did not deter him. After burning their longhouses and corn fields, the French marched back to Canada. The Mohawks then rebuilt their villages, reoccupied them, and all went on as before.[70] The French claim proved merely to be a futile gambit in their diplomatic skirmishes with the British.

Subsequently the French acquired a healthy respect for the martial prowess of the Iroquois. After the Five Nations, in the 1701 peace treaty, declared their intention to remain neutral in future Anglo-French hostilities, the French were extremely careful not to do anything that might cause them to abandon that stance.[71] When, in 1719, the French learned that the New York authorities intended to establish a fort at Niagara to give them access to the Northwest, and at the same time sever the French communication route through the Great Lakes to the Far West and Louisiana, the Governor-General of New France, Philippe de Rigaud de Vaudreuil, forestalled them by establishing a post there before the English of New York were able to move. Before proceeding, however, Vaudreuil was careful to obtain the sanction of the Senecas, who claimed the territory as theirs. He dispatched one of his officers—Chabert de Joncaire, who had been adopted into the Seneca nation—to request permission to build a house at Niagara. This the Senecas could not deny to one of their own, as Joncaire was.

Upon receiving the accord of the Seneca council, Joncaire swiftly garnered a squad of soldiers from Fort Frontenac and built his 'house'.[72] A few years later it was replaced by a massive stone building but, significantly, it was not constructed in the form of a fort but rather as a large manor house in order not to upset the Senecas. Had the Senecas refused their consent to Joncaire, the French would not have dared to make the move. As it was, when the New York authorities protested that the fort represented an invasion of British territory, the Iroquois told them to remain quiet and live in peace with the French. They also stated that they had 'given the French liberty of free Passage thru Lake Ontario.'[73] At that time the Iroquois still were, in North American terms, a power to be reckoned with, one the French feared and respected far more than they did the English colonies.[74]

It was under the cover of the war with the Iroquois that began in 1684 with their attacks on the French in the Illinois territory, a war that lasted until 1699, that the French expanded their influence throughout the West. Although this was ostensibly to enlist the support of the western nations, in reality it was a concerted drive by rival fur-trade factions to increase their trade. Posts were established around the northern shores of the Great Lakes, down Lake Michigan, and into the Mississippi Valley.[75] As the intendant Jean Bochart de Champigny put it: 'There is not a single nation within five or six hundred leagues of here where there are not some French with goods to trade with the Indians as soon as they trap their beaver.'[76] The predictable result was that the market for beaver in France became glutted. In desperation the Minister of Marine finally issued orders that all the western posts save Saint-Louis des Illinois were to be burned and abandoned. Saint-Louis was to be retained solely to prevent the Indian nations of the region from forming an alliance with the English. No more *congés* were to be issued for voyages to the West. In future the Indians were to bring their furs to trade at Montreal.[77] The Governor-General and the Intendant were quick to point out that to abandon the western posts while the war with the English and the Iroquois raged would merely invite the enemy to fill the political vacuum, win over all the Indian allies of the French, and bring on the ultimate destruction of New France.[78] The Minister was thereupon constrained to relax his Draconian edict and the western posts were maintained.[79] Four years later an abrupt shift in European power politics confirmed the wisdom, or in the long run the folly, of that reluctant decision.

In 1701, on the eve of the War of the Spanish Succession, Louis XIV made a decision that was to have drastic consequences for everyone in North America—French, English, Spanish, and Indian. On 31 May 1701 he signed a *mémoire* to Callières and Champigny, Governor-General and Intendant respectively at Quebec, stating in part: 'His Majesty has resolved to establish a settlement on the lower Mississippi . . . this has become an indispensable necessity to halt the progress that the colonial English have begun to make in the lands between their colonies and that river.'[80] In addition a settlement was ordered to be established at Detroit to maintain control of the Great Lakes. Significantly the lands here to be occupied were vacant. The founder of the new post, Antoine Laumet *dit* de Lamothe Cadillac, had to persuade Ottawa and Huron Indians to move there from Michilimackinac.[81] Here too there was no need for the French either to seize the territory by force or to offer monetary compensation to anyone. The French mission posts in the Illinois country were also ordered to be strengthened. They had been established with the agreement of the resident Indians, who saw no cause for concern at the presence among them of traders, hunters, and farmers. The way of life of these settlers differed little from that of the Illinois nation, and intermarriage was common.[82]

During the ensuing war the Iroquois honoured their treaty obligation and remained neutral. On the earnest advice of Champigny, who had been recalled to France to serve as Intendant at Le Havre and also as the Minister's adviser on Canadian affairs,[83] a tacit understanding was reached with New York that neither would attack the other unless attacked first. This was agreed to by the French for fear that an attack on New York would cause the Iroquois to give the British their military support.[84]

Against New England it was a different story. The New England authorities claimed that they had title to all the land up to the St Lawrence River and west along it to the border of New York.[85] To hold them well back from the St Lawrence, Governor-General Vaudreuil had to rely on the Abenaki. To make sure they remained at war with the English he launched a series of devastating raids by war parties composed of Canadians, Mission Iroquois, and Abenaki on New England towns along the coast and well inland. That on Deerfield, Massachusetts, in February 1704—which resulted in the sacking of the village, the killing of 47 villagers, and the capture of 111 who were taken back to Canada as prisoners—was typical.[86]

The Treaty of Utrecht that ended the war in 1713 saw France make sweeping territorial concessions in North America to avoid having to make them elsewhere. Newfoundland, part of Acadia, and Hudson Bay were yielded to Great Britain. In addition in Clause 15, which declared that all Indians were permitted to trade with both the English colonies and New France without molestation or hindrance, the Five Nations were described as being 'subject to the Dominion of Great Britain'.[87] This assertion was made without the knowledge of the Iroquois, and when the French subsequently challenged them on the point they specifically denied that they were the subject of any foreign power. In 1748 the Onondaga chief, Chachouintioni, declared that they had ceded their lands to no one, that the land was still theirs, given them by the Great Spirit. He declared that he spoke for all Five Nations in attendance. The Cayuga chief, Tomahae, repeated the same declaration and for proof that the Iroquois were not the subjects of the British King he pointed to their refusal to join the British in their current war with the French. The mere fact that they were in Canada discussing the issue indicated that they were an independent power. Tomahae also declared that he spoke for all the nations of the Confederacy and the forty-eight Iroquois delegates concurred.[88]

Despite the Iroquois rejection of British claims the French officials, in the years after 1713, had to make every effort to undo the harm caused by the concessions thoughtlessly made in the treaty. Cape Breton had been retained, along with fishing rights on the northeast coast of Newfoundland. The major threat to French interests was in the northern and western interior of the continent. The British overreached themselves when they insisted that the term 'ceded' Hudson Bay to His Britannic Majesty be replaced by 'restored', this to make explicit their assertion that they had always had the prior claim. The French readily agreed, then riposted by asserting that, by definition, the British could have restored to them only the territory that they had previously occupied, namely their posts on the shores of the Bay.[89] The French rejected out of hand British claims to all the lands that drained into the Bay, later defined as north and west of a line from Cap Perdrix at 58½° Lat. on the Labrador coast down through Lake Mistassini to the 49th parallel and westward along it to the Pacific.

The Hudson's Bay Company was brazenly claiming most of present-day Canada despite the fact that, with the exception of Henry Kelsey's voyage to the Saskatchewan River in 1690, no Englishman had seen more than the coastal strip of the Bay.[90] As with the French, the Indians were pleased to have the Bay posts there to provide competition for the French and did not see that they could ever constitute a threat to their interests. Before the conquest of Canada the company made only two attempts to establish a post inland—Henley House on the Albany River. The first post, built in 1743, was destroyed by the Indians twelve years later. When re-established in 1759 it was again destroyed in a matter of weeks.[91] Thus the Hudson's Bay Company could by no stretch of the imagination be deemed to have established British sovereignty over the lands it claimed. All it had, at best, was squatter's rights to its posts on the shores of the Bay.[92]

In Acadia after 1713 the Massachusetts authorities tried to lay claim to the lands of the Abenaki on the grounds that the King of France had ceded them to Great Britain by the Treaty of Utrecht. The Governor of Massachusetts also demanded that the Abenaki proclaim their new British monarch, take an oath of fidelity to him, and allow the English to settle among them on what was now regarded as British territory.[93] These claims the Abenaki vehemently rejected more than once. They declared that no king had ever taken possession of their lands, not by cession, conquest, or purchase. In the presence of French officials they declared that they had never been French subjects and that since no one could cede to another that which had never belonged to him, the French could not have ceded their lands to the English.[94]

Earlier during the war the French had rejected New England protests about the atrocities committed by the Abenaki during their raids on New England settlements, declaring that they could do nothing since the Abenaki were not French subjects.[95] Here was another example of the French 'janusian' attitude. They still claimed title to the lands of the Abenaki, but they did so merely to deny them to the English.[96] To the Abenaki they never would have dared make such a claim, for it would have alienated totally a vital ally who would have given them the same answer as they had given the English. The French had to support the Abenaki to keep the English from occupying territory within three days' march of the St Lawrence, which would have put the neck of New France in a noose. The Abenaki reminded the French that they had supported them in all their wars with the English, hence it was now their turn to come to the aid of their ally.[97] The French had good cause to fear that if they failed to provide the requested military support the Abenaki would be forced to make peace with the English on English terms and, as Governor-General Vaudreuil pointed out, they would then assuredly turn their wrath on the French. It would, he stated, be all too easy for them to devastate the French settlements along the south shore of the St Lawrence, from Gaspé to above Quebec.[98] By no stretch of the imagination could either the French, or the English, at that time have pretended to exercise sovereignty over the Abenaki and their land. Both powers wanted something from them; both feared that the other would acquire, if not the support of the Abenaki, then their acquiescence in the attainment of its aims.

A similar situation developed in the West, where the French were determined to prevent the English from occupying the lands west of the Appalachian Mountains to the Mississippi. They had no intention of occupying the territory themselves, and even if they had they lacked the means to do it.[99] Nor did they covet the fur trade of that region. The better furs were to be had to the north, where the French garnered the lion's share in competition with the Hudson's Bay Company.[100] To prevent the English from flooding over the mountains into the west the French had to enlist the aid of the Indian nations which, all too often, were their own worst enemies. The task for the French was to strive to keep those belligerent nations from constantly warring with one another and to weld them into an alliance, amenable to French direction, against the relentless encroachment of land-hungry speculators and settlers from the English colonies.[101]

From the French viewpoint, despite Clause 15 of the Treaty of Utrecht, the western nations had to be prevented by one means or another from having any dealings with the English colonials. To this end posts were established down the Mississippi Valley, on both sides of Lake Superior, at Lake of the Woods, on the Red and Assiniboine Rivers, and far up the Saskatchewan. The latter posts, forming the Mer de l'Ouest district, and those at Lakes Nipigon, La Carpe, and Timiskaming, were intended to reduce the flow of Indians and furs to the Hudson's Bay Company posts.[102] Fort Rouillé, near the Toronto portage, was built specifically to stop the Mississaugas from going to the New York post at Oswego.[103] In every instance these posts were established with the sanction of the Indians. In 1736 the Cree and Assiniboine demanded that La Vérendrye establish a post at the foot of Lake Winnipeg, declaring that he had promised them the post to supply their needs.[104]

Dr Toby Morantz, in discussing the relationship between the northern Cree and the Hudson's Bay Company, remarked that the Cree did not regard themselves as dominated by Europeans. They exercised considerable influence over the trading policies of the Company.

> Trade rituals, giving of presents, value of goods traded and their quality, respect of the factor toward the Indians, and the expansion of trade were all affected. The Indians had the upper hand for they could always take their furs to the opposition. It was a weapon they knew how to use well to their own advantage.[105]

The western posts of the French—all but the main bases at Niagara, Detroit, Michilimackinac, and eventually Grand Portage—consisted of little more than a three- to four-metre-high log palisade thirty-odd metres long on each side, enclosing four or five clay-chinked log cabins with bark roofs.[106] The 'presents' that the French were constrained to give the Indian nations every year were regarded by the latter as a form of rent for the use of the land where the posts stood and as a fee for the right to travel on the Indians' territory.[107] As early as 1650 Father Ragueneau, SJ, was, according to one contemporary account, made embarrassingly aware of this Indian customary law. While fleeing to Quebec from the Iroquois with a party of Hurons, he refused to pay the usual Ottawa River toll to the Algonquins of Allumette Island, declaring that the French were now the masters of the land and its people. The Algonquin chief, Le Borgne, promptly had the priest strung up in a tree by his armpits to teach him who was master there.[108]

In the 1680s, when Pierre-Charles le Sueur first travelled to the Sioux country, the Sioux described the territorial limits of their land and stated 'that it was not their custom to hunt on other peoples' territory without first being invited by those to whom the land belonged.'[109] In 1754 the Sioux complained bitterly to Capitaine Joseph Marin de Malgue, commandant at La Baie des Puants (Green Bay), that the Saulteux were trying to steal their land. They drew a map and explained that all the land from the mouth of the Wisconsin River to Lac Sangsue belonged to them, it having been granted them by the 'Master of Life'. Three years earlier, on making peace with the Saulteux at Marin's behest, they had allowed them to hunt at L'Aile du Corbeau, and the Saulteux subsequently claimed that the land was, in consequence, now theirs.[110] This pretence the Sioux vehemently denied. After the conquest of New France the British fur traders early learned that the Indians guarded access to their lands jealously. In a *mémoire* on the Indian trade the Montreal merchants stated: 'the Indians are so tenacious of their property, and jealous of other nations that they will not suffer them in passing through their lands to hunt for their support.'[111]

Ocassionally the Indians came to resent the presence of the French. Posts were destroyed or had to be abandoned hastily, as was the case with Fort la Reine on the Assiniboine in 1752.[112] During the Fox wars the Sioux posts had to be abandoned.[113] After being re-established at the request of the Sioux, they again had to be abandoned owing to the mounting hostility of the tribesmen. In fact the French had lots of practice with that particular post. In 1700 Pierre-Charles le Sueur had established the first Sioux post at the junction of the Minnesota and Blue Earth Rivers; three years later the garrison had to flee for their lives to Mobile.[114] The uprising of the Detroit Hurons and some Saulteux against the French in 1747 indicated all too clearly that their hold over the tribes was tenuous.[115]

Twice a year the fur and supply brigades voyaged to and from Montreal in convoy for security, with an officer of the colonial troops in command. One or two canoes was an invitation to pillage and, possibly, murder. Every *voyageur* was required by law to take a musket with him for self-defence and have it with him on his return on pain of three months in jail. The organization was that of a military expedition into enemy country and the casualties were not inconsiderable.[116] The French, despite their claims to sovereignty over the land west of the Appalachians, Iroquoia, and Hudson Bay, were in fact sovereign only inside their garrisoned forts, and beyond only within the range of their muskets.

As early as 1704 a gathering of western tribesmen, when challenged by French officers at Lake Erie and asked where they were taking their furs, defiantly replied: 'This land is not yours, it is ours, and we shall go wherever we please.'[117] Three years later the Intendant, Jacques Raudot, admitted to the Minister of Marine: 'with regard to the Indians, we can do no more than appeal to them not to go to the English for we cannot prevent them from so doing.'[118] A half-century later Governor-General François-Pierre de Rigaud de Vaudreuil sought to have an Onondaga of his choosing appointed a chief and member of the Council at the Iroquois mission post, La Présentation. The Iroquois were outraged at this attempted interference in their affairs. They informed Vaudreuil that although it was true that they had taken an oath of fidelity to the French, they were governed by a council made up of twelve village chiefs, six war chiefs, and twelve council women. Their spokesman added that when they had been regenerated in the same baptismal water as had christened the Governor-General, they had not renounced their freedom or the rights they held from the Master of Life. If one wished to deprive them of those rights then they would regard themselves as no longer bound by their oath; their agreement was a reciprocal one. 'It is for us alone to appoint our chiefs,' their spokesman declared. He then demanded to know why Vaudreuil sought to impose on them the Onondaga who was not even a Christian: 'My father, explain your words. They trouble us,' the spokesman bluntly requested. Vaudreuil was obliged to back down, with the face-saving statement that he thought it would be a good thing were his Onondaga nominee to be made a member of their Council.[119]

One area that France claimed for purely strategic reasons was Lake Champlain, but this had to be done without offending the Mohawks, who claimed that much of the area belonged to them. The lake and the Richelieu River flowing out of it to the St Lawrence had long been the main invasion route into Canada from New York. In 1708 the Minister of Marine instructed the Governor-General and the Intendant that the English could not be allowed to establish themselves near the lake.[120] In 1730, when Governor-General Beauharnois learned that the Lieutenant-Governor of New York intended to place settlers on Wood Creek, which flowed into Lake Champlain from the south, he replied by having Fort Saint-Frédéric built at the narrows of the lake near its southern end.[121] Two years later the plans to replace the wooden fort with a masonry structure were approved and the Quebec officials were instructed to use force if necessary to prevent the English from settling in the area.[122]

In 1739 the Mohawks obtained the erroneous information that the French intended to occupy Wood Creek. They reported this to the Albany authorities and declared that all the land around the lake as far north as Ochjargo belonged to them.[123] This was a dubious claim; they hunted in the area but had no villages there. The Mahicans had once occupied the region and in the 1730s the western Abenaki had established a village at Missisquoi Bay.[124] Since before Champlain's day no tribe had been able to dominate the region.[125] The Mohawks sent a delegation to discuss the issue with the Governor-General of New France. He informed them that the King of France claimed title to all the lands whose waters drained into the lake as far south as the portage to Lac Saint-Sacrement. He also stated that he would not allow the English to settle anywhere on those lands. Despite the fact that some sections on both sides of the lake had been conceded as seigneuries, but not settled, he declared that the French Crown's rights to the land from Crown Point to the head of the lake at the carrying place would be given as a deed of gift to the Mohawks and Abenaki to 'make use of it for a hunting Place for them and their Posterity . . .'. He also assured them that no French would be allowed to settle there.[126]

In the West, at the conclusion of the War of the Austrian Succession—a war that changed nothing, settled nothing, and had to be refought—the French, English, and Iroquois all claimed title to the entire Ohio Valley. The Iroquois claimed it by right of conquest;[127] the English of Virginia by virtue of their colonial charter and because they regarded the Iroquois as subjects of the British Crown;[128] and the French by virtue of La Salle's pretended prior discovery.[129] The French sought to deny the region to the English, not because they had any use for the land then or in the foreseeable future, but because the English coveted it and were they once to occupy the valley their potential military power would increase immeasurably and the water route from Canada to Louisiana then could be severed too easily.[130] Captain Pierre-Joseph de Céloron de Blainville was dispatched with 213 men in 1749 by Governor-General Roland-Michel Barrin, comte de la Galissonière, to map the route from Lake Erie down the Ohio, to claim the region for France, and to drive out any English traders encountered there.[131]

In 1753 a French military expedition began clearing a route from Lake Erie to the forks of the Ohio. A party of Virginians that had begun to build a fort was driven off and Fort Duquesne was hastily constructed.[132] When the Iroquois protested, they were bluntly told to accept the French presence, which was there for their protection against English encroachment, or be destroyed.[133] The French thus seized control of the region by force of arms, just as had the Iroquois three-quarters of a century earlier. During the ensuing hostilities that endured from 1754 to 1760 the Indian nations of the region—Shawnee, Delaware, Miami, Huron, Illinois, even many of the Six Nations Iroquois—initially fought with the French.[134] They did so because the French appeared to be the winning side, but also because they had been outraged over the years at the treatment they had received from American traders who had used rum to befuddle, cheat, and debauch them.[135] Worse still, they had been defrauded of vast tracts of land by Pennsylvania and New York.[136]

Once engaged in the war, they fought as independent sovereign powers, as allies of the French but in no way subservient to them; rather they regarded the French as their allies in a war being fought to protect their interests. They depended on the French for supplies and usually, but by no means always, accepted French tactical direction of the campaigns. They fought when and how they saw fit, greatly to the consternation at times of the French high command.[137] The British generals, throughout the war, demanded that it be fought according to eighteenth-century European rules and held the French responsible for the atrocities committed by their Indian allies.[138] They could not conceive that as the war was being fought for the Indians' lands, and much of it on their land, then Indian concepts of warfare, not European, would obtain.

The independence of these sovereign nations was made startlingly clear in 1758 when the government of Pennsylvania offered to restore to the Shawnees and Delawares the lands that had been taken from them by fraudulent means, in return for their ending hostilities. The initial stages of the resultant Easton Treaty were negotiated by Frederick Post with the Indians encamped across the Ohio River from Fort Duquesne. The officers of the French garrison who attended the meeting were not allowed to intervene, or even to speak. They had to watch in angry, frustrated silence as their erstwhile allies agreed to a separate peace and to withdraw from the war. At the conclusion of the negotiations a chief naïvely remarked to Post, 'Now Brother, we love you, but can't help wondering why the *English* and the *French* don't make it up with one another, and tell one another not to fight on our land.'[139]

In September 1760 the hopelessly outnumbered French forces, following on the defeat at Quebec the preceding year, were forced to surrender to the armies of Major-General Jeffery Amherst. Governor-General Vaudreuil drafted the terms of capitulation that he was prepared to accept. Amherst agreed to most of them, rejected some, and qualified others. One clause that he accepted with an inconsequential amendment was Article 40, which stated:

> The Savages or Indian allies of his most Christian Majesty, shall be maintained in the lands they inhabit; if they chuse to remain there: they shall not be molested on any pretence whatsoever, for having carried arms, and served his most Christian Majesty; they shall have, as well as the French, liberty of religion, and shall keep their missionaries. The actual Vicars General, and the Bishop, when the Episcopal see shall be filled, shall have leave to send them new Missionaries when they shall judge it necessary.

Amherst minuted the clause with the comment: 'Granted except the last article, which has already been refused'.[140]

The part of the article that Amherst did accept is highly significant. It was not revoked in the Treaty of Paris. In Article 4 of that treaty, by virtue of which France ceded to Great Britain 'Canada with all its dependencies', no mention was made of the Indian nations.[141] Article 40 of the Capitulation of

Montreal, not having been rescinded, therefore remained binding on Great Britain and also on whatever government subsequently acceded to the sovereignty then exercised by Britain—such as, for example, the Dominion of Canada, or as surrogate any of its provincial governments. Article 40 tacitly acknowledged that the Indians retained title to their lands; therefore any attempt to dispossess them or to dispose of their lands without their prior consent would constitute 'molestation' and be in breach of the article in question.

In 1763 the British blandly assumed that the Treaty of Paris had confirmed their old claims to sovereignty over the territory west of the Allegheny Mountains to the Mississippi. They also assumed that the territories north and west of the St Lawrence and Great Lakes, as well as the lands between the St Lawrence and New England and New York, had been dependencies of Canada, hence they had acquired sovereignty over them. They based these claims on the presumption that France had held title to the lands in question, despite the fact that prior to 1763 they had rejected all such assertions. In fact the French had never been able to exercise sovereignty in those territories. When, in 1715, the Abenaki had denied that they had ever been French subjects, the Canadian officials had not disputed the assertion; they had thereby tacitly admitted the truth of the Abenaki claim.[142]

Similarly in 1763 the British admitted that the Indians residing in the newly created Province of Quebec were not their subjects. In Article 60 of the Royal Instructions of Governor Murray, dated 7 December 1763, it was stated: 'And whereas Our Province of Quebec is in part inhabited and possessed by several Nations and Tribes of Indians, with whom it is both necessary and expedient to cultivate and maintain a strict Friendship and good Correspondence, so that they may be induced by Degrees, not only to be good neighbours to Our Subjects, but likewise themselves to become good Subjects to us.'[143]

Two things stand out in that policy statement: first, since it is hoped that eventually the Indian nations will be pleased to become the subjects of His Britannic Majesty, then clearly they were not, in 1763, considered to be his subjects; and since they were not considered to be the subjects of any other foreign power, then they were considered to have been independent, sovereign nations; second, this is confirmed by the phrase 'inhabited and *possessed*', [emphasis added] for if they are considered to have 'possessed' the land, then it has to be acknowledged that, under the circumstances, they held title to it.

The lands lying between the north side of the lower St Lawrence River and the territory claimed by the Hudson's Bay Company were also deemed to have been ceded to Great Britain by France in 1763. Yet when, in 1766, a dispute arose over exploitation of the resources at the old King's Domain of the French regime, Governor James Murray informed the Lords of Trade:

> The lands of the King's Domain were never ceded nor purchased by the French King, nor by his Britannic Majesty; but by compact with the savages inhabiting the said lands, the particular Posts or Spots of ground, whereon the Kings buildings are erected and now stand, were ceded to the French King, for the purpose of erecting storehouses & other conveniences for the Factors, Commis or servants employed to carry on the trade; and the savages residing within the limits of the Domain, & who resort to the said Posts of His Majesty at certain seaons of the year, were adopted as Domicile Indians under the sole and immediate protection of the King, & so remained till the reduction of the Province, & a Missionary was sent to reside constantly among them. The lands of the Domain therefore, are to all intents & purposes reserved, as hunting grounds to the savages, of which they are ever jealous, on the least appearance of an encroachment amongst themselves.[144]

Exactly the same could have been said of the French posts in the Northwest, although in both instances the Indians likely would have quarrelled with the notion that they had 'ceded' the 'spots of land' on which the trading-posts stood. In their view they had merely granted the French those spots of land during their pleasure and they expected compensation—'presents', virtually rent—in return. In 1761 General Jeffery Amherst, with his customary ignorance and arrogance, ordered the granting of presents to cease. The Indians were, he stated, not to be bribed, but punished when they failed to submit. The Indians were outraged. The old understanding that they had had with the French had been unaccountably broken.[145]

They rejected totally all British claims to sovereignty over their lands. The attitude and intentions of the Anglo-Americans, despite anything the royal officials might declare, were all too clear.[146] The response of the Great Lakes Indians was the so-called 'uprising' of Pontiac. In fact it was not an uprising since, by definition, such an act has to be against duly constituted authority, and this the British had not then established. It was rather a pre-emptive strike by the Indians to defend their lands from invasion and occupation by the Anglo-Americans. British posts were attacked and several captured. American frontier settlements were once again ravaged by heavy casualties; and, as in the preceding war, the American provincial assemblies sought to avoid voting money and supplies or raising troops for defence. Once again it was British regulars who had to do the fighting to defend those who were actually responsible for the hostilities.[147]

The reaction to the news of the Indian assaults by the British commander-in-chief, Amherst, was uncomprehending, savage, and ruthless. He instructed his subordinate commanders that the Indians were to be treated 'as the vilest race of beings that ever infested the earth, and whose riddance from it must be deemed a meritorious act, for the good of Mankind. You will therefore take no prisoners, but put to death all that fall into your hands.' He also instructed his field commander, Colonel Henri Bouquet: 'Could it not be contrived to send the small pox among the disaffected tribes?' Bouquet replied that he would make the attempt.[148] Whether or not he actually did is not known.[149] However, the commanding officer of Fort Pitt, Captain Simeon Ecuyer, like Bouquet a Swiss mercenary, replied to a Delaware demand that he surrender the fort with a present of two blankets and a handkerchief from the fort's smallpox ward. An epidemic raged through the villages of the Delawares, Shawnees, and Mingoes. Although there is a possibility that it began before Bouquet received his orders, the incident at Fort Pitt could only have extended and intensified the spread of that dread disease, to which the Indians had no resistance.[150]

Unable to support a long-drawn-out campaign without external logistic aid, such as they had previously received from the French, the Indians were forced to submit.[151] Now obliged to allow the British to reoccupy the old French posts, they still maintained that the French had neither conquered them nor purchased a foot of their land, hence the French could not have ceded to anyone what had never belonged to them.[152]

The British government, by the terms of the Royal Proclamation of October 1763, strove, for expediency's sake, to stop the usurpation of Indian lands by the American colonists. The Proclamation stated, unquivocally, that Indian lands could be ceded only to the Crown and not acquired by private purchase. Persons who had, by one means or another, acquired such lands were ordered to relinquish and depart from them forthwith.[153] Despite this order, land speculators were very active in London and the colonial capitals, striving by all means, licit and otherwise, to obtain title to some 2,400,000 acres in the Ohio Valley, ceded for a pittance by the Six Nations at Fort Stanwix in October 1768—a cession that was later bitterly protested by the Senecas, Shawnees, and Delawares.[154] Companies such as the Mississippi Company, the Walpole Company, and the Illinois Company employed every device available to gain their ends, eventually challenging the Crown's right to prevent their dealing directly with the Indian nations.[155] Meanwhile American squatters continued to flood in their tens of thousands onto the Indians' lands. Again the tribes began to prepare for war.[156] South of the Great Lakes the royal proclamation proved to be an exercise in futility.

With the advent of the American Revolution the British policy of striving to defend the Indians' right to their lands, *pro tempore*, went by the board. Ironically one cause of the Revolution was this attempt to thwart such avid land speculators as George Washington, his kinsmen the Lees, Benjamin

Franklin, Samuel Wharton, Phineas Lyman, and others later prominent in the revolutionary cause.[157]

In 1783, despite outraged but belated protests from the French foreign minister, Charles Gravier, comte de Vergennes, the Americans negotiated, behind the backs of their French allies and in contravention of their treaty, a separate peace with Great Britain whereby they were granted not only their independence but also the dubious, to say the least, British claim to the vast area between the Appalachian Mountains and the Mississippi.[158] The Indian nations in that vast area were thereby abandoned to certain despoliation by the Americans.

In May 1783 Brigadier Allan Maclean at Niagara reported to General Haldimand that the Indians were very uneasy over 'certain pretended boundaries'. He stated that they considered themselves a free people subject to no power upon earth. Having served the King of England faithfully as allies, not as his subjects, during the war with the Americans, they declared that he had no right whatsoever to grant their lands or their rights to the enemy. Maclean went on:

> They added that many years ago their ancestors had granted permission to the French King to build trading houses, or small forts on the water communications between Canada and the western Indians in the heart of their country for the convenience of trade only, without granting one inch of land but what these forts stood upon, and that at the end of the last war they granted leave to Sir William Johnson to hold these forts for their ally the King of England, but that it was impossible from that circumstance to imagine that the King of England should pretend to grant to the Americans all the whole country of the Indians lying between the Lakes and the fixed boundaries as settled in 1768.

Maclean added: 'I do from my soul pity these people.'[159] The Indian nations were then driven off their lands by the Americans and brought close to annihilation. By 1840 the Indians east of the Mississippi, with the exception of a few small enclaves, 'had either been removed to the trans-Mississippi or had died in the process of moving'.[160]

To the north, on what remained of British North America, the royal proclamation of 1763 was honoured for the time being, since there was no immediate rush of immigrants to seize the hunting lands of the northern Indians and Métis. Then in the nineteenth century things changed. External forces made their lands economically desirable. The Indian and Métis hunting societies, therefore, had to go, to make way for staid farmers, ranchers, and the exploiters of timber and mineral resources who would play a 'proper' role in the eastern market economy. Force was not used until late in the nineteenth century, but eventually the result was the same in Canada as south of the border. Destruction of the plains Indians' main food supply and economic resource, the buffalo,[161] an appalling flood of alcohol,[162] epidemics that decimated the Indian population some seven times in less than 150 years,[163] and finally sordid political and bureaucratic bungling and chicanery brought them low.[164]

Such were the means whereby sovereignty and title to the lands of the Indians were eventually acquired by the Crown in Canada. They certainly were not acquired by virtue of France's having ceded a non-existent title to the British Crown in 1763.

NOTES

THE HISTORY OF NEW FRANCE ACCORDING TO FRANCIS PARKMAN

[1] Francis Parkman, *Montcalm and Wolfe*, Centenary edn (Boston, 1922), I, p. 38.

[2] Francis Parkman, *The Old Regime in Canada*, Centenary edn (Boston, 1922), 467–8.

[3] Ibid., 281–2.

[4] Ibid., 347.

[5] Ibid., 333.

[6] Ibid., 312–13.

[7] Ibid., 355.

[8] At the risk of being wearisome, it might be pointed out that Parkman was unaware of the extent to which England subsidized, directly or indirectly, certain economic endeavours of her American colonies.

[9] Parkman, *Old Regime*, 24.

[10] Francis Parkman, *The Jesuits in North America*, Centenary edn (Boston, 1922), 552–3.

[11] Parkman, *Old Regime*, 421–5.

[12] Ibid., 426.

[13] Ibid., 427.

[14] Ibid., 153–4.

[15] Ibid., 164–5.

[16] Another example, in a different context, of Parkman's imputing of unworthy motives is to be found in *Montcalm and Wolfe*, II, 313. There he claimed, on the basis of no evidence whatsoever, that Vaudreuil's late arrival on the fateful battlefield of the Plains of Abraham at Quebec, 13 Sept. 1759, 'was well timed to throw the blame on Montcalm in case of defeat, or to claim some of the honour for himself in case of victory'.

[17] Parkman, *Old Regime*, 226.

[18] Ibid., 146–51.

[19] Ibid., 227–8.

[20] Ibid., 164.

[21] Parkman, *Montcalm and Wolfe*, I, 10–11, II, 45–50.

[22] Ibid., I, 19–20, II, 41–2, 401–4, 424.

[23] Ibid., I, 155, 167.

[24] Francis Parkman, *Count Frontenac and New France under Louis XIV*, Centenary edn (Boston, 1922), 19–20.

[25] Frontenac declared in his dispatch to Colbert: 'I never claimed thereby to form bodies that should subsist, knowing full well of what consequence that could be.' 13 Nov. 1673, Series Amérique, V, 346–7, Archives du Ministère des Affaires étrangères, Paris.

[26] Parkman, *Frontenac and New France*, 75.

[27] In 1680 Louis XIV informed Frontenac that New France 'runs the risk of being completely destroyed unless you alter both your conduct and your principles . . . .' For a discussion of this question, and Parkman's manner of dealing with it, see my *Frontenac: The Courtier Governor* (Toronto, 1959), 99–126, 153–6, 198–9.

[28] Parkman, *Frontenac and New France*, 459.

[29] Jean Delanglez, S.J., *Some La Salle Journeys* (Chicago, 1938), *passim*.

[30] Francis Parkman, *La Salle and the Discovery of the Great West* (Boston, 1899), 363. See also ibid., 348–9, where Parkman described the scheme La Salle proposed to the Court for founding a colony on the Gulf of Mexico and where he stated: 'This memorial bears some indications of being drawn up in order to produce a certain effect on the minds of the King and his minister . . .Such a procedures may be charged with indirectness; but there is a different explanation, which we shall suggest hereafter, and which implies no such reproach.' Thus, La Salle's 'indirectness' was here neatly dismissed. The only explanation that is later suggested was that La Salle's brain was 'overwrought'.

[31] Ibid., 431–2.

[32] Ibid., 432.

[33] Francis Parkman, *A Half Century of Conflict*, Centenary edn (Boston 1922), I, 223.

[34] Parkman, *Old Regime*, 23–4.

[35] Yet, to the Lachine massacre, perpetrated by the Iroquois on the Canadians, and an event of greater significance than the Deerfield raid, Parkman devoted only four pages. It would appear that much depended on whose scalp was being lifted. Compared Parkman's *Half Century of Conflict*, I, 55–93, and his *Frontenac and New France*, 185–9.

[36] Parkman, *Montcalm and Wolfe*, I, 118.

[37] Parkman, *Half Century of Conflict*, I, 248–9.

[38] Ibid., 260.

[39] Ibid., 268–9.

[40] Ibid., 346.

[41] This view is implicit in the statement by Robin W. Winks in his *Recent Trends and New Literature in Canadian History*, Service Center for Teachers of History, A Service of the American Historical Association, no. 19 (Washington, 1959), 28: '*The struggle for North America*. Little that is new has been said, and one suspects there is little new to be said, about the Old Régime in North America.'

THE ROLE OF THE CHURCH IN NEW FRANCE

[1] *Edits, Ordonnances Royaux, Déclarations et Arrêts du conseil d-Etat du Roi concernant le Canada* (Québec, 1854), 553.

[2] Lucien Campeau S.I., ed., *Monumenta Novae Franciae I: 1602–1616* (Rome and Québec, 1967), 4–5.

[3] Marcel Trudel, *Histoire de la Nouvelle-France II: Le comptoir: 1604–1627* (Montréal, 1966), 91.

[4] E.R. Adair, 'France and the Beginnings of New France', *The Canadian Historical Review* 25 (Sept. 1944).

[5] *Rapport de l'Archiviste de la Province de Québec*, Tome 41 (1963), 109–10.

[6] Dominion Bureau of Statistics, Demography Branch, 'Chronological List of Canadian Censuses'.

[7] Jean Delumeau, *Le Catholicisme entre Luther et Voltaire* (Paris, 1971), 256–7.

[8] Ibid.

[9] Ibid.

[10] Ibid., 270.

[11] Louis Pérouas, *Le Diocèse de la Rochelle de 1648 à 1724, Sociologie et Pastorale* (Paris, 1964), 202.

[12] Pierre Goubert, *The Ancien Regime: French Society, 1600–1750* (New York, 1974), 202.

[13] Robert Mandrou, *Magistrats et sorciers en France au XVIIe siècle* (Paris, 1968).

[14] Joyce Marshall, ed., *Word from New France: The Selected Letters of Marie de l'Incarnation* (Toronto, 1967).

[15] Guy Frégault, *Le XVIIIe siècle canadien: Etudes* (Montréal, 1968), 105.

[16] P.G. Roy, ed., *Inventaires des jugements et délibérations du Conseil Supérieur de la Nouvelle-France de 1717 à 1760*, 7 vols., (Beauceville, 1932–1935), 1:340–4, 346–7, 349–50.

[17] Frégault, *Le XVIIIe siècle*, 88.

[18] Noël Baillargeon, *Le Séminaire de Québec sous l'Episcopat de Mgr de Laval*, (Québec, 1972), 52–5.

[19] Archives Nationales, Paris, Series CIIA, Colonies 6:185, De Meulles au Ministre, Qué., 4 nov. 1683.

[20] Baillargeon, *Le Séminaire de Québec*, 103–19.

[21] Ibid., 117; Marcel Trudel, *Initiation à la Nouvelle-France* (Montréal, 1968), 255ff.

[22] Ibid.

[23] Henri-Raymond Casgrain, ed. *Collection des manuscrits du maréchal de Lévis*, 12 vols. (Montreal and Québec, 1889–95), vol. 6, *Journal du Marquis de Montcalm durant ses campagnes au Canada de 1756 à 1760* (Québec, 1895), 61.

[24] Trudel, *Initiation*, 255ff.

[25] Archives Nationales, Colonies, AN, CIIA 48:434, Jean Evesque de Québec au Ministre, Qué. 10 sept. 1726.

[26] Archives Nationales, Colonies, Series CIIA 50:23–24, Beauharnois et d'Aigremont au Ministre, Qué. 1 oct. 1728.

[27] P.G. Roy, *Inventaire des Ordonnances des intendants de la Nouvelle-France*, 3 vols. (Beauceville, 1917), 2:11; P.G. Roy, ed., *Inventaire des jugements et délibérations du Conseil Souverain* (Québec, 1932–35), 3:162; Archives du Séminaire de Québec, polygraphie 6, no. 31.

[28] Adolph Benson, ed., *Travels in North America by Peter Kalm*, 2 vols, (New York: Dover edition, 1966), 2:525.

[29] Archives du Québec à Montréal, Greffe F. Simmonet, 1750.

[30] Archives du Séminaire de Québec, polygraphie 6, no. 31.

[31] Olwen H. Tufton, *The Poor of Eighteenth-Century France 1750–1789* (Oxford, 1974), 3.

[32] Ibid., 131–76.

[33] Roy, *Ordonnances des Intendants*, passim; Archives Nationales, Colonies, Series B, 33:135; Ruette d'Auteil, *Mémoire de l'état présent du Canada* (1712).

[34] Archives Nationales, Colonies, Series F3, 7:101, Moreau de St-Méry, 'Hôpital à Montréal.'

[35] *Arrêts et Règlements du Conseil Supérieur de Québec, et Ordonnances et Jugements des Intendants du Canada* (Québec, 1855), 391–2.

[36] On this institution, see Micheline D'Allaire, *L'Hôpital-Général de Québec 1692–1784* (Montréal, 1970).

[37] Mgr. Henri Têtu, *Notices biographiques: Les Evèques de Québec* (Québec, 1889), 149.

[38] Archives Nationales, Colonies, Series CIIA, vol. 27, 'Abstraits des mémoires de Canada 1707', 59: *Nouvelle France: Documents Historiques: Correspondance échangée entre les autorités françaises et les gouverneurs et intendants* (Québec, 1893), 1:173.

[39] Archives Nationales, Colonies, Series CIIA, 91:32 Galissonière et Bigot au Ministre, Qué., 25 sept. 1748.

[40] W.J. Eccles, 'Social Welfare Measures and Policies in New France', *XXXVI Congreso Internacional de Americanistas 4* (Sevilla, 1966).

[41] *Edits, Ordonnances royaux, Déclarations et Arrêts du Conseil d'Etat du Roi concernant le Canada* (Québec, 1854), 1:288.

[42] *Ordonnances des Intendants et Arrêts portant règlements du Conseil Souverain* (Québec, 1806), 2:278–9.

[43] Archives Ministère de la Guerre, Series A1–3417, no. 137, Montcalm au Ministre, Montréal, 12 juin 1756.

[44] John McManners, *French Ecclesiastical Society under the Ancien Régime* (Manchester, 1960), 92–102.

[45] D'Allaire, *L'Hôpital-Général de Québec, 149–86.*

[46] *Rapport de l'Archiviste de la Province de Québec 1947–1948* Vaudreuil et Bégon au Ministre, Qué. 12 nov. 1712, 185.

[47] For a hostile description of Le Loutre's role, see Francis Parkman, *A Half Century of Conflict*, various editions.

[48] Archives Nationales, Colonies, C11A, vol. 26, Vaudreuil et Raudot au Ministre, Qué. 15 nov. 1707, 12; *Rapport de l'Archiviste de la Province de Québec 1939–1940*, 293.

[49] Archives Nationales, Colonies, Series C11A, 17:3ff, Callières et Champigny au Ministre, Qué. 20 oct. 1699.

[50] Archives nationales du Québec à Montréal, Greffe Adhémar, no. 1350, 15 sept. 1724.

[51] Ibid., Greffe Barrette, no 734, 22 dec. 1726; *Jugements et Délibérations du Conseil Souverain* 5:996–1000.

[52] *Rapport de l'Archiviste de la Province de Québec 1947–1948*, 301; Archives Nationales, Colonies, Series C11A 2:328; 18:64–6.

[53] Archives nationales du Québec à Montréal, Greffe J. David, no. 379, 31 juillet 1721.

[54] Hufton, *The Poor*, 321, gives figures showing an almost threefold rise in the illegitimacy rate.

[55] Archives Nationales, Colonies, Series C11A 65:248–53.

[56] See Hufton, *The Poor*, 318–51; William L. Langer, 'Checks on Population Growth: 1750–1850,' *Scientific American*, Feb. 1972.

[57] One finds innumerable *actes* for this form of adoption in the notarial *greffes*.

[58] Jacques Henripin, *La population canadienne au début du XVIIIe siècle* (Paris, 1954).

SOCIAL WELFARE MEASURES AND POLICIES IN NEW FRANCE

[1] *Rapport de l'archiviste de la Province de Québec, 1930–1931*, 9, Mémoire du Roy pour servir d'instruction à Talon. Paris, 27 mars 1665.

[2] *Edits, ordonnances royaux, déclarations et arrêts du conseil d'état du Roi concernant le Canada* (Québec, 1854), III, 50, Commission . . . pour M. de Champigny, 24 avril 1686.

[3] Paris, Archives Nationales, Colonies, Series C11A, XI, f. 292, Champigny au Ministre, Que., 12 nov. 1691.

[4] *Rapport de l'archiviste de la Province de Québec, 1927–1928*, 139; Mémoire du Roy au Gouverneur de Frontenac et à l'intendant Bochart Champigny.

[5] Ibid., *1928–1929*, 324, Mémoire du Gouverneur de Frontenac et de l'intendant Bochart Champigny au Ministre. (26 oct. 1696).

[6] *Ordonances des intendants et arrêts portant règlements du Conseil Supérieur de Québec.* Québec, 1806, II, 128 ff. Projets et règlements faits par Messrs de Tracy et Talon au sujet de l'établissement du pays du Canada . . .

[7] On the Canadian seigneurial system see Marcel Trudel, *Le régime seigneurial*, Brochure Historique no. 6, Publication de la Societé Historique du Canada. Ottawa, 1956.

[8] Projets et règlements faits par Messrs de Tracy et Talon . . . op. cit.

[9] *Jugements et délibérations du Conseil Souverain de la Nouvelle France* (Québec, 1885), I 201–6.

[10] Louise Dechêne, *Habitants et marchands de Montréal au XVIIe siècle* (Montreal, 1974), 61-3.

[11] For examples of such contracts see, *Jugements et délibérations du Conseil Souverain de la Nouvelle France*, I, 118.

[12] Ibid., I, 96.

[13] Ibid., II, 261.

[14] Paris, Archives Nationales, Colonies, Series C11A, XVII, ff. 106-110. Champigny au Ministre, Qué., 20 oct. 1699.

[15] *Jugements et délibérations du Conseil Souverain . . .*, II, 870-2.

[16] Ibid.

[17] Ibid., III, 219 ff.

[18] Ibid.

[19] Paris, Affaires Etrangères, Mémoires et documents, France, vol. 783, f. 128, 1626, Règlement fait pour les pauvres.

[20] Archives Judiciares de Montréal, Extrait des registres du Conseil Souverain, 22 fevrier 1698.

[21] Ibid.

[22] *Jugements et déliberations du Conseil Souverain . . .*, IV, 341.

[23] Archives Judiciares de Montréal, Documents 1698.

[24] Paris, Bibliothèque Nationale, Series F3 Moreau de St Méry, VI, 323, Concession par Mr. Dollier Superieur du Semre. de Montréal à Mr. Charon et ses associez . . . 28 oct. 1688; Paris, Archives Nationales, Colonies, Series C11A, XIV, 294, Champigny au Ministre, Qué., 25 oct. 1696.

[25] Ibid., XI, 539-40, Champigny au Ministre, Qué. 12 nov. 1691.

[26] *Arrêts et règlements du Conseil Supérieur de Québec et ordonnances et jugements des intendants du Canada* (Québec, 1854), 391-2.

[27] *Edits, ordonnances royaux . . .*, I, 271.

[28] *Arrêts et règlements du Conseil Supérieur . . .*, 310.

[29] *Inventaire des ordonnances des intendants de la Nouvelle France* (Québec, 1919), II, 203.

[30] *Arrêts et règlements du Conseil Supérieur . . .*, 395-6.

[31] Maude E. Abbot: *History of Medicine in the Province of Quebec* (Toronto, 1931), 25-6.

[32] *Jugements et délibérations du Conseil Souverain . . .* IV, 312-15.

[33] A.D. Kelly: 'Health Insurance in New France,' in *Bulletin of the History of Medicine*, XXVIII, Nov.-Dec. 1954.

[34] *Jugements et délibérations du Conseil Souverain . . .*, I, 436-7. (In this case, heard on 1 August 1667, a surgeon sued a citizen of Trois Rivières for non-payment of medical bills, for the treatment of the defendant, his family and servants, amounting to 465 *livres*. The defendant claimed to have a yearly medical contract and was required to produce proof.)

[35] *Ordonnances des intendants et arrêts portant règlements du Conseil Supérieur de Québec*, II, 278-9, 7 juin 1727.

[36] A.D. Kelly, op cit.

NEW FRANCE AND THE WESTERN FRONTIER

[1] A very interesting discussion of the significance of the metropolis in Canadian history is contained in the article by J.M.S. Careless, 'Frontierism, Metropolitanism, and Canadian History,' in *Canadian Historical Review*, XXXV (March 1954) 1-21.

[2] R. Glover, 'The Difficulties of the Hudson's Bay Company's Penetration of the West', in *The Canadian Historical Review*, XXIX, (Sept. 1948) 240-254.

[3] *Peter Kalm's Travels in North America*, (Adolph B. Benson ed., New York, 1966), I, 363-5, 373.

[4] Glover, op cit.

[5] On this 'Frenchification policy' see Jean Delanglez, *Frontenac and the Jesuits*, (Chicago, 1939), 36–8; W.J. Eccles, *Frontenac the Courtier Governor* (Toronto, 1959), 54–8. In 1709 the governor-general and the intendant, Vaudreuil and Raudot, stated that three years earlier they had forbidden the marriage of Frenchmen to Indian women because of the adverse social consequences. The King subsequently approved this decision. *Rapport de l'Archiviste de la Province de Quebec* (hereafter referred to as RAPQ), 1942–3, 420, Vaudreuil et Raudot au Ministre, Que., 14 nov. 1709; RAPQ 1946–7, 423, Mémoire du Roy à Vaudreuil et Raudot, Marly, 7 juillet 1711.

[6] The first such appointments were made in 1684 by LeFebvre de la Barre, Governor-General; Morel de la Durantaye being appointed to command at Michilimackinac and the Chevalier de Baugy at St Louis des Illinois. Paris, Archives Nationales (hereafter referred to as AN), CIIA, VI, 273–7, La Barre au Ministre, Que. 5 juin 1684.

[7] Reuben Gold Thwaites, *The Jesuit Relations and Allied Documents* (Cleveland, 1896–1901), vol. 65, 189–253. R.P. Carheil à Champigny, Michilimackinac, 30 aoust 1702. RAPQ 1965, 37, Fr. J.-F. de St-Cosme, Michilmackinac, 13 septembre 1698. The *Jesuit Relations* are replete with complaints on this score.

[8] AN. CIIA. X 66, Denonville à Seignelay, Que., 10 aoust 1688.

[9] P. Margry ed., *Mémoires et documents pour servir à l'histoire des origines francaises des pays d'outre mer: Découvertes et établissements des Francais dans l'ouest et dans le sud de l'Amérique septentrionale* (Paris, 1876), V, 83–5, Relation du Sr de la Mothe Cadillac.

[10] Richard J. Hooker ed., *The Carolina Backcountry on the Eve of the Revolution* (Chapel Hill, N.C., 1953) 26–8, 33, 121–2.

[11] AN F3, VI, 214, Arrest du Conseil d'Estat qui permet aux Gentilshommes de Canada de faire le Commerce du 10 mars 1685.

[12] RAPQ 1934–5, 52–4, Mme Bégon à son fils, Mtl., 28, 29 mars, 2 avril 1749.

[13] Richard Colebrook Harris, *The Seigneurial System in Early Canada* (Madison, Wisconsin, 1966), 79–81.

[14] AN. CIIA, VII 89–95, Denonville au Ministre, Que., 13 nov. 1685.

[15] Charlevoix, Francois-Xavier, Père de, *Histoire de la Nouvelle France*, Tome II, *Journal d'un voyage fait par ordre du Roi dans l'Amérique septentrionale adressé à Madame la Duchesse de Lesdiguières* (Paris, 1744), 247–9.

[16] On one manifestation of this characteristic, see the interesting comments in Fernand Ouellet, 'La mentalité et l'outillage, économique de l'habitant Canadien 1760 . . . in *Bulletin des Recherches Historiques* (1956), 131–6.

[17] AN. B. VIII, 88–9, Ordonnance du Roy, Versailles, 2 mai 1881.

[18] RAPQ 1947–8, 264, Vaudreuil au Ministre, Que., 16 sept. 1714, 273; Vaudreuil et Bégon au Ministre, Que., 20 sept. 1714.

[19] Guy Frégault, *La Guerre de la Conquête*. (Montreal and Paris, 1955), 218–27; L.H. Gipson, *The British Empire Before the American Revolution*, (N.Y., 1949), VII, 36–74.

[20] C.P. Stacey, *Quebec, 1759: The Siege and the Battle* (Toronto, 1959), 145–53.

[21] Alexander Ross, *The Fur Hunters of the Far West*, (London, 1855), II, 236–7. Quoted in P.B. Waite, *Canadian Historical Document Series, Vol. II, Pre-Confederation* (Toronto, 1965), 145.

A BELATED REVIEW OF HAROLD ADAMS INNIS'S
THE FUR TRADE IN CANADA

[1] All references are to the 1962 reprint of the revised 1956 edition, it being the most readily available today. The book was first published in 1930.

[2] Harold Adams Innis, *The Fur Trade in Canada* (Toronto, 1962), 83. The operative word in this statement is 'inadequately'. Professor Winks later noted (xiv), 'His only serious lack was failure to obtain access to the closed archives of the Hudson's Bay Company . . .' This implies that he attempted to gain access but was refused. It is difficult to see why this should have been since F. Merk was permitted to study documents in the archives of the company relevant to his work *Fur Trade and Empire*, published in 1931, and A.S. Morton made good use of those archives for his *History of the Canadian West to 1870-71*, published in 1939. Nor did Innis consult the great mass of fur trade documents in the Archives judiciaries de Montréal. He did make use of some of the correspondence between the royal officials at Quebec and the Ministry of Marine, but only the transcripts of the documents at the Public Archives of Canada. Had he consulted the original documents in Paris he would have discovered that a considerable number of them were not transcribed for Ottawa. A list of those not to be transcribed, mostly dealing with economic affairs, was affixed to the inside of the cover of each volume. A considerable proportion of them dealt with the fur trade.

[3] Innis, *Fur Trade*, 76, notes 132, 133.

[4] Ibid., 83.

[5] La Rochelle, Archives de la Chambre de Commerce, Anciennes archives, carton 27, Récapitulation de . . . marchandises entrées dans . . . La Rochelle, 1718-1761. Cited in A.J.E. Lunn, 'Economic Development in New France, 1713-1760' (unpublished PH D thesis, McGill University, 1942), 464-5. In 1715 Ruette d'Auteuil estimated the Canadian fur trade to be worth upwards of a million *livres* a year. See *Rapport de l'Archiviste de la Province de Québec, 1922-23*, 59-60. Fur and hide imports at La Rochelle, taken from the same source and for the same time span, are cited in Emile Garnault, *Le Commerce rochelais. Le Rochelais et le Canada* (La Rochelle 1893), 15-16. Emile Salone, *La Colonisation de la Nouvelle-France* (Paris 1905), 397-8, reproduces Garnault's figures with an amendment, the deduction of the entry for hides since these, he states, most likely came from the Antilles. Moose hides, deer, and seal skins, were, however, a not inconsiderable item in Canada's fur-trade exports. There is a fairly consistent but puzzling discrepancy between Garnault's figures and those cited by Dr Lunn.

[6] Dale Miquelon, *Dugard of Rouen* (Montreal and London, 1978), 87.

[7] Maurice Filion, *La pensée et l'action coloniale de Maurepas vis à vis du Canada 1723-1749* (Ottawa 1972), 82. See also Fernand Braudel et Ernest Labrousse, éds., *Histoire économique et sociale de la France* (Paris, 1970), II, 499ff.

[8] The same was true in Britain where, in the eighteenth century, furs accounted for less than half of one per cent of the total value of imports. See Murray G. Lawson, *Fur: A Study in English Mercantilism 1700-1775* (Toronto, 1943), 70, 72. His concluding sentence says it all: 'In short, in the eighteenth century . . . it was actually of no real importance either to the English or American economy.' Innis wrote a lengthy foreword to this work without noting that it contradicted much that he had written in his own study of the fur trade. That the cod exported from Louisbourg equalled or exceeded in value the furs exported from Canada is demonstrated by Christopher Moore. 'The Other Louisbourg; Trade and Merchant Enterprise in Ile Royale 1713-1758', *Histoire sociale/Social History*, XII, May 1979, 84.

[9] *Édits, Ordonnances royaux, Déclarations et Arrêts du Conseil d'État du Roi concernant le Canada* (Québec 1854), 5-11.

[10] Innis, *Fur Trade*, 63-4.

[11] Yves F. Zoltvany, 'Aubert de La Chesnaye, Charles', *Dictionary of Canadian Biography*, II (Toronto 1969), 29.

[12] See Stewart L. Mims, *Colbert's West India Policy* (New Haven, 1912). Innis does not appear to have consulted this work.

[13] For a more detailed discussion of the beaver crisis of 1696 see W.J. Eccles, *Frontenac: The Courtier Governor* (Toronto, 1959), 285–94.

[14] Here, as throughout his work, Innis failed to distinguish between beaver and other furs when citing the sources; to him they seemed synonymous. He also failed to distinguish between *livres* weight of fur and *livres* value, which renders much of this statistical information meaningless or misleading.

[15] Innis, *Fur Trade*, 115.

[16] Lawson, *Fur Trade*, ix.

[17] Innis, *Fur Trade*, 110. See also 391: 'The competition of cheaper goods contributed in a definite fashion to the downfall of New France and enabled Great Britain to prevail in the face of its pronounced militaristic development.'

[18] Ibid., 97, 106, 138, 167, 168–9, 175.

[19] Thomas Elliot Norton, *The Fur Trade in Colonial New York 1686–1776* (Madison, Wis., 1974), 56, 87, 124, 171–2.

[20] The burden of the evidence indicates clearly enough that, all things being equal, the Indians preferred to trade with the French. They appear to have traded with the English mainly to preserve that option and thereby oblige the French to keep their prices competitive. James Knight at York Fort wrote on 19 September 1714: 'One of the Indians came to me when I hoisted the Union flag: he told me he did not love to see that, he loved to see the white one, so there is many of the Indians has great friendship for the French here.' Publications of the Hudson's Bay Record Society, xxv: K.G. Davies, ed., *Letters from Hudson Bay 1703–40* (London 1965), 37 [hereafter HBC Records].

[21] Fernand Grenier, éd., *Papiers Contrecoeur et autres documents concernant le conflit anglo-français sur l'Ohio de 1745 à 1756* (Québec 1952), 264–5.

[22] Innis, *Fur Trade*, 97, 106, 138, 167, 168–9, 175.

[23] Ibid., 111.

[24] See W.J. Eccles, 'The Battle of Quebec: A Reappraisal', in The French Colonial Historical Society, *Proceedings of the Third Annual Meeting*, 1977.

[25] Innis, *Fur Trade*, 114.

[26] Ibid., 166.

[27] The Bay Company did establish Henley House in 1743 some 120 miles inland on the Albany River, but it proved almost impossible to maintain and in 1755 the staff was massacred by local Indians infuriated by the bad treatment they had received. Not until 1766 did the company succeed in re-establishing the post. See E.E. Rich, *The Fur Trade and the North West to 1857* (Toronto 1967), 105–8, 140.

[28] Innis, *Fur Trade*, 47, 52–3, 97, 109, 166.

[29] Ibid., 138, 167.

[30] Arthur J. Ray and Donald Freeman, *'Give us Good Measure': An Economic Analysis of Relations between the Indians and the Hudson's Bay Company before 1763* (Toronto, 1978), 41–51.

[31] Innis, *Fur Trade*, 47.

[32] HBC Records, 611; Ray and Freeman, *'Give Us Good Measure'*, 161.

[33] *Rapport de l'Archiviste de la Province de Québec 1923–24*, 44–5, Mémoire sur l'Etat de la Nouvelle-France 1757, Bougainville.

[34] Innis, *Fur Trade*, 190. The reference is to J. Carver, *Travels Through the Interior Parts of North-America in the Years 1766, 1767, and 1768* (London, 1778), 110–12. The relevant passage states, after mentioning Indian complaints of the shoddy quality of the goods they had obtained at the Bay: 'The length of their journey to the Hudson's Bay factories, which they informed me, took them up three months during the summer heats to go and return, and

from the smallness of their canoes they could not carry more than a third of the beavers they killed. So that it is not to be wondered at, that these Indians should wish to have traders come to reside among them.'

[35] See the map in Ray and Freeman, '*Give us Good Measure*', 46, which gives dates for the freeze-up and the required dates of departure from York Factory for the Indians to return to their tribes before the rivers froze. Some of the dates given appear to be in error.

[36] Innis, *Fur Trade*, 164.

[37] Ray and Freeman, '*Give us Good Measure*,' 33. Elsewhere they make statements that qualify or refute this assertion. See, for example, '. . . the Indian's . . . per capita transport capacity remained fixed at a relatively low level' (129). See also 179, 197, 235, 239–40.

[38] Lawson, *Fur*, 87–92, 108, 136; Innis, *Fur Trade*, 138.

[39] Innis, *Fur Trade*, 52–3, 78, 109, 110, 179.

[40] Ibid., 391.

[41] Ibid., 172, citing Public Archives of Canada, CO 42, II, 363–4.

[42] Ibid., 172–3.

[43] Walter L. Dorn, *Competition for Empire* (New York, 1940), 254.

[44] Braudel et Labrousse, éds, *Histoire*, 499–528.

[45] HBC Records, 278–84. James Isham, York Fort, 20 July 1739. That the Canadian traders checked the goods shipped west carefully is confirmed by C. Nolan Lamarque, Livre de comptes, Archives nationales du Québec à Montréal.

[46] HBC Records, William Bevan and others, Moose River, 20 Aug. 1734, 196. See also Thomas White, York Fort, 9 Aug. 1734, 194–5.

[47] Ibid., Rowland Waggoner and others, Albany Fort, 15 Aug. 1739, 285; Richard Staunton and others, Moose Fort, 17 Aug. 1739, 306; Thomas McCliesh, Albany Fort, 16 July 1716, 44.

[48] Innis, *Fur Trade*, 85, 112.

[49] HBC Records, 325; see also 43, 75, 232, 306.

[50] Ibid., Thomas McCliesh, Albany Fort, 16 July 1716, 43. See also 89, 99, 142, 149.

[51] Ibid., 44, 81, 99, 148, 150, 191, 232.

[52] Ibid., Thomas McCliesh, Albany, 16 July 1716, 44.

[53] Innis, *Fur Trade*, 85.

[54] E.E. Rich, *The History of the Hudson's Bay Company 1670–1870, 1:1670–1763* (London 1958), 547; HBC Records, 205.

[55] Archives du Séminaire de Québec, Fonds Verreau, boîte 1, no 13, Duquesne à Contrecoeur, Mtl, 30 avril 1753.

[56] HBC Records, Thomas McCleish, York Fort, 8 Aug. 1728, 136.

[57] Innis, *Fur Trade*, 137.

[58] Norton, *Fur Trade in Colonial New York*, 112.

[59] Lunn, 'Economic Development', 157–63. The Canadian traders, however, catered to Indian needs and preferences more astutely than did the British. Surcoats were made in Montreal and shipped to the west without sleeves attached; these last were shipped separately in three lengths so that the Indian customers could be sure of a good fit. Similarly, hatchets, axes, and 'casse têtes' were made with round eye holes, making it much easier to replace a broken handle in the bush. A factor at Fort Albany reported in 1727 that he was returning 170 hatchets 'all flat eyed which will not trade, they having lain upon account this ten years to my knowledge'. HBC Records, 125.

[60] Paris, Archives nationales, Colonies, CIIA [hereafter AN CIIA], vol. 91, ff. 67–71, Galissonière et Bigot au ministre, Qué., 20 oct. 1748. They complained of some recent shipments of heavy and overly expensive cooking pots but stated that they were taking steps to prevent a recurrence. Their dispatch was written at the height of the war, just after the loss of Louisbourg

had resulted in a chronic shortage of trade goods. This had led to the defection of the western allies and attacks on the French posts. The governor-general and intendant further declared that good-quality trade goods at modest prices were essential, otherwise the trade would go to the English 'et les Mettra En Estat de tourner Contre nous Toutes les Nations dont l'alliance a Esté cy devant nôtre plus ferme apuy et le fleau des Colonies angloises. C'Est principalement dans cette Vue que nous insistons sur cet article.' This makes explicit that the fur trade was considered an economic means to a political and military end. Innis cited this document (85) as evidence of the superiority of British trade goods, failing to note the circumstances and ignoring the political context.

[61] AN CIIA, vol. 103, ff. 437–41, Mémoire.

[62] See the itemized invoices of such shipments in the Livre de comptes de C. Nolan Lamarque, Archives nationales du Québec à Montréal.

[63] Innis, *Fur Trade*, 138.

[64] Lawson, 108.

[65] Lunn, 'Economic Development', 455, 464–5.

[66] Lawson, *Fur*, 34.

[67] Norton, *Fur Trade in Colonial New York*, 100–3, 122, 124.

[68] The same trend developed in other commercial fields. France, by the 1740s, had succeeded in eliminating English goods from the Levant and her textiles from the Portuguese market, was making great inroads in the Spanish colonies, and took the lion's share of the fish on the Grand Banks. As French overseas trade increased by leaps and bounds that of England stagnated. See Roland Mousnier et Ernest Labrousse, *Histoire générale des civilisations*, v: *Le XVIIIe siècle* (Paris 1955), 213; Dorn, *Competition for Empire*, 122–30. These economic factors were a main reason for England's seeking a spoiling war with France in 1744 and again a decade later. As Pares put it: 'These are the ambitions of the respectable tradesman who hopes to increase his custom by hiring the racketeer to destroy his neighbour's shop.' Richard Pares, *War and Trade in the West Indies, 1739–1763* (Oxford, 1936), 181, also 61–4, 180. See also E.E. Rich and C.H. Wilson, *The Cambridge Economic History of Europe*, IV: *The Economy of Expanding Europe in the Sixteenth and Seventeenth Centuries* (Cambridge, 1967), 536–7. Innis, however, without citing any evidence, stated: 'At the end of the period (1749) English products had made substantial inroads on the French market in Spain, Portugal, Italy and Germany' (*Fur Trade*, 101).

[69] *The Papers of Sir William Johnson* (Albany, 1925), I, 72; IV, 559.

[70] John J. McCusker, *Money and Exchange in Europe and America, 1600–1775: A Handbook* (Chapel Hill, NC, 1978).

[71] New York prices are those given by Sir William Johnson, those at Montreal are from Le Livre de comptes de C. Nolan Lamarque. For clarity the Montreal prices were converted into sterling at the current exchange rate of ten pence to the *livre tournois*.

[72] Innis, *Fur Trade*, 112–13.

[73] Ibid., 102, 112, 386.

[74] Ibid., 60 n l, 113. See also 115: 'The direct relation between the fur trade and the colonial administration as carried out from France, or in the colony, was unique. The paternalism of the French *regime* was characteristic of a colony dependent on the fur trade.' And again, 390 as well as pp. xi, xiii of this preface to Lawson.

[75] Innis, *Fur Trade*, 115.

[76] Ibid., 390.

[77] Ibid., 391.

[78] AN CIIA, v, ff 297–8, Duchesneau à Seignelay, Qué., 13 nov. 1681; x, ff. 65–7, Denonville à Seignelay, Qué., 10 août 1688.

[79] Hubert Charbonneau et Yolande Lavoie, 'Introduction à la reconstitution de la population

du Canada au xviie siècle: Étude critique des sources de la période 1665-1668,' *Revue d'histoire de l'Amérique français*, XXIV, 4, mars 1971, 485-511.

80 Innis, *Fur Trade*, 166.

81 See, for example, 190, 192-3, 195-8, 228-30, 237-42, 249ff, 258-9.

82 Ibid., 154, 159-60, 289. For the significance of the York boat, and other factors that Innis ignored, see R. Glover, 'The Difficulties of the Hudson's Bay Company's Penetration of the West,' *Canadian Historical Review*, XXIX, Sept. 1948, 240-54.

83 Innis, *Fur Trade*, 387.

84 Ibid., 241-2.

85 Lawson, *Fur*, x.

86 Guy Frégault, *Le Grand Marquis* (Montréal, 1952), 317ff.

87 Lawson, *Fur*, x. See also Innis, *Fur Trade*, 110.

88 Ibid., 393.

89 Ibid., 67.

90 Ibid., 386.

91 Ibid., 388.

92 It is rather ironic that although there was no conflict in New France between settlement and the fur trade—Innis to the contrary—that conflict was quite pronounced in colonial New York. See Sung Bok Tim, *Landlord and Tenant in Colonial New York* (Chapel Hill, NC, 1978), 75-6.

93 Innis, *Fur Trade*, 178.

94 See Eccles, *Frontenac*, 334-6; *France in America* (New York, 1972), 178-81; Frégault, *Le Grand Marquis*, 329ff.

95 Innis, *Fur Trade*, 393.

96 Ibid., 392.

97 Ibid., 391.

98 Ibid., 401-2.

99 W.J. Eccles, 'The Role of the American Colonies in Eighteenth Century French Foreign Policy', *Atti del I Congresso Internazionale di Storia Americana* (Genova, 1976), 163-73.

THE FUR TRADE AND EIGHTEENTH-CENTURY IMPERIALISM

1 On the Huron-Iroquois conflict see Bruce G. Trigger, *The Children of Aataentsic: A History of the Huron People to 1660*, 2 vols (Montreal, 1976), and John A. Dickinson, 'Annaotaha et Dollard vus de l'autre côté de la palissade', *Revue d'histoire de l'Amérique française*, XXXV (1981), 163-78.

2 The best study of this early period is Marcel Trudel, *The Beginnings of New France, 1524-1663*, trans. Patricia Claxton (Toronto, 1973). The period of 1663-1701 is covered in W.J. Eccles, *Canada under Louis XIV, 1663-1701* (Toronto, 1964). The latter work is now somewhat dated.

3 In order of conquest or dispersal these tribes were the Mahicans, 1628; Hurons, 1649; Neutrals, 1651; Eries, 1653-7; and Susquehannocs, 1676.

4 Mémoire de Henri Tonty, Nouvelles Acquisitions, vol. 7485, f. 103, Bibliothèque Nationale, Paris; Duchesneau au ministre, 13 nov. 1680, c11A, vol. 5, ff. 39-40, Archives Nationales, Colonies, Paris.

5 W.J. Eccles, *Frontenac: The Courtier Governor* (Toronto, 1959), 82-4, 107-10; François Vachon de Belmont, *Histoire du Canada, D'après un manuscrit à la Bibliothèque du Roi à Paris* (Québec, 1840), 14.

6 Belmont, *Histoire du Canada*, 15-16; Eccles, *Frontenac*, 167-71; Presens des Onontaguez à Onontio à la Famine le Cinq Septembre 1684, Le febvre de la barre, c11A vol. 6, ff. 299-300.

[7] Le roy au Sr. de Meules, 10 mars 1685, B, vol. II, f. 96, Archs. Nationales.

[8] Eccles, *Frontenac*, 157–97, 244–72.

[9] Ibid., 328–33.

[10] Ibid., 334–7; Marcel Giraud, *Histoire de la Louisiane française*, I: *Le règne de Louis XIV (1698–1715)* (Paris, 1953), 13–23.

[11] M. Tremblay à M. Glandelet, 28 mai 1701, Lettres, Carton O, no. 34, Archives du Séminaire de Québec.

[12] Giraud, *Histoire de la Louisiane*, I, 39–43.

[13] Yves F. Zoltvany, *Philippe de Rigaud de Vaudreuil: Governor of New France, 1703–1725* (Toronto, 1974), 39–41.

[14] Ibid., 40, 86–7; Champigny au ministre, 8 août 1688, C11A, vol. 10, ff. 123–4; Callières et Champigny au ministre, 5 oct. 1701, ibid., vol. 19, ff. 6–7. That this fear was soon to be realized is made clear in d'Iberville's journal for 1702 where he mentions his accepting furs from Canadian *coureurs de bois* for shipment to France. See Richebourg Gaillard McWilliams, trans. and ed., *Iberville's Gulf Journals* (University, Ala., 1981), 165, 178.

[15] Charles Edwards O'Neill, *Church and State in French Colonial Louisiana: Policy and Politics to 1732* (New Haven, Conn., 1966), *passim*.

[16] Rapport de l'Archiviste de la Province de Québec 1938–9 (hereinafter RAPQ), 69, Ministre à Vaudreuil, Versailles, 17 juin 1705.

[17] Beauharnois et d'Aigremont au ministre, 1 Oct. 1728, C11A, vol. 50, ff. 31–3; minister to La Jonquière and Bigot, 4 May 1749, State Historical Society of Wisconsin, *Collections*, XVIII (1908), 25–6; Beauharnois to the minister, 18 Oct. 1737, Michigan Pioneer and Historical Society, *Historical Collections*, XXXIV (1905), 146–7.

[18] For a revealing commentary on the working of a typical fur-trade company of the period see Meuvret au Lt. Joseph Marin de la Malgue [Commandant, la Baie des Puants], 15 mai 1752, Fonds Verreau, Boite 5, no. 38 1/2, Archs. Sém. Québec. See also Acte de Société, 23 mai 1726, Jean Le Mire Marsolet de Lignery, Guillaume Cartier, Greffe J-B, Adhemar, no. 1854, Archives Nationales du Québec à Montréal.

[19] Pierre-Jacques Chavoy de Noyan to the minister, 18 Oct. 1738, Mich. Pioneer Hist. Soc., *Hist. Colls.*, XXXIV (1905), 158–9; Le Conseil de Marine à MM de Vaudreuil et Bégon, 20 oct. 1717, C11A, vol. 37, ff. 378–9; Beauharnois et Hocquart au ministre, 5 oct. 1736, ibid., vol. 65, ff. 57–8; Greffe J., David, 28 avril 1723, Archs. Québec (Mtl.), is but one of hundreds of permits that specify the obligations to the crown of those allowed to trade in the west. See also ibid., Greffe J-B, Adhemar, no. 1257, 23 mai 1724, and no. 1211, 8 mai 1724; Beauharnois et d'Aigremont au ministre, 1 oct. 1728, C11A, vol. 50, ff. 31–3; Wilbur R. Jacobs, *Dispossessing the American Indian: Indians and Whites on the Colonial Frontier* (New York, 1972), 194, n. 38; and Zoltvany, *Vaudreuil*, 174–5.

[20] Zoltvany, *Vaudreuil*, 166–8, 196–209.

[21] Canada. Conseil. MM de Vaudreuil et Bégon, 26 oct. 1720, C11A, vol. 41, ff. 390–1.

[22] Parole de toute la Nation Abenaquise et de toute les autres nations sauvages ses alliés au gouverneur de Baston au sujet de la Terre des Abenaquise dont les Anglois s'Emparent depuis la Paix . . . fait à KenasK8K au bas de la Rivière de Kenibeki Le 28 juillet 1721, F3 Moreau de St. Méry, vol 2, ff. 413–16, Archs. Nationales.

[23] Mémoire du Roy à MM de Beauharnois et Dupuy, 29 avril 1727, *Nouvelle-France. Documents historiques. Correspondance échangée entre les autorités française et les gouverneurs et intendants*, I (Québec, 1893), 64.

[24] E.E. Rich, *The History of the Hudson's Bay Company, 1670–1870*, I: *1670–1763* (London, 1958), 423–5, 482–6; 'Memorial of the Governor and Company of Adventurers of England Trading into Hudson's Bay to the Council of Trade and Plantations', in W. Noel Sainsbury *et al.*, eds, *Calendar of State Papers, Colonial Series, America and the West Indies* (London,

1860–), XXXI, no. 360; Mr Delafaye to the Council of Trade and Plantations, 4 Nov. 1719, ibid., no. 443; Observations et réflexions servant de réponses aux propositions de Messieurs les Commissaires anglais au sujet des limites a régler pour la Baie d'Hudson, RAPQ 1922-3, 95-6.

25 Rich, *Hudson's Bay Company*, I, 554, 434, 556, 575, and *The Fur Trade and the Northwest to 1857* (Toronto, 1967), 118.

26 Lawrence J. Burpee, ed., 'The Journal of Anthony Hendry, 1754–55', Royal Society of Canada, *Proceedings and Transactions*, 2d Ser., XIII, Pt. ii (1907), 352–3.

27 Rich, *Hudson's Bay Company*, I, 482, 526, 529; Arthur J. Ray, 'Indians as Consumers in the Eighteenth Century', in Carol M. Judd and Arthur J. Ray, eds, *Old Trails and New Directions: Papers of the Third North American Fur Trade Conference* (Toronto, 1980), 255–71; W.J. Eccles, 'A Belated Review of Harold Adams Innis, *The Fur Trade in Canada'*, *Canadian Historical Review*, LX (1979), 427–34.

28 Mémoire ou Extrait du Journal Sommaire du Voyage de Jacques Legardeur Ecuyer Sr de St Pierre . . . chargé de la Descouverte de la Mer de l'Ouest, Fonds Verreau, Boite 5, no. 54, Archs. Sém. Québec.

29 The population figures for these settlements are revealing: Detroit in 1750, 483; Illinois in 1752, 1,536; lower Louisiana in 1746, 4,100.

30 Denonville et Champigny au ministre, 6 nov. 1688, C11A, vol. 10, f. 8, et le ministre à Denonville, 8 jan. 1688, B, vol. 15, f. 20, Archs. Nationales.

31 Similarly the Iroquois specifically rejected British claims that they were subjects of the British crown. See Acte authentique des six nations iroquoises sur leur indépendance (2 nov. 1748), *Rapport de l'Archiviste*, 1921-2, unnum. plate following 108.

32 D'Iberville au ministre, 26 fév. 1700, C13A, vol. I, f. 236, Archs. Nationales; Pièces détachées judiciares 1720: Archs. Québec (Mtl.), Vaudreuil à Beauharnois, 9 nov. 1745, Loudon Collection, Henry E. Huntington Library, San Marino, Calif.: Ordonnance de Beauharnois, 8 juin 1743, Fonds Verreau, Boite 8, no. 96, Archs. Sém. Québec, Duquesne à Contrecoeur, 12 juin 1753, ibid., Boite I, no. 19; Duquesne à Contrecoeur, 24 juin 1754, Fernand Grenier, ed., *Papiers Contrecoeur et autres documents concernant le conflit anglo-français sur l'Ohio de 1745 à 1756* (Québec, 1952), 193.

33 On this controversial issue see Ray, 'Indians as Consumers', in Judd and Ray, eds, *Old Trails and New Directions*, 255–71, and Eccles, 'Belated Review of Innis', *Canadian Hist., Rev.*, LX (1979), 419–41.

34 Rich, *Hudson's Bay Company*, I, 545.

35 Calvin Martin, *Keepers of the Game: Indian-Animal Relationships and the Fur Trade* (Berkeley, Calif., 1978), 63–4; André Vachon, 'L'eau de vie dans la société indienne', Canadian Historical Association, *Report* (1960), 22–32.

36 Ray, 'Indians as Consumers', in Judd and Ray, eds, *Old Trails and New Directions*, 255–71.

37 Arthur S. Morton, eds, *The Journal of Duncan M'Gillivray of the North West Company at Fort George on the Saskatchewan, 1794-5* (Toronto, 1929), 47.

38 Beauharnois et Hocquart au ministre, 12 oct. 1736, C11A, vol. 65, ff. 49–51; Observation de la Conseil de la Marine, 1 juin 1718, ibid., vol. 39, ff. 242–6. See also Reuben Gold Thwaites, ed., *The Jesuit Relations and Allied Documents: Travels and Explorations of the Jesuit Missionaries in New France, 1610-1791* (Cleveland, Ohio, 1896–1901), *passim*.

39 Eccles, *Frontenac*, 66.

40 For a brief overview of this contentious issue see ibid., 61–8.

41 Peter Schuyler to Gov. Donagan, 2 Sept. 1687, E.B. O'Callaghan *et al.*, eds. *Documents Relative to the Colonial History of the State of New-York* . . . (Albany, N.Y., 1856–87), III, 479, hereafter cited as *N.-Y. Col. Docs.*; Propositions made by four of the Chief Sachems of

the 5 Nations to his Excell. Benjamin Fletcher . . . in Albany, 26 Feb. 1692/3, ibid., IV, 24; 27 Dec. 1698, Peter Wraxall, *An Abridgement of the Indian Affairs . . . Transacted in the Colony of New York, from the Year 1678 to the Year 1751*, ed. Charles Howard McIlwain (Cambridge, Mass., 1915), 31; Relation de ce qui s'est passé de plus remarquable en Canada . . . 1695, F3 Moreau de St. Méry, vol. 7, ff. 370-2, Archs. Nationales; Vaudreuil au ministre, 25 oct. 1710, *Rapport de l'Archiviste*, 1946-7, 385; Vaudreuil et Bégon au ministre, 20 sept. 1714, ibid., 1947-8, 275-6; Beauharnois et Hocquart au ministre, 12 oct. 1736, C11A, vol. 65, ff. 44-6.

[42] Eccles, 'Belated Review of Innis', *Canadian Hist. Rev.*, LX (1979), 434.

[43] Thomas Elliot Norton, *The Fur Trade in Colonial New York, 1686-1776* (Madison, Wis., 1974), 100-3, 122, 124.

[44] Jean Lunn, 'The Illegal Fur Trade out of New France, 1713-1760', Canadian Hist. Assn., *Report* (1939), 61-76; Wraxall, *New York Indian Records*, ed. McIlwain, *passim*.

[45] Le Ch^{er} Dailleboust à Madame d'Argenteuil, 5 jan. 1715, Collection Baby, g 1/12, Université de Montréal, Montréal, Que.; Ordonnance de Gilles Hocquart, 25 avril 1738, C11A, vol. 69, ff. 180-3; Pierre-Georges Roy, ed., *Inventaire des Ordonnances des Intendants de la Nouvelle-France, conservées aux Archives provinciales de Québec*. I (Beauceville, Que., 1919), 160-1, 222; J.W. De Peyster à Jean Lidius, 23 sept. 1729, NF 13-17, Procédures Judiciares, III, ff. 389-93, Archs. Québec (Mtl.); Myndert Schuyler à Jean Lidius, 15 oct. 1729, ibid.; Extrait des Registres du Conseil Supèrieur de Québec, 28 sept. 1730, ibid, ff. 385-8.

[46] Lunn, 'Illegal Fur Trade', Canadian Hist. Assn., *Report* (1939), 61-76.

[47] Vaudreuil et Bégon au ministre, 12 nov. 1712, *Rapport de l'Archiviste*, 1947-8, 183-4; Mémoire du Roy pour servir d'instructions au Sieur marquis de Beauharnois, gouverneur et lieutenant-général de la Nouvelle-France, 7 mai 1726, *Nouvelle-France. Documents historiques*, I, 57; Report of Messrs. Schuyler and Dellius' Negotiations in Canada, 2 July 1698, *N.-Y. Col. Docs.*, IV, 347; Bellomont to Council of Trade and Plantations, 24 Aug. 1699, Sainsbury *et al.*, eds, *Calendar of State Papers Colonial, America and West Indies* XVII, 406.

[48] Beauharnois to Maurepas, 21 Sept. 1741, *N.-Y. Col. Docs.*, IX, 1071.

[49] Arthur H. Buffinton, 'The Policy of Albany and English Westward Expansion', *Mississippi Valley Historical Review*, VIII (1922), 327-66.

[50] For contemporary British comment on the superior skills of the Canadian traders see *American Gazetteer . . .* (London, 1762), II, s.v. 'Montreal': 'The French have found some secret of conciliating the affections of the savages, which our traders seem stranger to, or at least take no care to put it in practice.' See also Burpee, ed., 'Journal of Anthony Hendry', Royal Soc. Canada, *Procs. and Trans.*, 2d Ser., XIII, Pt. ii (1907), 307.

[51] Johnson to the Lords of Trade, 16 Nov. 1765, C.O. 5/66, f. 296, Public Record Office. I am indebted to Dr Francis P. Jennings for providing me with this piece of evidence.

[52] For a specific instance of this see the entry for Teganissorens in David M. Hayne, ed., *Dictionary of Canadian Biography*, II (Toronto, 1969), 619-23.

[53] Wraxall, *New York Indian Records*, ed. McIlwain, III.

[54] Zoltvany, *Vaudreuil*, 168-9; Wraxall, *New York Indian Records*, ed. McIlwain, 132-5.

[55] Percy J. Robinson, *Toronto during the French Régime: A History of the Toronto Region from Brulé to Simcoe, 1615-1793*, 2d ed. (Toronto, 1965), 66.

[56] Wraxall, *New York Indian Records*, ed. McIlwain, 161.

[57] Ibid.

[58] Mémoire touchant du droit françois sur les Nations Iroquoises, 12 nov. 1712, C11A, vol. 33, f. 284. The Iroquois admitted to the Albany commissioners that the French had five

posts on the south side of Lake Ontario, from Niagara to Cayouhage, east of Oswego. See 10 Sept. 1720, Wraxall, *New York Indian Records*, ed. McIlwain, 130–1.

[59] On Anglo-French relations at this time see Paul Vaucher, *Robert Walpole et la politique de Fleury (1713–1742)* (Paris, 1924).

[60] Zoltvany, *Vaudreuil*, 199.

[61] Wraxall, *New York Indian Records*, ed. McIlwain, 113, Charles Thomson, *An Enquiry into the Causes of the Alienation of the Delaware and Shawanese Indians from the British Interest . . .* (London, 1759), 56, 76, 114, 118–22; Wilbur R. Jacobs, ed., *The Appalachian Indian Frontier: The Edmond Atkin Report and Plan of 1755* (Columbia, S.C., 1954), *passim.*

[62] Duquesne à Contrecoeur, 30 avril 1753, Fonds Verreau, Boite 1, no. 13, Archs. Sém. Québec.

[63] 14 mars 1721, 25 avril 1726, Roy, ed., *Inventaire des Ordonnances des Intendants*, I, 196, 282; Hocquart au ministre, 25 oct. 1729, c11A, vol. 51, f. 264; Vaudreuil, Beauharnois, et Raudot au ministre, 19 oct. 1705, *Rapport de l'Archiviste*, 1938–9, 87–8.

[64] Mémoire sur les postes de Canada . . . en 1754 . . ., *Rapport de l'Archiviste*, 1927–8, 353.

[65] Extrait Général des Revenues des Compagnies Entretenues en la Nouvelle-France . . . 1750, D2C, vol. 48, f. 130, Archs. Nationales.

[66] Many of the *voyageurs* hired to serve in the west had notarized contracts, a copy of which had to be preserved in an official register by the notary. Unfortunately, many *voyageurs* were instead hired *sous seing privé*, that is, with a written contract not drawn up by a notary. A few of the latter type of contract have survived by accident or because they were submitted as evidence in legal proceedings. Many men may well have been hired with a mere verbal understanding of the terms of service. Statistical studies based on the notarized contracts alone therefore cannot help but be misleading since there is no way of knowing what proportion of the total number of *voyageurs* employed in any given year the contracts represent. See Gratien Allaire, 'Les engagements pour la traite des fourrures, évaluation de la documentation', *Revue d'histoire de l'Amérique française*, XXXIV (1980), 3–26.

[67] W.J. Eccles, *France in America* (New York, 1972), 178–9.

[68] La Chauvignery à [Contrecoeur], 10 fév. 1754, Fonds Verreau, Boite 1, no. 77, Archs. Sém. Québec.

[69] As early as 1708 François Clairambault d'Aigremont, sent to investigate conditions in the west, stated in a momentous report to the minister that the French could not take enough precautions to conserve the trade north of Lake Superior, since the furs at Detroit and those of the region to the south were not worth much. The reluctance of the Canadian fur traders to engage in trade in the Ohio country is made plain in Gov.-Gen. Duquesne's correspondence with Claude-Pierre Pécaudy de Contrecoeur, commandant at Fort Duquesne. Le Sr d'Aigremont au Ministre Pontchartrain, 14 nov. 1708, c11A, vol. 29, f. 175; Grenier, ed., *Papiers Contrecoeur*, 126, 128, 209, 224, 248–9, 253.

[70] Galissonière au ministre, 1 sept. 1748, c11A, vol. 91, ff. 116–22.

[71] Donald H. Kent, *The French Invasion of Western Pennsylvania, 1753* (Harrisburg, Pa., 1954), 12; Sylvester K. Stevens and Donald H. Kent, eds, *Wilderness Chronicles of Northwestern Pennsylvania . . .* (Harrisburg, Pa., 1941), 56; Duquesne à Contrecoeur, 8 sept. 1754, Grenier, ed., *Papiers Contrecoeur*, 250; Duquesne à Rouillé, 31 (sic) nov. 1753, c11A, vol. 99, ff. 139–43; Duquesne à Rouillé, 29 sept. 1754, ibid., ff. 242–3; Duquesne à Rouillé, 7 nov. 1754, ibid., f. 259.

[72] By Oct. 1753, of over 2,000 men who had left Montreal the previous spring and summer only 880 were fit for service. Duquesne à Marin, 16 nov. 1753, Grenier, ed., *Papiers Contrecoeur*, 81; Ministre à Duquesne 31 mai 1754, B, vol. 99, f. 199, Archs. Nationales; Kent, *French Invasion*, 64.

[73] Duquesne à Contrecoeur, 1 juillet 1754, Grenier, ed., *Papiers Contrecoeur*, 207–8.

[74] In Apr. 1754 Capitaine de Contrecoeur warned the Indians who were trading with the English at their post on the Ohio that he intended to drive the English out. If the Indians chose to support the enemy, they too would be crushed; it was up to them to decide whether or not they wished to be destroyed. Paroles de Contrecoeur aux Sauvages, Grenier, ed., *Papiers Contrecoeur*, 116–17. See also Duquesne à Contrecoeur, 15 avril 1754, ibid., 113–16.

[75] Duquesne à Contrecoeur, 14 Aug. 1754, ibid., 248; Duquesne to the minister, 31 Oct. 1754, *N.Y. Col. Docs.*, x, 269; Thomas Pownall, cited in Louis De Vorsey, Jr., *The Indian Boundary in the Southern Colonies, 1763–1775* (Chapel Hill, N.C., 1961), 56–7.

[76] Thomson, *Enquiry into the Causes, passim*; Journal de Chaussegros de Léry, *Rapport de l'Archiviste*, 1927–8, 409–10.

[77] For French and British casualties see Grenier, ed., *Papiers Contrecoeur*, 390–1.

[78] Ministre à Duquesne, 31 mai 1754, B, vol. 99, f. 199, Archs. Nationales.

[79] Vaudreuil au ministre, 13 oct. 1756, c11A, vol. 101, ff. 117–19.

[80] Duquesne à Marin, 20 juin, 10 juillet 1753, Fonds Verreau, Boite 5, nos. 62, 66:6, Archs. Sém. Québec; Duquesne à Contrecoeur, 22 juillet, 6 août 1753, ibid., Boite 1, nos. 27, 28; Varin à Contrecoeur, 18 août 1753, ibid., Boite 5, no. 311.

[81] Mémoire sur les sauvages du Canada jusqu'à la Rivière de mississippi . . . Donné par M. de Sabrevois en 1718, c11A, vol. 39, f. 354; Varin à Contrecoeur, 17 mai, 1 juin, 26 juillet, 1753, Fonds Verreau, Boite 4, nos. 501, 502, 307, Archs. Sém. Québec; Varin à de la Perrière, 21 oct. 1754, ibid., Boite 8, no. 78; Contrecoeur à Douville, 14 avril 1755, Grenier, ed., *Papiers Contrecoeur*, 310–11.

[82] Duplessis Faber à Lavalterie, 16 avril 1756, BABY, no. 137; Péan à Contrecoeur, 15 juin 1754, Fonds Verreau, Boite 1, no. 80, Archs. Sém. Québec; Varin à Contrecoeur, 4 fév. 1753, ibid., no. 294; Varin à (?), 10 mai 1753, ibid., no. 300; Contrecoeur à Douville, 14 avril 1755, Grenier, ed., *Papiers Contrecoeur*, 310; La Perrière à Contrecoeur, 20 avril 1755, ibid., 321; Benoist à Contrecoeur, 30 juin 1755, ibid., 370–3; Saint-Blin à Contrecoeur, au for [sic] de la riviere au beouf [sic] le 3 juilietts [sic] 1755, ibid., 374–5; Journal de Joseph-Gaspard Chaussegros de Léry, 1754–5, *Rapport de l'Archiviste, 1927–1928*, 385.

[83] Vaudreuil au ministre, 13 oct. 1756, c11A, vol. 101, ff. 117–19.

[84] Thomson, *Enquiry into the Causes*, 108–14.

[85] Ibid., 138–60.

[86] Niles Anderson, 'The General Chooses a Road', *Western Pennsylvania Historical Magazine*, XLII (1959), 138, 249, quotation on 396.

[87] Lee Kennett, *The French Armies in the Seven Years' War: A Study in Military Organization and Administration* (Durham, N.C., 1967), 3–13.

[88] H. Carré acidly remarked, in describing the chaos that reigned in the Ministry of Marine, 'enfin le lieutenant de police Berryer, sous l'administration duquel s'effondra la marine. A la fin, il suspendit les travaux des ports et vendit à des particuliers le matériel des arsenaux. Choiseul, son successeur, relèvera la marine, mais trop tard pour le succès de la guerre engagée' (*La Règne de Louis XV (1715–1774)*, in Ernest Lavisse, ed., *Histoire de France* . . ., VIII, Pt. ii [Paris, 1909], 272).

[89] W.J. Eccles, 'The Battle of Quebec: A Reappraisal', French Colonial Historical Society, *Proceedings of the Third Annual Meeting* (Athens, Ga., 1978), 70–81.

[90] 28 Dec. 1758, c11A, vol. 103, ff. 453–5; Guy Frégault, *La guerre de la conquête* (Montréal, 1955), 365–72.

[91] Mémoire du duc de Choiseul, déc. 1759, Manuscrits français, Nouvelles Acquisitions, vol. 1041, ff. 44–63, Bib. Nationale.

[92] One interesting aspect of this attitude, as manifested in New England, is discussed by F.W. Anderson, 'Why Did Colonial New Englanders Make Bad Soldiers? Contractual Principles

and Military Conduct during the Seven Years' War', *William and Mary Quarterly*, 3d Ser., XXXVIII (1981), 395–417.

93 Rich, *Fur Trade and the Northwest*, 115, and *Hudson's Bay Company*, I, 554, 572, 575–86.

94 Beauharnois au ministre, 17 oct. 1736, C11A, vol. 65, f. 143.

95 MG7, I, A–Z, Fonds français, MS 12105, Mémoire de Le Maire 1717, f. 83, Public Archives of Canada.

96 Conférence avec les Onondagués et Onneiouts, 28 juillet 1756, et Conférence, 21 déc. 1756. C11A, vol. 101, ff. 55–61, 263.

LA MER DE L'OUEST: OUTPOST OF EMPIRE

1 H.P. Biggar, ed., *The Works of Samuel de Champlain* (Toronto, 1925), 326–45.

2 *Dictionary of Canadian Biography* (Toronto, 1966), vol. 1, 516–18, 'Jean Nicollet de Belleborne'.

3 Public Archives of Canada (hereafter PAC) transcript. documents St-Sulpice, Paris, Registre 25, vol. 1, pt. 1, Relation de la découverte de la Mer du Sud . . . R.P. Dablon, S.J., 1 aoust 1674.

4 See Marcel Trudel, *Atlas de la Nouvelle-France. An Atlas of New France* (Québec, 1968), 126–7, Carte de Mr Guillaume Delisle . . . 1717. Sur la Mer de l'Ouest.

5 Archives Nationales, Colonies, Paris (hereafter AN), F3 Moreau de St Méry, vol. 2, f. 11, Mémoire de Canada. De la Chesnaye, 1695; ibid., vol. 7, f. 7, Antoine Raudot au Ministre, 1710; ibid., vol. 2, f. 215, Mémoire touchant le Canada et l'Acadie envoyé par M. de Meulle.

6 See W.J. Eccles, *Frontenac: The Courtier Governor* (Toronto, 1959), 273–94, 334–7.

7 Dominion Bureau of Statistics, Demography Branch, Ottawa, *Chronological List of Canadian Censuses; Historical Statistics of the United States. Colonial Times to 1957* (Washington, D.C.: Department of Commerce, 1960).

8 AN D2C, vol. 48, f. 130, Extrait Général des Revues des Compagnies Entretenues en la Nouvelle-France . . . 1750.

9 On fur-trade statistics, see the *caveat* contained in the article by Gratien Allaire, 'Les engagements pour la traite des fourrures; évaluation de la documentation', *Revue d'histoire de l'Amérique française*, vol. 34, juin 1980, 3–26.

10 AN C11A, vol. 93, f. 11, Observations sur les Réponses fournies par la Compagnie des Indes au Mémoire et à la Lettre Envoiée de Canada en 1748 . . .

11 E.E. Rich, *The Fur Trade and the Northwest to 1857* (Toronto, 1967), 82–3.

12 During the Seven Years' War the Seneca, Cayuga, and Onondaga sent frequent war parties against frontier settlements in Virginia and Pennsylvania. *Rapport de l'Archiviste de la Province de Québec 1923-1924* (hereafter RAPQ), 250, Journal de l'expédition d'Amérique commencée en l'année 1756. Bougainville; AN C11A, vol. 101, f. 265, Conference. Cinq Nations, Mtl., 21 déc. 1756; Carl Van Doren and Julian P. Boyd, eds, *Indian Treaties Printed by Benjamin Franklin* (Philadelphia, 1938), 220.

13 In 1748 Governor-General La Galissonière informed the minister that the nations at La Baie and the Pouteouatimis of St Joseph, angered by the short supply of trade goods occasioned by the Anglo-French war, blamed it on the leaseholders of the posts and demanded that trade be opened to all who obtained a permit from the authorities at Quebec. Galissonière stated that he had been obliged to concur lest the Indians should go to the English. AN C11A, vol. 91, ff 230–33, La Galissonière au ministre, Qué., 23 oct. 1748. Galissonière's successor La Jonquière, and the intendant Bigot confirmed the decision the following year. C11A, vol. 93, f 42, La Jonquière et Bigot au Ministre, Qué., 9 oct. 1749.

14 See Wilbur R. Jacobs, *Indian Diplomacy and Indian Gifts: Anglo-French Rivalry along the Ohio and Northwest Frontier 1748-1763* (Stanford, Calif., 1950).

[15] RAPQ 1963, vol. 41, 304, Marin à son beau frère, M. Deschambeau, 1 juin 1754; *Dictionary of Canadian Biography* (Toronto, 1969), vol. 2, 619–23, 'Teganissorens'.

[16] Archives du Séminaire de Québec (hereafter ASQ), Fonds Verreau, Boite 8, no. 85, Beauharnois à de la Perrière, Mtl., 25 juillet 1745; AN C11A, vol. 65, ff. 52–3, Beauharnois et Hocquart au Ministre, Qué., 12 oct. 1736; Journal de . . . Bougainville, op. cit., 260.

[17] Archives nationales du Québec à Montréal (hereafter ANQM), Greffe J. David, no. 173, 11 août 1720; ibid., no. 215, 16 sept. 1720; Antoine Champagne, *Les La Vérendrye et le poste de l'Ouest* (Québec, 1968), 157, n 10; E.B. O'Callaghan, ed., *Documents Relating to the Colonial History of New York* (Albany, 1856–83) (hereafter NYCD), vol. 10, 245–51, M. de Longueuil to M. de Rouillé, 21 avril 1752.

[18] Lawrence J. Burpee, ed., *Journals and Letters of Pierre Gaultier de Varennes de La Vérendrye and His Sons* (Toronto: Champlain Society, 1927), 427; Champagne, *Les La Vérendrye*, . . . 293–6.

[19] See, for example, the declaration of an assembly of Sable, Ottawa, Huron, and Saulteux to the French at Lake Erie in 1704, 'Cette terre n'est pas à vous, elle est à Nous . . .'. Cited in E.E. Rich, *The History of the Hudson's Bay Company 1670–1870* (London, 1958), vol. 1, 482.

[20] Champagne, op. cit., 89; AN, F3, Moreau de St Méry, vol. 7, ff. 146–50, R.P. Guigas S.J., à Beauharnois, dattée de la Mission de St Michel arcange au fort de Beauharnois chez les Scioux, 13, 29 May 1728; AN C11A, vol. 51, f. 24, Beauharnois et Hocquart au Ministre, Qué., 25 oct. 1729; ibid., vol. 93, f. 42, Jonquière et Bigot au Ministre, Qué., 9 oct. 1749.

[21] W.J. Eccles, *The Canadian Frontier 1534–1760* (Albuquerque, 1969), 151–4.

[22] RAPQ 1926–27, 287, R.P. Nau à Madame Aulneau, Sault St-Louis, 3 oct. 1735.

[23] RAPQ 1947–48, 299, Mémoire du Roi à Vaudreuil et Bégon, Paris, 15 juin 1716; ibid., 330, Vaudreuil au Conseil de Marine, Qué., 14 oct. 1716.

[24] Marcel Giraud, *Histoire de la Louisiane française, vol. I. Le règne de Louis XIV* (Paris, 1953), 14–18.

[25] J.S. Bromley, ed., *The New Cambridge Modern History*, VI . . . (Cambridge, 1971), 40–1.

[26] H. Carré in Ernest Lavisse, ed., *Histoire de France* (Paris, 1909), VIII-2, 176–7.

[27] *Dictionary of Canadian Biography* (Toronto, 1974), vol. 3, 593–600, 'Michel Sarrazin'; W.J. Eccles, *Canada under Louis XIV, 1663–1701* (Toronto, 1964), 139–40.

[28] J.C. Dubé, *Claude-Thomas Dupuy, Intendant de la Nouvelle-France*, 1678–1738 (Montréal, 1968), 298.

[29] *Dictionary of Canadian Biography*, III, 262–3, 'Jean-Baptiste Gosselin': AN C11A, vol. 76, f. 22, Hocquart au Ministre, Qué., 25 oct. 1741; AN D2D, carton 1, Canada. Demandes particulières.

[30] Adolph B. Benson, ed., *The America of 1750: The Travels in North America by Peter Kalm* (New York, 1966), vol. 1, 375–6.

[31] *Nouvelle-France. Documents historiques. Correspondance échangée éntre les autorités françaises et les gouverneurs et intendants* (Québec, 1893), vol. 1, 148–9, Le Conseil de Marine, 29 sept. 1717.

[32] AN C11A, vol. 37, f. 376, Conseil de Marine 7 déc. 1717.

[33] Ibid., vol. 41, f. 235, Conseil de Marine, avril 1720.

[34] Pierre-Athanase Margry, *Mémoires et documents pour servir à l'histoire des origines françaises des pays d'outremer. Découvertes et établissements des français dans l'ouest et dans le sud de l'Amérique septentrionale, 1614–1754* (Paris, 1879–88), vol. 6, 525. Le Père Charlevoix à son Altesse Sérénissimé Monseigneur le comte de Toulouse, Paris, 20 jan. 1723.

[35] RAPQ 1926–7, R.P. Nau S.J., au R.P. Richard, Provinciale de la Province de Guyenne, Qué., 20 oct. 1734.

[36] Antoine Champagne, op. cit., chap. 7, 10, 11, 13, 15.

[37] As early as 1710 the intendant Antoine Raudot had reported to the minister that some Frenchmen had voyaged as far as the country of the Assiniboine, which at that time would have been Lake Winnipeg, and that those Indians had apparently traveled as far as the western ocean. That sea would, he added, have been discovered long since but for the profits being made from the furs of the region, which kept the French from proceeding further. This refrain was to be repeated by royal officials for the ensuing four decades. Raudot obviously believed that the Mer de l'Ouest was within easy reach of the western posts. Margry, op. cit., vol. 6, 14, lettre 50, Raudot au Ministre, Qué., le . . . 1710; see also RAPQ 1926-7, 286, R.P. Nau au R.P. Bonin, Sault St-Louis, 2 oct. 1735.

[38] ASQ, Fonds Verreau, Boite 5, no. 38 1/2, Meuvret au Capitaine Le Gardeur de St Pierre, Que., 15 mai 1752.

[39] AN C11A, vol. 95, f. 91, Jonquière et Bigot au Ministre, Qué., 18 aoust 1750.

[40] RAPQ 1963, vol. 41, 237-308, Journal de Marin, fils, 1753-4. (Ed., R.P. Ant. Champagne, C.R.I.C.)

[41] See, for example, the repeated plaintive request of Captain Celoron de Blainville, commandant at Niagara in 1744, to M. Pierre Guy, a Montreal merchant, for a barrel of wine, followed by—'Rendé moy toutes les nouvelles de France et celle du pays'. Archives de l'Université de Montréal, Collection Baby, boite 125, Céloron à Pierre Guy, Niagara 22 juliette [sic] 1744.

[42] RAPQ 1934-5, 52, 54, Mme Bégon à son gendre, Mtl. 28, 29 mars, 2 avril 1749.

[43] AN B, vol. 10, ff. 17-18, Reglement que le Roy veut estre observé pour le payement des officiers de marine . . . dans la Nouvelle-France, Versailles, 10 avril 1684; AN C11A, vol. 17, Mémoire sur la reforme des Troupes en Canada. 1700.

[44] Huntingdon Library, Loudoun Papers, Rigaud à Vaudreuil, Trois Rivières, 27 mai 1752; Jean Meyer, *La noblesse bretonne au XVIIIe siècle* (Paris, 1972), 39; AN C11A, vol. 105, ff. 137-8, Vaudreuil au Ministre, 30 juin 1760.

[45] RAPQ 1926-7, 287, R.P. Nau à Madame Aulneau, Sault St-Louis, 3 oct. 1735.

[46] RAPQ 1927-8, 340-1, Mémoire sur les postes du Canada adressé à M. de Surlaville en 1754 par le Chevalier de Raymond.

[47] ASQ. Fonds Verreau, Boite 5, no. 26, De la Jonquière à Le Gardeur de St Pierre, Qué., 17 avril 1750.

[48] Ibid., Carton 3, no. 205, Etat de ce qui est accordé annuellement aux Commandants des postes du Roy; *Inventaire des Ordonnances des Intendants de la Nouvelle-France conservées aux Archives provinciales de Québec* (Québec, 1919), III, 109, 23 août 1748.

[49] Ant. Champagne, op. cit., 179-181.

[50] ASQ, Fonds Verreau, Boite 5, no. 54, Mémoire ou extrait du Journal Sommaire au voyage de Jacques Legardeur . . . Sr. de St Pierre. . . .

[51] Archives de l'Université de Montréal, Collection Baby, Portneuf à? du Fort Rouillé le 20 d'aoust 1751.

[52] Journal Sommaire du voyage de Jacques Legardeur . . . Sr. de St Pierre . . . loc. cit.; ibid., Fonds Verreau, Carton 5, no. 33, Mémoire pour servir d'instruction au Sr Legardeur de St-Pierre . . . commandant aux Forts La Reine, Dauphin, Maurepas . . . La Jonquière, Mtl., 27 mai 1750; AN C11A, vol. 71, f. 35, Beauharnois au Ministre, Qué., 30 juin 1739.

[53] AN C11A, vol. 35, ff. 5-6. Ramezay et Bégon au Ministre, Qué., 13 sept. 1715; ibid., vol. 43, f. 324, Conseil, de M. de le Marqs de Vaudreuil, 6 oct. 1721; ibid., vol. 93, ff. 143-4, La Galissonière au Ministre, le 26 juin 1749; ANQM, Greffe J. David, no. 173, 215, 11 août 1720, 16 sept 1720; ASQ, Fonds Verreau, Boite 1, no. 19, Duquesne à Contrecoeur, Mtl., 12 juin 1753; Fernand Grenier, ed., *Papiers Contrecoeur et autres documents concernant le conflit anglo-français sur l'Ohio de 1745 à 1756* (Québec, 1952), 193.

[54] Ant. Champagne, op. cit., 182-6.

[55] Journal de Marin, fils . . . op. cit., 251 ff.

[56] Ibid., 253, 295.

[57] AN, F3 Moreau de St Méry, vol. 14, f. 14, Ordonnance de M. de la Jonquière, 27 fev. 1751.

[58] AN C11A, vol. 42, ff. 158–60, Extrait du Mémoire de M. Le Marquis de Vaudreuil pour servir d'Instruction au Sr. Dumont . . . 26 aoust 1720.

[59] Thomas Elliot Norton, *The Fur Trade in Colonial New York 1686–1776* (Madison, Wis., 1974), 56, 87–90; AN C11A, vol. 76, f. 334, Mémoire sur le commerce du Canada, 1741; ASQ, Fonds Verreau, Boite 1, no. 13, Duquesne à Contrecoeur, Mtl., 30 avril 1753.

[60] AN C11A, vol. 19, f. 228, Vaudreuil au Ministre, Mtl., 1 oct. 1701.

[61] E.E. Rich, *The History of the Hudson's Bay Company 1670–1870, Volume I: 1670–1870* (London, 1958), 526–7; Glydwr Williams, 'The Puzzle of Anthony Henday's Journal, 1754–55', *The Beaver*, Winter 1978, 42, citing Robson's Memoirs, *An Account of Six Years' Residence in Hudson's Bay*.

[62] Examples of such contracts are to be found in the hundreds in the Notarial Greffes at the Archives nationales du Québec à Montréal.

[63] ASQ Fonds Verreau, Boite 10, no. 45, Beauharnois à De Muy, Mtl., 28 mai 1732; ibid., Carton 5, no. 13, Beauharnois à St-Pierre, Mtl., 22 juillet 1742.

[64] ANQM. Greffe J. B. Adhemar, no. 1148, 14 avril 1724.

[65] *Inventaire des Ordonnances des Intendants de la Nouvelle-France* . . . II, 146–7.

[66] AN F3, Moreau de St-Méry, vol. 11, f. 176, Ordonnance de M. d'Aigremont, Qué., 20 oct. 1728.

[67] L.J. Burpee (ed.), *Journals and Letters of Pierre Gaultier de Varennes de la Vérendrye and his Sons* (Toronto, 1926), 451–2.

[68] ASQ Fonds Verreau, Boite 5, no. 12, Beauharnois à St-Pierre, Mtl., 28 aoust 173 . . . (last figure of the date torn off). Jacques Le Gardeur de Saint-Pierre was commandant at the Poste de Scioux from 1734 to 1737.

[69] RAPQ 1923–4, 51, Mémoire sur l'état de la Nouvelle-France 1757. Bougainville.

[70] ANQM. Greffes J. David, no. 212, J.B. Adhemar, no. 1539, 1847, 1858, 2250, 2225.

[71] ASQ Fonds Verreau, Carton 5, no. 53, La Galissonière à M. de St-Pierre. . . . Qué. 4 sept. 1748.

[72] Fernand Grenier, op. cit., 77–8, 83–4.

[73] ASQ Fonds Verreau, Boite 5, no. 54, Mémoire ou extrait du Journal Sommaire du voyage de Jacques Legardeur . . . de St-Pierre. . . .

[74] A.S. Morton, *A History of the Canadian West to 1870–71* (London, 1939), 237–8; J.B. Brebner, *The Explorers of North America, 1492–1806* (London, 1933), 1964 edition, 323; Ant. Champagne, op cit., 419.

[75] Mémoire pour servir d'instruction au Sr. le Gardeur de St-Pierre . . . loc. cit.

[76] Mémoire ou Extrait du Journal Sommaire du voyage de Jacques Legardeur . . . de St-Pierre . . . loc. cit.

[77] A.S. Morton, op. cit., 237.

[78] L.J. Burpee, *The Search for the Western Sea* (Toronto, 1908), 278, n 1.

[79] L.J. Burpee, ed., 'York Fort to the Blackfeet Country. The Journal of Anthony Henday, 1754–55', in *Transactions of the Royal Society of Canada*, sec. 2, 1097, 338.

[80] Mémoire ou Extrait du Journal Sommaire du voyage de Jacques Legardeur . . . de St-Pierre . . . loc. cit.

[81] For examples of the patronizing manner with which the French officers addressed the Indians in their councils, see 'Journal de Marin, fils', op. cit., *passim*.

[82] L.J. Burpee, ed., *Journals and letters of Pierre Gaultier de Varennes de La Vérendrye and his sons* (Toronto, 1926), 138.

[83] On the vastly superior stature and physique of the Indians compared to the French, see the

comments by Bougainville in Journal de M. de Bougainville, 1757, op. cit., 267–8. In 1734 Father Nau, S.J., writing to the Provincial of Guyenne, remarked that the Iroquois of Sault St Louis were much bigger than the French, closer to six feet tall than to five. RAPQ 1926–7, 268, The average height of Frenchmen in the eighteenth century was reckoned to be five feet one inch to five feet two, French measure, which would be five feet four inches and a bit to five feet six, English measure. In the French army fusiliers were required to be five French feet two inches and the cavalry five feet four. Objections were raised to this requirement on the grounds that over half the male population was thereby excluded from military service. See André Corvisier, *L'Armée française de la fin du XVIIe siècle au ministère de Choiseul. Le Soldat*, tome second (Paris, 1964), 637–51.

[84] Ant. Champagne, op. cit., 191–2.

[85] Mémoire ou Extrait du Journal Sommaire du voyage de Jacques Legardeur . . . de St-Pierre . . . loc. cit.

[86] Burpee, 'York Fort To the Blackfeet Country. The Journal of Anthony Henday, 1754–55', op. cit., 351.

[87] Burpee, *Journals and letter of . . . La Vérendrye*, . . . 256–7, n 2.

[88] The 'Mémoire pour servir d'instruction au Sr Le Gardeur de St-Pierre . . .', loc. cit., issued by Governor-General La Jonquière in May 1750, speaks of the necessity to follow in La Vérendrye's footsteps to the height of land in the high mountains beyond which lay the great saltwater that the Indians spoke of and which led to the sea. Le Gardeur de St-Pierre, in his journal, speaks of pushing on to the Rocky Mountains where de Niverville established Fort La Jonquière, but he says nothing of a large body of saltwater. Obviously they then knew that there was no Mer de l'Ouest east of the Rocky Mountains.

[89] On this policy, see W.J. Eccles, *The Canadian Frontier 1534–1760* (Albuquerque, 1974), 154–6.

[90] AN B, vol. 99, f. 199. Ministre à Duquesne, Versailles, 31 mai 1754.

THE SOCIAL, ECONOMIC, AND POLITICAL SIGNIFICANCE OF THE MILITARY ESTABLISHMENT IN NEW FRANCE

[1] Gustave Lanctot, 'Les Troupes de la Nouvelle France', Canadian Historical Association Report, 1926, 40–4. See also E.M. Faillon, *Histoire de la Colonie Française en Canada* (3 vols, Villemarie, 1866), III, 13–20, wherein is given a nominal roll of these militia companies.

[2] Lanctot, 'Les Troupes de la Nouvelle France'.

[3] The importance attached to the Canadian command by Louis XIV can be gauged by the military rank of Tracy. There were four grades of general officers, *maréchal de France, lieutenant-général, maréchal de camp, brigadier*.

[4] See W.J. Eccles, *Canada Under Louis XIV 1663–1701* (Toronto, 1964), 39–44.

[5] Paris, France, Archives Nationales, Colonies, D2C, vol. 47, 1–2.

[6] *Rapport de l'Archiviste de la Province de Québec* 1930–31, 70 (hereinafter RAPQ); Archives du Séminaire de Québec, Lettres, Carton N, no. 482.

[7] Joyce Marshall, ed., *Word from New France: The Selected Letters of Marie de l'Incarnation* (Toronto, 1967), 314.

[8] R.G. Thwaites, ed., *Jesuit Relations and Allied Documents* (73 vols., Cleveland, 1896–1901), V, 170.

[9] Archives Nationales, Colonies, B, vol. I, 105.

[10] The estimated population was 2,500 in 1663, 3,215 in 1666. In 1667 Jean Talon had a census taken; his total was 3,918 (Dominion Bureau of Statistics, Demography Branch, 'Chronological list of Canadian Censuses,' 3). These figures are likely too low. See the

comments on that score in Jacques Mathieu, 'La vie à Québec au milieu du XVII siècle. Etude des sources', *Revue d'Histoire de l'Amérique française*, XXIII, 3 déc. 1969, 404–24.

[11] On the origins of the office of intendant see Edmond Esmonin, *Etudes sur la France des XVIIe et XVIIIe siècles* (Paris, 1964), 13–112.

[12] RAPQ 1947–8, 278. Vaudreuil et Bégon au Ministre, Qué., 20 sept. 1714.

[13] Cameron Nish, *Les Bourgeois-gentilshommes de la Nouvelle France 1729–1748* (Montreal, 1968), 155–6, seems to imply that the seigneurial class dominated the commissioned ranks of the militia. The ranks above captain, perhaps, but the few seigneurs who were captains of militia appear to be exceptions that prove the rule. In 1712 the Minister of Marine instructed Governor-General Vaudreuil that the seigneurs were to abandon their claim that the *capitaines de milice* must communicate to them the orders they received from the governor or intendant (see RAPQ 1947–8, 146). Moreover, the *capitaines de milice* served as police officers, arresting suspected criminals on orders of the intendant, a task that a seigneur would have considered beneath his dignity. It was ordered that *capitaines de milice* had the right to occupy 'le banc le plus honorable' in their parish church, after that of the seigneur. There would have been no need for such an *ordonnance* had the seigneurs served as militia captains. See P.G. Roy, ed., *Inventaire des ordonnances des intendants de la Nouvelle-France conservées aux Archives provincials de Québec* (Beauceville, 1919), 161; and also RAPQ 1947–8, 242; RAPQ 1946–7, 385.

[14] Archives Nationales, Colonies C11A, vol. 27, 169. This offers additional proof that the *capitaines de milice* were not of the seigneurial class, whose members would have scorned non-commissioned rank in the regulars. A plea the preceding year, 1706, that militia men crippled on active service be paid a small pension was likewise rejected. See RAPQ 1938–9, 158; RAPQ 1939–40, 366.

[15] Only two occasions have been found when the militia objected strongly to serving on a campaign, that of 1739 against the Chickasaws in Louisiana, and the invasion of the Ohio valley in 1753.

[16] Archives Nationales, Colonies, C11A, vol. 27, 169, Raudot au Ministre, Québec, 10 nov. 1707. See also Archives du Québec, NF 13.8 Procédures judicaires IV, 1730–51, 359–2*v*, wherein a certain Constantin, in 1737, wrote the intendant to inform him of an attempted murder in his district, and opened his letter by stating that it was his duty as *capitaine de milice* of Saint Augustin to investigate all accidents and 'regler la police sur les Contestations' that might occur between *habitants* of the district.

[17] See the stern rebuke received by Denonville when the minister of marine, Seignelay, learned that the Governor-General had corresponded with Louvois, minister of war, on a very innocent civil matter (Transcript, Public Archives of Canada, Archives Nationales, Colonies, B, vol. 13, 209–310).

[18] Lee Kennet, *The French Armies in the Seven Years' War* (Durham, NC, 1967), 55–6.

[19] Archives Nationales, Colonies, C11A, vol. 9, 105–7.

[20] For regulations governing the billeting of troops on the *habitants* see P.G. Roy, ed., *Ordonnances, commissions etc., etc., des intendants et gouverneurs de la Nouvelle-France* (Québec, 1924), 105–6, 126–8.

[21] Louise Dechêne, ed., *La Correspondance de Vauban relative au Canada* (Ministère des Affaires culturelles, Quebec, 1968), 19. In 1740 a sergeant was given permission to establish a tar works. See Roy, ed., *Inventaire des ordonnances des intendants . . .*II, 293. On the general subject of the *Troupes de la Marine* as a source of labour, see W.J. Eccles, *Frontenac: The Courtier Governor* (Toronto, 1959), chap. 12.

[22] Adolph B. Benson, ed., *The America of 1750: Peter Kalm's Travels in North America* (Dover edition, New York, 1966), I, 381–3.

[23] E.B. O'Callaghan, ed., *Documents Relating to the Colonial History of New York* (15 vols, Albany, 1856–83), IV, 701.

[24] Ibid., 681.

[25] In a paper read at the International Colloquium on colonial history held at the University of Ottawa in November 1969, Dr Wilcomb E. Washburn of the Smithsonian Institution pointed out that the torture of prisoners was part of the Indian's ethical framework; that 'the warrior represented courage and was expected to demonstrate it as effectively in being killed by his enemies as in killing them'. The Canadians came to accept this as a condition of war in the North American environment.

[26] J. Mitchell, *The Contest in America between Great Britain and France* (London, 1757), 137–8 [quoted in J.K. Steele, *Guerillas and Grenadiers* (Toronto, 1969), 72].

[27] Archives Nationales, Colonies, C11A, vol. 47, 94–5; vol. 9, 31; vol. II, 143, 192–3.

[28] Archives Nationales, Colonies, D2C, vol. 47, 253, Mémoire Contenant les noms des officiers des troupes qui sont en Canada . . .

[29] The brothers Le Moyne are good examples. So too are the three sons of Charles Legardeur de Tilly. See Bibliothèque Nationale, Collection Clairambault, vol. 849, 108.

[30] Archives du Séminaire de Québec, Fonds Verreau, Carton 5, no 62, Duquesne à Marin, Montréal, 20 juin 1753.

[31] Archives Nationales, Colonies D2C, vol. 48, 19, 7 mars 1733, Canada. Remplacements d'officiers de guerre.

[32] Ibid., Duquesne à Marin, Montréal, 20 juin 1753.

[33] Ibid., vol. 47, 325, 333, 382. Enseignes Vacante 1719.

[34] Ibid., C11A, vol. 50, 140, Beauharnais au Ministre, Québec, 1 oct. 1728.

[35] Ibid., vol. 85, 357.

[36] Cadets were paid 6 *livres* 15 *sols* a month; *enseignes en second*, 25 *livres*; *enseignes a l'éguillette*, 40 *livres*; *lieutenants*, 60 *livres*; *capitaines*, 90 *livres*. The *livre* was equal to one shilling sterling in the early eighteenth century, declining to ten pence by the 1750s.

[37] RAPQ 1939–40, 375.

[38] In 1709 the Marquise de Vaudreuil crossed to France to defend her husband at the Court against his critics. A remarkable woman, she quickly won the favour of the Minister and was appointed assistant governess to the children of the Duc de Berry, Louis XIV's grandson. Her influence in Canadian affairs was very great. See l'Auteuil, Mémoire de l'état présent du Canada, 1712, RAPQ 1922–3, 50.

[39] RAPQ 1946–7, 376.

[40] Ibid., 409.

[41] Archives Nationales, Colonies, C11A, vol. 50, 6–7, Beauharnois et d'Aigremont au Ministre, Québec, 1 oct. 1728; ibid., vol. 51, 244, Hocquart au Ministre, Québec, 25 oct. 1729.

[42] Ibid., D2C, vol. 47, 270–1, 303, 319, 405, 417, 423, 431.

[43] Ibid., vol. 48, 70.

[44] One has only to peruse Volume II of the *Dictionary of Canadian Biography* (Toronto, 1969), to note the prevalence of this social mobility. A few random examples of families that followed the path are Le Moyne, Boucher, Charly St Ange, Marin, Hertel, Charest.

[45] Richard Colebrook Harris, *The Seigneurial System in Early Canada* (Madison, 1966), 38, 62.

[46] It is not without significance that in 1705 Governor-General Vaudreuil succeeded in obtaining royal sanction to grant the officers a month's leave in May and a month in September to allow them to oversee the seeding and harvest on their seigneuries. See RAPQ 1938–9, 42, 98, 120, 170.

[47] Adam Shortt and Arthur G. Doughty, *Documents Relating to the Constitutional History of Canada 1759–1791* (Ottawa, 1918), 1, 211.

[48] 'Chronological List of Canadian Censuses' (Dominion Bureau of Statistics, Ottawa, nd).

[49] Archives Nationales, Colonies, CIIA, vol. 36, 100, Vaudreuil au Comte de Toulouse, 1717.

[50] To eliminate this guess work a quantitative and qualitative study of the colony's population will have to be made. This will require a close analysis of such sources as the notarial *greffes* and the judicial records, as well as the more obvious official correspondence. Only in this way will a reasonably accurate picture of the social fabric of the colony emerge. In this connection, see Mathieu, 'La vie à Québec au milieu du XVII siècle'.

[51] Shortt and Doughty, *Documents*, 1, 79, General Murray's report of the state of the government of Quebec in Canada, 5 June 1762.

[52] See Eccles, *Frontenac: The Courtier Governor*, 273–94.

[53] Ibid., 334–7.

[54] See Guy Frégault's article 'La compagnie de la colonie' in his *Le XVIIIe siècle canadien: Etudes* (Montréal, 1968).

[55] See Yves F. Zoltvany, 'The Frontier Policy of Philippe de Rigaud de Vaudreuil 1713–1725', *Canadian Historical Review*, XLVIII, 3, Sept. 1967.

[56] Archives Nationale, Colonies, CIIA, vol. 50, 31–3.

[57] One clause in the instructions given to Le Gardeur de St Pierre, commandant at the Mer de l'Ouest, read '. . . il aura pour principal objet de maintenir toutes les nations de ces postes dans les interests du Roy et de la nation française, et faire de son mieux pour les détacher du commerce et des liaisons qu'ils peuvent avoir avec les Anglois', Archives du Séminaire de Québec, Fonds Verreau, Carton 5, no 33.

[58] Archives Nationales, Colonies, D2C, vol. 47, 402.

[59] RAPQ 1934–5, 52, 54, Mme Bégon à son gendre, Montréal, 28, 29 mars, 2 avril 1749. See also RAPQ 1927–8, 334, Mémoire sur les postes du Canada . . . par le chevalier de Raymond.

[60] On these aspects of a post commandant's responsibilities see RAPQ, tome 41, 1963 Journal de Marin, fils, 1753–4; and, archives du Séminaire de Québec, Fonds Verreau, Carton 5, nos 24, 33, 54.

[61] *Nouvelle France: Documents Historiques. Correspondance échangée entre les autorités françaises et les gouverneurs et intendants* (Québec, 1893), I 148–9.

[62] RAPQ 1927–8, 353, Mémoire sur les postes du Canada . . . par le chevalier de Raymond.

[63] Archives Nationales, Colonies, CIIA, vol, 85, 3–5.

[64] Guy Frégault, *Le Grand Marquis: Pierre de Rigaud de Vaudreuil et la Louisiane* (Montréal, 1962), 264–5.

[65] Ibid., 406–7.

[66] Benson, ed., *The America of 1750*, I, 343–6.

[67] Ibid., 374–392.

[68] Arthur G. Doughty, ed., *An Historical Journal of the Campaigns in North America For the years 1757, 1758 and 1759, by Captain John Knox* (Champlain Society Publications, Toronto, 1914), III, 605.

[69] A great many visitors or newcomers to the colony in the eighteenth century were struck by this phenomenon. Here, too, what is needed is a thorough study of the notarial and judicial records to establish what the living standards actually were. To put them in a clear perspective they would then have to be compared with living standards in France, and in the English colonies. Great care will have to be exercised in the analysis of this quantitative data. For example, that a man died leaving little but debts does not prove that his scale of living had been low, the reverse might well have caused the debts.

[70] See Harris, *The Seigneurial System in Early Canada*, 63–7.

[71] Cameron Nish, in his book *Les Bourgeois-gentilshommes de la Nouvelle-France*, 118–24, asserts the contrary, but in a most unconvincing fashion. Professor R.C. Harris, in contrast,

produces sound arguments to demonstrate that speculation in land was virtually negligible. See *The Seigneurial System*, 56–62.

[72] RAPQ 1922–3, 59–60.

[73] Jean Hamelin, *Economie et société en Nouvelle-France* (Quebec, 1960), 51–7.

[74] In 1715, thirty-two individuals hired *voyageurs* at Montreal, to transport goods to the West. Some of them may have been French merchants, or the agents of French traders. The number of *voyageurs* hired and of hirers increased very rapidly over the succeeding years. See 'Répertoire des engagements pour l'ouest conservés dans les archives judiciares de Montréal (1670–1778)', RAPQ 1929–30, 195–466. Unfortunately the répertoire does not give the residence of the employers or the *voyageurs*.

[75] See Kennet, *The French Armies in the Seven Years' War*, 89–98; and Frégault, *Le XVIIIᵉ siècle canadien*, 289–363.

[76] RAPQ 1922–3, 43.

[77] RAPQ 1946–7, 389.

[78] R. Lamontagne, *Aperçu structural du Canada au XVIIIᵉ siècle* (Montreal, 1964), 91.

[79] Archives Nationales, Colonies, C11A, vol. 85, 354. Extrait des payements faits au Sr Dejauniers, entrepreneur des fortifications de Québec, depuis le 20ᵉ aoust 1754, jusqu'au 21 mars 1746.

[80] Ibid., vol. 65, 203–6.

[81] Ibid., vol. 85, 388.

[82] RAPQ 1923–4, 57, 64. In his article, 'Les finances canadiennes', *Le XVIIIᵉ siècle canadien*, 336, Frégault gives statistics for military expenditures during the years 1744 to 1751, showing a climb from nearly half a million *livres* to almost a million and a quarter. In 1748 Bigot arrived at Quebec, two years later military expenditures doubled. It is doubtful if the Canadians derived much benefit from the increase, but even so, Bougainville's comment on the habitants' possession of silver utensils indicates that some of this wealth was filtering down through Canadian society. At least this data indicates that military expenditure was then a more important factor in the economy than the fur trade.

[83] See note 30 above.

[84] These reports are to be found in Archives Nationales, Colonies, series D2C.

[85] Leonard W. Labaree, *Royal Government in America* (New York, 1930), 134 ff.

[86] But see, George F.G. Stanley, *New France. The Last Phase 1744–1760* (Toronto, 1968), 272.

[87] This raises an interesting point that, in passing, deserves elucidation. When the governorship of Montreal fell vacant in 1755 Vaudreuil made a strong plea that his brother, Rigaud, governor of Trois Rivières, be given the appointment since this, he claimed, had come to be regarded as the normal succession. The Minister was reluctant to appoint Rigaud because in the event of the sudden demise of the governor-general it was customary for the governor of Montreal to take over in the interim, and Rigaud clearly lacked the qualities needed for the post. It was therefore proposed to appoint a young *Capitaine de Vaisseau* governor of Montreal, who would there gain the administrative experience needed to succeed Vaudreuil. Vaudreuil, however, seeing his brother's advancement in jeopardy, opposed the suggestion strongly. He declared that if Rigaud were passed over he should be granted an honourable retirement. He also argued that the Canadian upper class would thereby be greatly offended and their zeal for the service reduced. There might have been some truth in this last, or there might not. In fact, reasons could be advanced for the opposite being more likely to be true. In any event, Vaudreuil was pleading a special case, hence his statement requires corroboration from other sources.

The issue was finally referred to the King for a decision, with the very revealing comment by a senior official that were Rigaud to be given the appointment, 'il n'y aura pas d'inconvenient à craindre pour le Commandement general de la Colonie, supposé que le Mis de Vaudreuil vienne à manquer pendant que son frère sera Gouverneur de Montréal puisque par des lettres Patentes expediées dès l'année dernière, ce Commandement est donné au Sr. Mis de Montcalm: arrangement qui est tenu secret, les lettres Patentes étant renfermées dans un paquet, dont l'Intendant est le depositaire, et qui ne doit être ouvert qu'en cas de mort du Mis de Vaudreuil' (see, Archives Nationales, Colonies, D2C, vol. 48, 276–7, 1 May 1757, Canada Remplacement d'off[rs] de guerre Gouvernments particuliers).

[88] Archives de la Guerre, Vincennes, Series A1, vol. 3417, f. 10. Montreuil au Ministre, Mtl. 10 oct. 1755; ibid., f. 140. Montreuil à ? Mtl. 12 juin 1756; ibid., f. 208. Montcalm au Ministre, Mtl. 28 aoust 1756; ibid., vol. 3457, f. 163. M de Vaudreuil le 23 oct. 1756; ibid., #37, Ministre à Montcalm, Versailles, 10 avril 1757; ibid., vol 3498, #14, Copie d'une Lettre Ecrite à Monsieur de Moras, de Québec le 19 février 1758; Casgrain op. cit., v, *Lettres de Bourlamaque au chevalier de Lévis*, 207–10. Montcalm à Bourlamaque, Mtl. 7 mars 1758; Archives Nationales, Colonies, Series C11A, vol. 103, ff. 319–20, Vaudreuil au Ministre, Mtl. 20 oct. 1758; RAPQ 1944–1945, 154, Doreil au Ministre, Qué. 12 aoust 1758; Casgrain op. cit., *Lettres du marquis de Vaudreuil au Chevalier de Lévis*, VIII, 127, Vaudreuil à Lévis, 16 oct. 1759.

[89] Henri-Raymond Casgrain, ed., *Collection des Manuscrits du Maréchal de Lévis en Canada de 1756 à 1760* (Montréal and Québec, 1887–95), II: *Lettres du Chevalier de Lévis concernant la guerre du Canada (1756–1760)*, 387–8.

[90] See Eccles, *Frontenac: The Courtier Governor*, 334–7.

[91] See Roland Mousnier et Ernest Labrousse, *Histoire générale des civilizations*, v: *Le XVIIIe siècle* (Paris 1955), 213; Paul Vaucher, *Robert Walpole et la politique de Fleury (1731–1742)* (Paris, 1924), 298–302.

[92] See E.E. Rich, ed. *The Cambridge Economic History of Europe* (Cambridge, 1967), IV, 536–7.

[93] See W.J. Eccles, *The Canadian Frontier 1534–1760* (New York, 1969), 154–6.

[94] Ibid.

[95] Ministère des Affaires Etrangères, Mémoires et Documents, Espagne, vol. 574, 26–7, Choiseul au marquis d'Ossun, à Versailles, 2 juin 1760; 122–4, à Fontainebleau, 19 oct. 1762; 132, à Paris, 23 fev. 1762; 149–50, à Versailles, 17 mai 1762; ibid., Mémoires et Documents, Angleterre, vol. 445, 21–4, Choiseul à M. de Bussy, Versailles, 4 juil. 1761.

[96] Bibliothèque Nationale, Manuscrits français, Nouvelles acquisitions, vol. 1041, 44–63.

[97] The abandonment of Canada to Britain to achieve this end was advocated in December 1758 by a senior official in the Ministry of Marine, the marquis de Capellis. See Guy Frégault, *La Guerre de la Conquête* (Montréal, 1955), 318–20.

[98] Fernand Ouellet, *Histoire économique et sociale du Québec 1760–1850* (Montréal, 1966), 57.

[99] C.P. Stacey, *Canada and the British Army 1840–1871* (London, 1936; revised edition 1963), 11.

[100] Hansard, New Series, XIX, 7 July 1828, 1628–30; ibid., 3rd Series, C, 25 July 1848, 831–2.

THE BATTLE OF QUEBEC: A REAPPRAISAL

[1] Field-Marshal Viscount Montgomery of Alamein, *A History of Warfare*, (London, 1968), 320.

[2] Archives du Ministère de la Guerre, Vincennes, Series A1, vol. 3540, ff. 136–7, M. de Montgay à . . . Mtl., 17 mai 1759; ibid., f. 39, Malartic à . . . Mtl., 9 avril 1759; ibid., ff. 138–9; Lévis à . . . Mtl., 17 mai 1759; ibid., f. 115, Montreuil à Mgr . . . Mtl., 6 mai 1759.

[3] Archives du Séminaire de Québec, Séminaire 7, no. 72C, Journal de l'Abbé Richer, 22 aoust.

[4] Archives du Ministère de la Guerre, Vincennes, Series A1, vol. 3540, no. 103, Bigot au Ministre de la Guerre, Mtl., 15 oct 1759.

[5] Public Archives of Canada, Murray Papers, MG23, GII-1, vol. 1, 30, Murray to Amherst, Que., 19 May 1760.

[6] Ibid., 8–9, Thos. Ainslie to James Murray, Louisbourg, 28 Oct. 1759.

[7] C. P. Stacey, *Quebec 1759. The Siege and the Battle*, (Toronto, 1959), 184–91. The dispatch is here printed *in toto*.

[8] Christopher Hibbert, *Wolfe at Quebec*, (London, 1959), 104.

[9] Archives du Ministère de la Guerre, Vincennes, Series A1, vol. 3540, f. 128, Journal de M. Malartic 1758-9; ibid., 149, Situation des huit Bataillons d'Infanterie françaises servant en Canada d'Après la Revue qui en a été faitte en Mai; *Rapport de l'Archiviste de la Province de Québec 1920-1921*, 155, Journal du Siège de Québec, du 10 mai au 18 septembre 1759; Archives Nationales, Paris, Colonies, Series F3, Moreau de St Méry, vol. 15, f. 334, Bigot au Ministre, Qué., 15 oct. 1759.

[10] Ibid.; H.-R. Casgrain, ed., *Collection des manuscrits du Maréchal de Lévis*, vol. VI, 214.

[11] Ibid., vol. IX, 48-9.

[12] Ibid., vol. VI, 183.

[13] Archives Nationales, Paris, Colonies, Series C11A, vol. 104, f. 193, 1759 Journal tenu à l'armée; Casgrain, op. cit., vol. V, 41-2.

[14] Archives du Ministère de la Guerre, Vincennes, Series A1, vol. 3574, f. 112, Evenemens du Canada depuis le Mois d'Octobre 1759 Jusqu'au mois de Septembre 1760; Casgrain, op. cit., vol. IX, 56.

[15] Journal de M. Malartic 1758-9, loc. cit.; Casgrain, op. cit., vol. V, 349.

[16] Public Archives of Canada, MG 23, GII-1, series 2-7, P. MacKellar's Short Account of the Expedition against Quebec, 20.

[17] Casgrain, op. cit., vol. VI, 163.

[18] Ibid., vol. V, 343.

[19] Archives du Ministère de la Guerre, Vincennes, Series A1, vol. 3405, no. 217.

[20] 1759 Journal tenu a l'armée, op. cit., f. 187.

[21] Archives Nationales, Paris, Colonies, Series C11A, vol. 104, f. 332, Mémoire du Sieur de Ramezay.

[22] Casgrain, op. cit., vol. IV, 96.

[23] Stacey, op. cit., 102.

[24] Sir Julian S. Corbett, *England in the Seven Years' War*, (London 1918), vol. I, 454, n. 1; Hibbert, op. cit., 126.

[25] Stacey, op. cit., 97-8.

[26] See in particular Stacey, op. cit., 162-78, 'Generalship at Quebec'.

[27] Ibid., 154.

[28] Ibid., 137.

[29] Ibid., 154.

[30] *New York Review of Books*, 25 Jan. 1973.

[31] Capt. John Knox, *An Historical Journal of the Campaigns in North America*, (Champlain Society edition, Toronto, 1914–16), 99–101.

[32] Stacey, op. cit., 135; Archives Nationales, Paris, Series F3, Moreau de St Méry, vol. 15, ff. 286-8, Vaudreuil au Ministre, Mtl., 5 oct. 1759; Archives du Ministère de la Guerre, Vincennes, Series A1, vol. 3540, no. 103, Bigot au Ministre, Mtl., 15 oct. 1759.

[33] A great deal has been written on the weakness of the Quebec fortifications. Montcalm was scathing in his comments, but he always sought to make his situation appear far worse than it actually was. The engineering officer Pontleroy was equally critical, but he was not distinterested, he sought the post of chief engineer for the colony, claiming that such an

appointment was needed since all the colony's forts would have to be rebuilt and he was the obvious man to do it. According to his, and Montcalm's, rubric a fortified place that the French held was indefensible, but the moment the enemy occupied it, it became, *ipso facto*, impregnable. The other serving engineering officer in Canada, Desandrouins, a competent man of integrity, submitted a *mémoire* in 1778 on what forces would be required were the French to send an expedition to retake Quebec. He gave a good description of the fortifications, stated that they mounted 180 large guns, plus a large number of mortars, and made it plain that the fortifications of Quebec were indeed formidable. See Casgrain, op. cit., vol. IV, 322-4.

34 Francis Parkman, who went over the battlefield in 1879, noted in his *Montcalm and Wolfe* that, from the British line Quebec was hidden from sight by the Buttes à Neveu. He failed, however, to appreciate the military significance of the fact. Since his day the ridge has been reduced in height and levelled by the construction of buildings and, on the St Lawrence side, of a covered reservoir under what is today the battlefield park.

35 Archives Nationales, Paris, Colonies, Series F3, Moreau de St Méry, vol. 15, ff. 284-5, Vaudreuil au Ministre, Qué., 5 oct. 1759; ibid., ff. 337-40, Bigot au Ministre, Mtl., 15 oct. 1759.

36 Ibid., Series CIIA, vol. 104, ff. 168, 175-6, 179-80, 196, Journal tenu à l'Armée.

37 Corbett, op. cit., vol. I, 431.

38 William Charles Henry Wood ed., *The Logs of the Conquest of Canada*, (Champlain Society edition, Toronto, 1909), 315-16.

39 Knox Journal, op. cit., 99-101.

40 P. MacKellar, op. cit., 34.

41 Robert S. Quimby, *The Background to Napoleonic Warfare: The Theory of Military Tactics in Eighteenth Century France*, (New York, 1957).

42 G.F.G. Stanley, *New France. The Last Phase 1744-1760*, (Toronto, 1968), 248.

43 Staccy, op. cit., 164.

44 Stacey, op. cit., 245-9.

THE ROLE OF THE AMERICAN COLONIES IN EIGHTEENTH-CENTURY FRENCH FOREIGN POLICY

1 *Rapport de l'Archiviste de la Province de Quebec 1946-1947*, 377.

2 Adolph B. Benson, ed., *The America of 1750. Peter Kalm's Travels in North America*, 2 vols., (New York, 1966), vol. I, 139-40.

3 Gustave Schelle, ed., *Oeuvres de Turgot et documents le concernant*, Paris, 1913-1933, vol. I, 141.

4 Guy Frégault, *Le XVIIIe siècle canadien. Etudes*, (Montreal, 1968), 289 ff.

5 W. J. Eccles, *Frontenac. The Courtier Governor*, (Toronto, 1959), 334-7; Marcel Giraud, *Histoire de la Louisiane française. Le règne de Louis XIV*, (Paris, 1953), 13-23.

6 Paris, Archives Nationales, Colonies, CIIA, vol. 99, ff. 103, 247-8, 260. For earlier Canadian opposition to French expansion south of the Great Lakes see W.J. Eccles, op. cit., 336.

7 Paris, Archives Nationales, Colonies, CIIA, vol. 91, ff. 116-23.

8 Guy Frégault, *La guerre de la conquête*, (Montreal, 1955); George F. G. Stanley, *New France. The Last Phase 1744-1760*, (Toronto, 1968); Lee Kennett, *The French Armies in the Seven Years' War*, (Durham, North Carolina, 1967), xiv. The conquest of Canada cost Britain £80,000,000. The total of the budgets of Canada 1755-60 was 115,556,767 *livres*, equivalent to £4,814,865, Frégault, op. cit., 283.

9 C. P. Stacey, *Quebec 1759. The Siege and the Battle*, (Toronto, 1959); *Dictionary of Canadian Biography*, vol. III, (Toronto, 1974), Introductory Essay, xv-xxiii, Montcalm article, 458-69.

10 Paris, Archives Nationales, Colonies, B, vol. 112, ff. 280, 296.

[11] G. Frégault, op. cit., 319-20.

[12] Paris, Bibliothèque Nationale, Manuscrits français, Nouvelles Acquisitions, vol. 1041, ff. 44-63.

[13] Paris, Affaires Etrangères, Angleterre, vol. 445, ff. 21-4.

[14] Ibid., Espagne, vol. 574, ff. 122-4, 132, 149-50.

[15] Ibid., Angleterre, vol. 449, ff. 216, 262.

[16] See, W. J. Grant, 'Canada versus Guadeloupe. An Episode of the Seven Years' War', *American Historical Review*, vol. 17, 1912, 735-43; G. Frégault, op. cit., 401-27; Vincent T. Harlow, *The Founding of the Second British Empire 1763-1793. Volume One. Discovery and Revolution*, (London, 1952), 162-98; Sir Lewis Namier, *England in the Age of the American Revolution*, (London, 1930), 273-82.

[17] Quoted in Sir Julian S. Corbett, *England in the Seven Years' War*, (London, 1918), vol. 2, 173.

[18] G. Frégault, op. cit., 303-18.

[19] Zenab Esmat Rashed, *The Peace of Paris 1763*, (Liverpool, 1951), 209.

[20] A. T. Mahan, *The Influence of Seapower upon History*, (New York, 1957), 292-9.

[21] L. Kennett, op. cit., 138 ff.

[22] Robert S. Quimby, *The Background to Napoleonic Warfare: The Theory of Military Tactics in Eighteenth Century France*, (New York, 1957), 162 ff.

[23] Fernand Braudel et Ernest Labrousse eds, *Histoire économique et sociale de la France*, vol. II, (Paris, 1970), 76.

[24] W. J. Eccles, *France in America* (New York, 1972), 181-2.

[25] In 1759 the Minister of Marine informed the Governor General of New France that several supply convoys were leaving for Quebec from various French ports; additional supplies were being sent in neutral ships from neutral ports. He then added, 'Qu'il a cru aussi devoir profiter des offres qui lui ont été faites de quelques navires anglois pour la même opération'. See Henri-Raymond Casgrain, ed., *Collection des manuscrits du maréchal de Lévis*, vol. 3, *Lettres de la cour de Versailles au baron de Dieskau, au marquis de Montcalm et au chevalier de Lévis*, (Québec, 1890), 138-9; See also Richard Pares, *War and Trade in the West Indies 1739-1763*, (London, 1936), 394-468.

[26] Robert J. Chaffin, 'The Townshend Acts of 1767', in *The William and Mary Quarterly*, Third Series, vol. XXVII, n. 1, Jan. 1970, 91; V. Harlow, op. cit., 188.

[27] Ibid., 178-9.

[28] Ibid., 162-98; Joseph J. Malone, *Pine Trees and Politics*, (London, 1964), 134-43; R.G. Albion, *Forests and Sea Power*, (Cambridge, Mass., 1926), 281-315.

[29] Etienne-François duc de Choiseul, *Mémoires du duc de Choiseul, 1719-1785*, (Paris, 1904), 393.

[30] Baron Marc de Villiers du Terrage, *Les dernières années de la Louisiane Française*, (Paris, 1904).

[31] Pierre H. Boule, 'French Reactions to the Louisiana Revolution of 1768', in John Francis McDermott, ed., *The French in the Mississippi Valley*, (Carbondale, Ill., 1965).

[32] Marcel Trudel, *Louis XVI, Le Congrès americain et la Canada 1774-1789*, (Quebec, 1949), 131-6.

[33] Ibid., 120.

[34] R. Arthur Bowler, *Logistics and the Failure of the British Army in America, 1775-1783*, (Princeton, N.J., 1975).

[35] Piers Mackesy, *The War for America 1775-1783*, (London, 1964), 510.

[36] Ibid., 278.

[37] Ibid., appendix, for dispositions of the British army 1775-1782.

[38] Ibid., 384, 424.

[39] Ibid., 384–5.

[40] M. Trudel, op. cit., 131–41, 196.

[41] Ibid., 214.

[42] Ibid., 217, n. 81.

[43] Sir John Fortescue ed., *The Correspondence of King George III from 1760 to December 1783*, 6 vols, (London, 1927–8), vol. 6, 154, n. 3978.

SOVEREIGNTY-ASSOCIATION, 1500–1783

[1] Marcel Trudel, *The Beginnings of New France 1524–1663* (Toronto, 1973), 82–4.

[2] *Supreme Court of Canada Reports*, vol. XIII, 643–50, *St Catharine's Milling and Lumber Co.*, v *The Queen*, 1887; *House of Lords, Judicial Committee of the Privy Council*, vol. XIV, Appeal Cases, 1888, 46–61. In this all too frequently cited case Chief Justice Taschereau, of the Supreme Court of Canada, declared to the Judicial Committee that the King of France, in the 600 seigneuries extending from the Atlantic to Lake Superior, never recognized an Indian title to the land. There were, in fact, only 245 seigneuries in Canada during the French regime, the most westerly being La Petite-Nation, some 20 miles west of the mouth of the Ottawa River, and it was not settled. See Marcel Trudel, *Atlas de la Nouvelle-France/An Atlas of New France* (Quebec, 1968), 175–9; Richard Colebrook Harris, *The Seigneurial System in Early Canada* (Madison, WI 1968), endpaper. Moreover, the French kings most certainly did recognize Indian land title and sovereignty.

[3] Robert J. Berkhofer, Jr, *The White Man's Indian: Images of the American Indian from Columbus to the Present* (New York, 1978), 127–45.

[4] Ch.-André Julien, *Les voyages de découverte et les premiers établissements (XVe–XVIe siècles)* (Paris, 1948), 30–3; Pierre Renouvin, ed., *Histoire des relations internationales*, II; Gaston Zeller, *Les temps modernes: I De Christophe Colomb à Cromwell* (Paris, 1953), II 35–9, 45–6; Charles Gibson, *Spain in America* (New York, 1966), 14–23; David B. Quinn, *North America from Earliest Discovery to First Settlements: The Norse Voyages to 1612* (New York, 1977), 104–5, 110–12. For the text of the Treaty of Tordesillas see Frances Gardiner Davenport, *European Treaties Bearing on the History of the United States and Its Dependencies* (Washington 1934), I, 84–100.

[5] Julien, *Les voyages de découverte*, 114–17.

[6] Alden T. Vaughan, ' "Expulsion of the Salvages": English Policy and the Virginia Massacre of 1622', *The William and Mary Quarterly*, 3rd Series, XXXV (Jan. 1978), 58. See also K. G. Davies, *The North Atlantic World in the Seventeenth Century* (Minneapolis, 1974), 285–6; William S. Simmons, 'Cultural Bias in the New England Puritans' Perception of Indians,' *The William and Mary Quarterly*, 3rd Series, XXXVIII (Jan. 1981), 56–72.

[7] A. Roger Ekirch, ' "A New Government of Liberty": Hermon Husband's Vision of Backcountry North Carolina 1755', *The William and Mary Quarterly*, 3rd Series, XXXIV (Oct. 1977), 642.

[8] Alden T. Vaughan, *New England Frontier: Puritans and Indians 1620–1675* (rev. edn, New York, 1979), 104–20; Neal Salisbury, *Manitou and Providence: Indians, Europeans, and the Making of New England, 1500–1643* (New York, 1982), 101–9, 190–215. See also Francis Jennings, *the Invasion of America: Indians, Colonialism and the Cant of Conquest* (Chapel Hill, NC, 1975), a controversial work that gives pause for serious thought.

[9] Allen W. Trelease, *Indian Affairs in Colonial New York: The Seventeenth Century* (Ithaca, NY, 1960), 40–1; Berkofer, *The White Man's Indian*, 130.

[10] Vaughan, *New England Frontier*, 107–9.

[11] On fraudulent land claims see Peter Wraxall, *An Abridgement of the Indian Affairs . . . in the Colony of New York . . . 1678 to 1751*, C. H. McIlwain, ed. (Cambridge, MA, 1915),

passim; Charles Thomson, *An Enquiry into the Causes of the Alienation of the Delaware and Shawanese Indians from the British Interest* (London, 1759), *passim*. Other references on this topic could be added almost *ad infinitum*.

[12] Dennis Lloyd, *The Idea of Law* (London, 1965), 153–4, 157, 165.

[13] Francis N. Thorpe, ed., *The Federal and State Constitutions, Colonial Charters and Other Organic Laws of . . . the United States of America* (Washington, DC, 1909), VII.

[14] Ibid., 3795.

[15] Fernand Grenier, ed., *Papiers Contrecoeur et autres documents concernant le conflit anglo-français sur l'Ohio de 1745 à 1756* (Québec, 1952), 57, 217; Theodore Calvin Pease, *Anglo-French Boundary Disputes in the West, 1749–1763* (Springfield, IL, 1936), xlii, lix–lx, 14, 73, 377; Jean Delanglez, *Some La Salle Journeys* (Chicago, 1938), 3–39.

[16] See H.P. Biggar, ed., *A Collection of Documents Relating to Jacques Cartier and the Sieur de Roberval* (Ottawa, 1930), 128–31, 178–85, for Cartier's commission for his third voyage and Roberval's commission.

[17] Ibid., 42, grant of money to Cartier for his first voyage, 'pour descouvrir certain ysles et pays où l'on dit qu'il se doibt trouver grand quantité d'or et autres riches choses . . .'. See also 77, letter from Lagarto to John the Third, King of Portugal, 22 Jan. 1539.

[18] H.P. Biggar, ed., *The Works of Samuel de Champlain* (Toronto, 1922), I, 180–5. On his 1603 voyage to Canada Champlain was led to believe that rich veins of copper and silver had been found in a bay appropriately named Baie des Mines.

[19] Robert Le Blant and René Baudry, eds, *Nouveaux documents sur Champlain et son époque (1560–1622)* (Ottawa, 1967), 1, 74, 407–14, 137–43; Trudel, *The Beginnings of New France*, *passim*.

[20] Andrew Hill Clark, *Acadia: The Geography of Early Nova Scotia to 1760* (Madison, WI, 1968), 24–31, 67–9, 158–62.

[21] In 1714, after the cession of part of the area to Great Britain, the Acadian population was estimated to be less than 4,000 *Chronological List of Canadian Censuses*, Dominion Bureau of Statistics, Ottawa.

[22] Le Blant and Baudry, *Nouveaux documents*, 407–14.

[23] Trudel, *The Beginnings of New France*, 43–53.

[24] J. V. Wright, *Quebec Prehistory* (Toronto, 1979), 64–75.

[25] Bruce G. Trigger, *The Children of Aataentsic: A History of the Huron People to 1660* (Montreal and London, 1976), II, 270; Trudel, *The Beginnings of New France*, 185.

[26] *Edits, Ordonnances Royaux, Déclarations et Arrêts du Conseil d'Etat concernant le Canada* (Québec, 1854), 5–11, Acte pour l'établissement de la Compagnie des Cent Associés . . . .

[27] Ibid., 20–3, Concession d'une grande partie de l'Isle de Montréal . . .

[28] Ibid., 24–6., Ratification de la concession de l'Isle de Montreal . . .

[29] Ibid., 28–9, . . . traité faite . . . entre la dite Compagnie et le député des habitans de la Nouvelle-France.

[30] W.J. Eccles, *Canada under Louis XIV 1663–1701* (Toronto, 1964), 97; Jean Delanglez, *Frontenac and the Jesuits* (Chicago, 1939), 35–65.

[31] *Rapport de l'Archiviste de la Province de Québec pour 1943–1944* (hereafter RAPQ) 1–16, La Seigneurie de Sillery; Marcel Trudel, *Les débuts du régime seigneurial* (Montréal, 1974), 52, 171.

[32] Jean Longnon, ed., *Mémoires de Louis XIV* (Paris, 1927), 197; Marcel Marion, *Dictionaire des institutions de la France aux XVIIe et XVIIIe siècles* (Paris, 1968), 489–93; Roland Mousnier, *Les institutions de la France sous la monarchie absolue* (Paris, 1974), I, 510–15.

[33] *Edits, Ordonnances Royaux, Déclarations et Arrêts . . .* 7–8—Acte pour l'établissement de la Compagnie des Cent Associés.

[34] Ibid., 31-2.

[35] Delanglez, *Frontenac and the Jesuits*, 35-65; H. Charbonneau and Y. Landry, 'La politique démographique en Nouvelle-France,' *Annales de démographie historique* (1979), 29-57.

[36] *Collection de manuscrits contenant lettres, mémoires et autres documents historiques relatifs à l'histoire de la Nouvelle-France, recueillis aux archives de la province de Québec ou copiés à l'étranger* (Québec, 1873), I, 175, Le Roy à Courcelle.

[37] Delanglez, *Frontenac and the Jesuits*, 35-47.

[38] W.J. Eccles, *Frontenac: The Courtier Governor* (Toronto, 1959), 54-8.

[39] RAPQ 1930-1, 43, Colbert à Talon, Versailles, 5 jan. 1666; RAPQ 1926-7, 87, Lettre du Roi au Governeur Frontenac, Paris, 15 avril 1676, AN CIIA, vol. 4, f. 82, Ordonnance du Roy, St Germain-en-Laye, 12 mai 1678.

[40] AN CIIA, vol. 3, f. 97, Au Roy. Mémoire sur le Canada. Talon. Qué, 10 nov. 1670. Addition au présent mémoire, Talon, 10 nov. 1670.

[41] AN, B, vol. 3, ff. 12-24, Colbert à Talon, [1671]; ibid., vol. 7, f. 31, Le Roy à Frontenac, St Germain, 12 avril 1676.

[42] John Bartlet Brebner, *The Explorers of North America, 1492-1806* (London, 1933); RAPQ 1930-1, 157-8, Mémoire de Talon au Roi sur le Canada, 2 nov. 1671.

[43] Ministère des Affaires Etrangères, Paris. Public Archives of Canada (hereafter PAC) transcripts, Série Amérique, vol. V, part 2, 13. Copie du Procès verbal de la prise de possession du Sr de Saint-Lusson, 16 mai 1671; RP J Tailhan, SJ, ed., *Mémoire sur les moeurs, coustumes et relligion des sauvages de l'Amérique septentrionale par Nicolas Perrot* (Montréal, 1973), 126-8, 292-4; Reuben Gold Thwaites, ed., *The Jesuit Relations and Allied Documents* (Cleveland, 1899), LV, 105-15.

[44] A later example of this propensity occurred in 1742 when the chevalier de La Vérendrye, while on his epic trip across the western plains to the Bighorn Mountains, built a stone cairn near the future site of St Pierre, South Dakota, and beside it buried a lead plaque bearing the arms of France, brought from Quebec, to signify the taking of possession of the land. He noted in his journal, 'Je posait sur une éminence, près du fort, une plaque de plomb aux armes et inscriptions du Roy et des pierres en pyramide pour Monsieur le Général. Je dis aux Sauvages, qui n'avaoient pas connaissance de la plaque de plomb que j'avois mise dans la terre, que je mettois ces pierres en mémoires de ce que nous étions venus sur leurs terres.' Lawrence J. Burpee, ed., *Journals and Letters of Pierre Gaultier de Varennes de La Vérendrye and His Sons* (Toronto, 1927), 427; Antoine Champagne, *Les La Vérendrye et le poste de l'ouest* (Québec, 1968), 293.

[45] William W. Warren, *History of the Ojibway Nation* (Saint Paul, 1885; Minnesota Historical Society Collections, 1974), 130-2.

[46] N. Perrot, *Mémoire sur les moeurs*, 295.

[47] Ministère des Affaires Etrangères, Paris, Série Amérique, V, 288-9, Au Roy. Mémoire sur le Canada, Talon. Qué., 2 nov. 1671. In a lengthy memoir on the fur trade written in 1695, de Lagny, the Intendant de Commerce, wrote: 'Ce fut à l'arrivée de M. Talon en Canada que sous pretexte des découvertes les voyages dans la profondeur des terres furent autorisés et qu'il permet ce commerce et pour son compte.' AN CIIA, vol. 13, f. 400, Colonies, fév. 1695. Commerce du Castor de Canada.

[48] In 1748 the nations trading at La Baye complained to Governor General Galissonière that the leaseholder was charging too much for his goods. He immediately assured them that in future the post would not be leased to a monopolist but that the trade would be carried on by the issuing of *congés* to free traders. Galissonière did this out of fear that were he not to do so the Indians would go over to the English. AN CIIA, vol. 93, f. 42, Jonquière et Bigot au Ministre, Qué., 9 8bre 1749. See also Grenier, *Papiers Contrecoeur*, 265, Duquesne à

Contrecoeur, Qué., 21 oct. 1754. Governor General Duquesne here ordered Capitaine Contrecoeur, commandant at Fort Duquesne, to have the price of trade goods fixed to put an end to the Indians' complaints that they were being cheated.

49 RAPQ 1946-7, 398. Vaudreuil au Ministre, Qué., 3 nov. 1710; ibid., 427, Mémoire du Roi à MM de Vaudreuil et Raudot, Marly, 7 juillet 1711; AN C11A, vol. 102, f. 276, 1er 9bre 1757. Canada.

50 RAPQ 1939-40, 446. Vaudreuil et Raudot au Ministre, Qué., 14 nov. 1708.

51 AN C11A, vol. 29, f. 165v. Le Sr Daigremont, 14 nov. 1708.

52 When three soldiers who had murdered a Seneca chief and robbed his cache of furs were convicted and executed before a large assembly of visiting Iroquois and western Indians the tribesmen were appalled, regarding it as barbaric that three should be put to death for the murder of one. The Iroquois declared that they would have preferred to receive ten belts of wampum as compensation rather than see the three soldiers die. In cases of murder the Indians always demanded *wergeld* in order to avoid a blood feud. See Etienne-Michel Faillon, *Histoire de la colonie française en Canada* (Ville-Marie 1865-6), III, 324-5. See also Joyce Marshall, ed. and trans., *Word from New France: The Selected Letters of Marie d l'Incarnation* (Toronto, 1967), 240; and the case that unfolds in Archives Nationales du Québec à Montréal (hereafter ANQM), Pièces judiciares, 15 aoust-9 sept. 1722, wherein the Sault Saint-Louis Iroquois refused to allow one of their warriors to stand trial for the murder of a Canadian because he and his companions had been intoxicated at the time. The Governor-General had to intervene and order the prisoner released, whereupon the Iroquois promised to make due retribution to the widow and child of the victim.

53 AN C11A, vol. 99, ff. 257-8, Duquesne au Ministre, Qué 7 8bre 1754.

54 ANQM, Documents judiciares, 25 jan. 1719. Information contre Jacques Detaillis.

55 *Arrêts et réglements du Conseil Supérieur de Québec et ordonnances et jugements des Intendants du Canada* (Québec, 1855), 70.

56 RAPQ 1947-8, 241. Le Roi à Vaudreuil et Bégon, Versailles, 19 mars 1714.

57 André Lachance, *La justice criminelle du Roi au Canada au XVIIIe siècle* (Québec, 1978), 16-17.

58 AN C11A, vol. 34, ff. 27-32, Vaudreuil et Bégon au Ministre, Québec, 15 nov. 1713. See also ANQM, Pièces judiciares, 15 aoust-9 sept. 1722. In this case a Canadian was killed and another wounded by five or six inebriated Iroquois in Montreal. One of them was apprehended and imprisoned for interrogation. At the insistence of the Sault Saint-Louis Iroquois council the Governor-General was obliged to have the prisoner released after questioning to establish the facts of the case. Vaudreuil stated that he had to do so to calm the irate Indians, who would not permit the imprisonment of their people. The same thing had happened in a similar case previously and he had, on that occasion, declared that it was necessary 'd'agir a l'avenir avec beaucoup de precaution avec les Sauvages pour les menager'. A Canadian and his wife who, in the later case, had sold the liquor to the Iroquois were fined 500 *livres*, a year's wages for a skilled artisan.

59 ANQM, Documents judiciaires, 25 jan. 1719. Information contre Jacques Detaillis.

60 Ibid., 13 mai 1700, procès de François Noir; ibid., 14 mai 1700, procès de Jean Cuillerier; ibid., 10 fév. 1719; ibid., 25 juillet 1719; ibid., 9 avr. 1721; ibid., 27 juin-22 juillet 1721; ibid., 13-31 juillet 1721.

61 RAPQ1926-7, 282-3, RP Nau au RP Bonin, Sault Saint-Louis, 2 oct. 1735.

62 Edmond B. O'Callaghan, Berhold Fernow, eds, *Documents Relative to the Colonial History of the State of New York* (Albany, 1856-87), (hereafter NYCD), IV, 908-11, deed from the Five Nations to the King of their beaver hunting ground, 19 July 1701.

63 Ibid., 122, answer of the Five Nations to the Governor of Canada, Onondaga, 4 Feb. 1694/5.

[64] Ibid., 337-8, Comparative Population of Albany and of the Indians in 1689 and 1698; *Calendar of State Papers, Colonial Series, America and the West Indies* (hereafter CSPAWI) (London, 1860–); 1699, 135, Earl of Bellomont to Council of Trade and Plantations, New York, 13 Apr. 1699; Ibid., 1700, 543, Council of Trade and Plantations to Mr Secretary Vernon, Whitehall, 4 Oct. 1700; ibid., 615, Bellomont to Council of Trade and Plantations, New York, 24 Oct. 1700.

[65] AN C11A, vol. 29, f. 152, D'Aigremont au Ministre, Qué., 14 nov. 1708; Leroy V. Eid, 'The Ojibwa-Iroquois War: The War the Five Nations Did Not Win', *Ethnohistory*, XXVI (Fall 1979), 297-324; Victor Konrad, 'An Iroquois Frontier: The North Shore of Lake Ontario during the Late Seventeenth Century', *Journal of Historical Geography*, VII (1981), 129-44.

[66] Bruce G. Trigger, ed., *Handbook of North American Indians: Northeast* (Washington, 1978), XV, 588-93; Delf Norona, ed., 'Joshua Fry's Report on the Back Settlements of Virginia', (8 May 1751), *The Virginia Magazine of History and Biography*, LVI (Jan. 1948), 22-41; AN C11A, vol. 50, f. 43, Beauharnois et D'Aigremont au Ministre, Qué., 1 oct. 1728; AN F3, Moreau de Saint-Méry, vol. 12, f. 40, Mémoire du Roy aux Srs Beauharnois et Hocquart, Versailles, 22 avr. 1732.

[67] CSPAWI 1681-5, 422-3, no. 1059, Apr. 1683. Draft of a memorial in answer to Monsieur de la Barre; ibid., 1685-8, 645, no. 2091, Memorial for the French Ambassador; NYCD, IV, 908-11, deed from the Five Nations to the King of Their Beaver Hunting Ground, 19 July 1701.

[68] AN C11A, vol. 103, ff. 31-3. Acte Authentique des Six Nations Iroquoises sur leur Indépendance, 2 nov. 1748. See also AN C11A, vol. 39, f. 241. Conseil de Marine, juin 1718, Canada, for an example of the Iroquois' ability to work both sides of the street. The Five Nations having sent His Majesty a wampum belt to assure him of their fidelity, the Regent approved their being sent a gift in return—2,000 pounds of gunpowder and 4,000 musket balls.

[69] AN B, vol. 11, f. 104, Le Ministre à Mr. Barillon, Versailles, 10 mars 1685.

[70] CSPAWI 1699, no. 1109, 588. Copy of the Treaty Made with the Iroquois by M. de Tracy on 13 Dec. 1655; AN C11A, vol. 2, ff. 270-1, Prise de Possession des forts Dagnié, 17 oct. 1666.

[71] AN F3 Moreau de Saint-Méry, vol. 8, ff. 278-9, Assemblée faite par M. Lechevalier de Callières de tous les nations Iroquoises . . . Mtl 7e aoust 1701; *Nouvelle-France: Documents historiques, Correspondance échangée entre les autorités françaises et les gouverneurs et intendants* (Québec, 1893), I, 44-5, Mémoire du Roy aux Srs Chevalier de Callières et de Champigny, Versailles le 31 mai 1701; RAPQ 1938-9, 24-5, Vaudreuil au Ministre, Mtl., 3 avr. 1704; ibid., 29, Le Roy à Vaudreuil et Beauharnois, Versailles, 14 juin 1704; ibid., 160-1, Vaudreuil au Ministre, Qué., 4 nov. 1706; RAPQ 1939-40, 445, MM de Vaudreuil et Raudot au Ministre, Qué., 14 nov. 1708; RAPQ 1946-7, 453, Vaudreuil au Ministre, Qué., 8 nov. 1711.

[72] Yves F. Zoltvany, *Philippe de Rigaud de Vaudreuil: Governor of New France 1703-1725* (Toronto, 1974), 168-70. Earlier, when Canadian officials proposed establishing a post at Toronto to stop the Mississaugas and Amicoués from trading their furs with the Iroquois, the King agreed only on condition that the Iroquois gave their prior consent. See RAPQ 1947-8, 300. Mémoire du Roi à Vaudreuil et Bégon, Paris, 15 juin 1716.

[73] Peter Wraxall, *An Abridgement of the New York Indian Records* C.H. McIlwain, ed., (Cambridge, MA, 1915), 161.

[74] Vaudreuil, who knew better than most, wrote: 'Il est de notre interet Monseigneur de n'avoir aucune guerre avec cette nation tant qu'il nous sera possible et les cinq villages Iroquois sont plus a craindre que toutte la nouvelle angleterre.' RAPQ 1946-7, 453. Vaudreuil au Ministre, Qué., 8 nov. 1711. See also RAPQ 1939-40, 455, MM de Vaudreuil et Raudot au Ministre, Qué., 14 nov. 1708.

[75] Eccles, *Frontenac*, 273–94.

[76] AN CIIA, vol. 13, f. 198, Mémoire pour le Castor. Champigny, Qué., 26 oct. 1694.

[77] Eccles, *Frontenac*, 285–8.

[78] Ibid., 289–91.

[79] AN B, vol. 19, ff. 240–2, Mémoire du Roy pour les Srs comte de Frontenac et de Champigny, Versailles, 27 avr. 1697.

[80] AN B, vol. 22, ff. 231–2/245–6, Mémoire du Roy au Srs Chevalier de Callières . . . et de Champigny, Versailles, 31 mai 1701.

[81] Zoltvany, *Vaudreuil*, 38–41.

[82] Natalie Maree Belting, *Kaskaskia under the French Regime* (Urbana, IL, 1948); AN F3, Moreau de Saint-Méry, vol. 11, ff. 180–1, Arrest de la Chambre du Conseil en Canada, 18 déc. 1728.

[83] PAC transcripts, AN B, vol. 22–4, 368, Ministre à M. de Champigny, Versailles, 4 juin 1701; ibid., B, vol. 27–33, 437–9, Ministre à M. de Champigny, Versailles, 2 juin 1706; Francis H. Hammang, *The Marquis de Vaudreuil: New France at the Beginning of the Eighteenth Century* (Brussels, 1938), 21–2.

[84] Ibid., 120–2, 176; AN CIIA, vol. 21, f. 52, Vaudreuil au Ministre, Qué., 14 oct. 1703; RAPQ 1939–40, 423, Vaudreuil au Ministre, Qué., 28 juin 1708.

[85] *Nouvelle-France: Documents Historiques*, I, 89, Instruction particulière pour M. de Vaudreuil, Versailles, 1 avr. 1755; Theodore Calvin Pease, ed., *Anglo-French Boundary Disputes in the West 1749–1763* (Springfield, IL, 1936), xxxiii–xxxiv, 42–7—Lord Halifax on French encroachments, 15 Aug. 1753; Trudel, *Atlas de la Nouvelle-France/An Atlas of New France*, 139.

[86] RAPQ 1922–3, 95–6, Observations et réflexions servant de réponses aux propositions de Messieurs les commissaires au sujet des limites à régler pour la Baie d'Hudson [1720]; Max Savelle, 'The Forty-Ninth Degree of North Latitute as an International Boundary, 1719: The Origin of an Idea', *Canadian Historical Review*, XXXVIII (Sept. 1957), 183–201.

[87] Frances Gardiner Davenport, *European Treaties Bearing on the History of the United States and Its Dependencies, 1698–1715* (Washington, 1934), III, 193–214.

[88] RAPQ 1921–2, between 108–9, Acte authentique des six nations iroquoises sur leur indépendance (2 nov. 1748).

[89] RAPQ 1922–3, 95–6, Observations et réflexions servant de réponses aux propositions de Messieurs les commissaires anglais au sujet des limites a régler pour la Baie d'Hudson.

[90] CSPAWI, 1719–20, no. 360, Memorial of Governors, Hudson's Bay Company, no. 443 (1719), 4 Nov., Whitehall.

[91] Charles A. Bishop, 'The Henley House Massacres,' *The Beaver* (Summer 1976), 36–41.

[92] Elaine Allan Mitchell, *Fort Timiskaming and the Fur Trade* (Toronto, 1977), 209. Two Canadian governments later disputed the Hudson's Bay Company's claims to Rupert's Land. In 1856 the Honourable Philip Van Koughnet, president of the Executive Council of Canada, declared that 'no charter could give to a body of men control over half a continent' and that he would not rest 'until that Charter was abolished'. Eleven years later, at the first session of the federal parliament of the Dominion of Canada, the Honourable William McDougall, Minister of Public Works, on 4 Dec. 1867, declared in Parliament that the government was not prepared to heed the Hudson's Bay Company's demands for a large payment by Canada for the lands in question. The government proposed, he declared, 'to claim this country as being part of New France, as having been ceded to the English government in 1760 [*sic*], and as having remained in that position from that time down to the present.' See Alexander Begg, *History of the North-West* (Toronto, 1894), I, 330–42.

[93] AN CIIA, vol. 35, f. 113, Bégon au Ministre, Qué., 25 7 bre 1715; ANF3, Moreau de Saint-

Méry, vol. 2, ff. 413–6, Parole de toute la Nation Abenaquise . . . au gouverneur de Baston . . . 28 juillet 1721.

94 Ibid., II, ff. 410–12, Parole des Abenakis au Roy, sur ce que les Anglois depuis la paix d'Utrecht s'emparent de leurs terres; NYCD, X, 253, Propositions of the Abenakis of St Francis to Captain Phineas Stevens, Delegate from the Governor of Boston . . . See also L.F.S. Upton, *Micmacs and Colonists: Indian-White Relations in the Maritimes 1713– 1867* (Vancouver, 1979), 37.

95 AN C11A, vol. 31, ff. 121–5 (Vaudreuil). Lettre à M. Nicholson du 14 jan. en réponse à la sienne du 11 oct. 1710.

96 *Nouvelle-France: Documents Historiques*, I, 89, Instruction Particulière pour M. de Vaudreuil, Versailles, 1er avr. 1755.

97 AN C11A, vol. 43, ff. 372–7, Mrs de Vaudreuil et Bégon au Ministre, Qué., 8 8bre 1721.

98 AN C11A, vol. 39, ff. 160–2, Vaudreuil au Conseil Marine, 31 oct. 1718.

99 AN C11A, vol. 91, ff. 116–23, De La Galissonière au Ministre, Qué., 1 sept. 1748.

100 W.J. Eccles, 'The Fur Trade and Eighteenth Century Imperialism', *The William and Mary Quarterly*, 3rd Series, XL, July 1983, 341–62; W.J. Eccles, 'A Belated Review of Harold Adams Innis, *The Fur Trade in Canada'*, *Canadian Historical Review*, LX (Dec. 1979), 419–41.

101 BN, Collection Clairambault, vol. 882, f. 137, La Mothe Cadillac [à M. de Lagny, Michili-mackinac 1695]; AN C11A, vol. 24, ff. 3–5, Vaudreuil au Ministre, Qué., 28 avr. 1706; ibid., vol. 39, f. 212, Vaudreuil au Conseil de Marine, 12 8bre 1717; ibid., ff. 149–155, Vaudreuil au Conseil, Qué., 30 oct. 1718; ibid., vol. 71, f. 35, Beauharnois au Ministre, Qué., 30 juin 1739; Archives du Séminaire de Québec (hereafter ASQ), Fonds Verreau, Carton 5, no. 33, Mémoire pour servir d'instruction au Sr le Gardeur de Saint-Pierre . . . La Jonquière, Mtl, 27 may 1750; Archives Université de Montréal, Collection Baby (hereafter Baby) Céleron de Blainville à [M. de Lavalterie, commandant, Niagara] Detroit, le 26 jan. 1752; AN F3, Moreau de Saint-Méry, vol. 14, ff. 36–7, Le Ministre à Duquesne, 16 juin 1752.

102 Champagne, *Les La Vérendrye*, 99–104; ANQM, Congés et Ordonnances 1721–30, Charles, marquis de Beauharnois, 9 juillet 1729; Baby, G 1/3 Congé de la Barre au Sr D'Argenteuil, 1683; AN F3 Moreau de Saint-Méry, vol. 14, f. 14, Ordonnance de M. de la Jonquière, 27 fév. 1751.

103 AN C11A, vol. 93, f. 43, Jonquière et Bigot au Ministre, Qué, 9 8bre 1749.

104 Champagne, *Les La Vérendrye*, 191–2.

105 Toby Morantz, 'The Fur Trade and the Cree of James Bay', in Carol M. Judd and Arthur J. Ray, eds, *Old Trails and New Directions: Papers of the Third North American Fur Trade Conference* (Toronto, 1980), 54.

106 RAPQ 1926–7, 289, RP Aulneau au RP Bonin, Fort Saint-Charles, 30 avr. 1736; RAPQ, XLI, 1963, 263, Journal de Marin fils; Lawrence J. Burpee, ed., 'Journal of Anthony Henday'. in *Transactions of the Royal Society of Canada*, (1907), 431–4; Champagne, *Les La Vérendrye*, 152–3.

107 Wilbur R. Jacobs, *Dispossessing the American Indian* (New York, 1972), 50–7; Wilbur R. Jacobs, *Wilderness Politics and Indian Gifts* (Lincoln, NB, 1966); RAPQ, XLI, 1963, Journal de Marin fils, *passim*.

108 Trigger, *The Children of Aataentsic* II, 785. The source of the account of this incident is Tailhan, ed., *Mémoire sur les moeurs, coustumes et relligion des sauvages de l'Amérique septentrionale*, 95. Perrot mistakenly names RP Allemand as the victim. See 245, n. 11. Other examples of toll charges being levied on the Ottawa in the first half of the seventeenth century are mentioned in Gabriel Sagard, *Le grand voyage au pays des Hurons*, George M.

Wrong, ed. (Toronto, 1939), 257. Sagard also mentioned that the Montagnais levied tolls on their rivers (257). The Huron and Nipissing permitted no one to cross their territory to trade in that early period. See R.G. Thwaites, ed., *The Jesuit Relations and Allied Documents* (Cleveland, 1896–1901), VII, 215; VIII, 21, 83; IX, 275; X, 77; XV, 151; XXI, 171, 241. I am indebted to Conrad Heidenreich for the above references.

[109] Pierre Margry, *Mémoires et documents pour servir à l'histoire des origines françaises des pays d'outre mer: Découvertes et établissements des Français dans l'ouest et dans le sud de l'Amérique septentrionale* (Paris, 1876), VI, 78, Extrait du Mémoire de M. Le Chevalier Beaurien sur la Louisiane. Voyage de le Sueur chez les Sioux.

[110] RAPQ, XLI, 1963, 280–1, Journal de Marin fils; ibid., 295–8. A M. le Général. Lettre du 1er juin 1754.

[111] PAC transcripts, Shelburne MSS: MG 23, A4, vol. 12, 138–9, Montreal fur merchants, memorial on the Indian trade, sent by Governor Carleton to the Board of Trade, 20 Sept. 1767. Included with Mar. 1766 dispatches.

[112] ASQ, fonds Verreau, Boite 5, no. 54. Mémoire ou Extrait du Journal Sommaire du voyage de Jacques Legardeur . . . Sr de Saint-Pierre . . . .

[113] Ibid., Boite 11, no. 36–1/2. Relation des aventures de M. de Boucherville a son retour des Scioux.

[114] Jay Higginbotham, *Old Mobile: Fort Louis de la Louisiane 1702–1711* (Mobile, AL, 1977), 111.

[115] W.J. Eccles, *The Canadian Frontier 1534–1760* (Albuquerque, NM, 1969), 151–4.

[116] A.S. Morton, *A History of the Canadian West to 1870–71* (London, 1939), 252–3; Adolph B. Benson, ed., *The America of 1750: Peter Kalm's Travels in North America* (New York, 1966), II, 561: AN C11A, vol. 35, Ramezay et Bégon au Ministre, Qué., 13 7bre 1715; ANQM, Pièces judiciares, 11 mars 1720; AN C11A, vol. 43, f. 324, Conseil. M. le Marqs de Vaudreuil, 6 8bre 1721; Champagne, *Les la Vérendrye* 157, n10; Huntingdon Library, Loudoun Collection, Vaudreuil à Beauharnois, Nouvelle Orléans, 9 nov. 1745; AN C11A, vol. 93, ff. 143–4, Galissoniére au Ministre, le 26 juin 1759; ASQ, Fonds Verreau, Boite 5, no. 26, Congé. De La Jonquière à Le Gardeur de Saint-Pierre, Qué., 17 avr. 1750. Vu par Bigot; Grenier, *Papiers Contrecoeur*, 193: ANQM, Greffe J. David, no. 173, 11 aoust 1720; ibid., no. 215, 16 sept. 1720; ASQ Fonds Verreau, Boite 8, no 96, Ordonnance de Beauharnois, Mtl, le 8 juin 1743; Baby G 1/22 Ordonnance de Beauharnois, 31 mai 1738.

[117] Quoted in E.E. Rich, *The History of the Hudson's Bay Company 1670–1870* (London, 1958), I, 482.

[118] AN C11A, vol. 26, ff. 221v–222R, Raudot au Ministre, Qué., 12 nov. 1707.

[119] RAPQ 1939–40, 260; Journal de l'Expédition d'Amérique commencé en l'Année 1756, du 26 avr. 1757.

[120] RAPQ, 1939–40, 413. Mémoire du Roi à MM de Vaudreuil et Raudot, Versailles, 6 juin 1708.

[121] Frances G. Halpenny, ed., *Dictionary of Canadian Biography*, III (Toronto, 1974), Beauharnois de la Boische, 45; AN F3, Moreau de Saint-Méry, vol. 12, f. 40, Mémoire du Roy aux Srs Beauharnois et Hocquart, Versailles, 22 avr. 1732.

[122] Ibid., f. 140, Mémoire du Roy aux Srs Beauharnois et Hocquart, Versailles, 12 mai 1732.

[123] Wraxall, *New York Indian Records*, 212–13, Albany, 7 June 1739; ibid., 11 July 1732.

[124] Thomas Charland, OP, 'Un village d'Abenaquis sur la rivière Missisquoi' in *Revue d'Histoire de l'Amérique Française*, XV (Dec. 1961), 319–32.

[125] Biggar, *The Works of Samuel de Champlain*, II, 90–1. Champlain remarked of the lake in 1609: 'Ces lieux ne sont habitez d'aucuns sauuages [sic], bien qu'ils soient plaisans, pour le subiect de leurs guerres, & se retirent des riuires le plus qu'ils peuuent au profont des terres, afin de n'estre si tost surprins.'

[126] Wraxall, *New York Indian Records*, 215, Albany, 26 Oct. 1739.

[127] *Nouvelle-France: Documents Historiques*, I, 89, Instruction Particulière pour M. de Vaudreuil, Versailles, 1er avr. 1755; Grenier, *Papiers Contrecoeur*, 53-7, Conseil tenu par les Tsonnontouans venus de la Belle Riviére, du 2e 7bre 1753.

[128] Guy Frégault, *La guerre de la conquête* (Montreal and Paris, 1955), 114.

[129] ASQ, Fonds Verreau, Boite 1, no. 11, Duquesne à Contrecoeur, Mtl, 14 avr. 1753; Grenier, *Papiers Contrecoeur*, 96, Duquesne à Contrecoeur, Mtl, 30 jan. 1754; ibid., 98-9, Duquesne à St-Pierre, Mtl, 30 jan. 1754; *Nouvelle-France: Documents Historiques*, 89, Instruction Particulière pour M. de Vaudreuil, Versailles, 1er avr. 1755.

[130] AN C11A, vol. 91, ff. 116-23, Galissonière au Ministre, Qué., 1 sept. 1748; Pierre Margry, *Mémoires et documents*, VI, 727-8, Jonquière au Ministre, Qué., 20 sept. 1749.

[131] George F. G. Stanley, *New France: The Last Phase 1744-1760* (Toronto, 1968), 37-41; *Collections of the State Historical Society of Wisconsin*, XVIII, 57, Céloron de Blainville's Journal, 9 Nov. 1749.

[132] Lawrence Henry Gipson, *The British Empire before the American Revolution: Zones of International Friction. North America South of the Great Lakes Region 1748-1754* (New York, 1939), IV, 302-10.

[133] Grenier, *Papiers Contrecoeur*, 116, Paroles de Contrecoeur aux Sauvages, 16 avr. 1754.

[134] War parties of Onondaga, Cayuga, and Seneca are specifically mentioned as having served with the Canadians in raids on Anglo-American settlements. See *Minutes of the Provincial Council of Pennsylvania*, VIII, 182, 185; Carl Van Doren and Julian P. Boyd, eds, *Indian Treaties Printed by Benjamin Franklin* (Philadelphia, 1938), 220; AN C11A, vol. 101, f. 265, Conférence. 5 Nations. Mtl, 21 déc. 1756; RAPQ 1923-4, 250, Journal de l'expédition d'Amérique commencée en l'année 1756. 8 fév. 1757. Bougainville.

[135] Wraxall, *New York Indian Records, passim*; Charles Thomson, *An Enquiry into the Causes of the Alienation of the Delaware and Shawanese Indians from the British Interest*, 16-57.

[136] Thomson, *Enquiry*, 16-57.

[137] Their attack on the surrendered garrison at Fort William Henry in 1757 is a case in point. See also the plaintive statement of Capitaine de Contrecoeur after the crushing defeat of Major-General Edward Braddock's army near Fort Duquesne in 1755: 'Tous les sauvages du Détroit et de Michilimackinac sont partis le lendemain de l'action, sans que j'aye pu les arrester.' See AN F3, Moreau de Saint-Méry, vol. 14, f. 120. Extrait. Contrecoeur à M. de Vaudreuil, Fort Duquesne, 14 juin 1755. In a similar vein see AN C11A, vol. 101, ff. 117-19, Vaudreuil au Ministre, Mtl, 13 8bre 1756; AN F3, Moreau de Saint-Méry, vol. 15, ff. 75-9, Vaudreuil au Ministre, Mtl, 15 sept. 1757.

[138] The British, in contrast to the French, throughout the war were able to secure the services of only some fifty Stockbridge Indians, whose role is barely mentioned in the massive documentation of this war. The British thus were able to adopt a 'holier than thou' attitude toward the French. See Stanley McCrory Pargellis, *Lord Loudoun in North America* (New Haven, 1933), 301; John Clarence Webster, ed., *Journal of William Amherst in America, 1758-1760* (Toronto, 1931), 68; Henri-Raymond Casgrain, ed., *Collection des manuscrits du Maréchal de Lévis*, X, 14, Bernier à Lévis, Qué., 10 oct. 1759; ibid., 18-19, Bernier à Lévis, 20 oct. 1759.

[139] Thomson, *An Enquiry into the Causes of the Alienation*, 138-46, 163-6.

[140] Adam Shortt and Arthur G. Doughty, eds, *Documents Relating to the Constitutional History of Canada 1759-1791* (Ottawa, 1918), 1, 20, 33.

[141] Ibid., 99-101, 115-17.

[142] AN F3, Moreau de Saint-Méry, vol. 2, ff. 413-16, Parole de toute la Nation Abenaquise et de toutes les autre nations sauvages ses alliés au gouverneur de Baston . . . .

[143] Shortt and Doughty, *Documents Relating to the Constitutional History of Canada*, I, 199. Instructions to Governor Murray, St James's, 7 Dec. 1763.

[144] As cited in Brian Slattery, 'The Land Rights of Indigenous Canadian Peoples, as Affected by the Crown's Acquisition of Their Territories' (D. Phil. thesis, Oxford University, 1979), 224. The Domaine du Roy, or Traitte de Tadoussac, encompassed the territory from a point opposite the eastern end of Ile-aux-Coudres, downstream to 2 leagues (5 miles) below Sept Iles, and inland stretching within an east-west line from the western point at Ile-aux-Coudres to the height of land, and on the downstream side, from Cap-aux-Cormorans beyond Lake Mistassini to Hudson Bay. Included were the posts at Tadoussac, Chicoutimi, Lac Saint-Jean, Nekoubau, Mistassini, Papinachoix, Naskapie, Rivière Moisy, Sept Iles, and Malbaie. AN F3, Moreau de Saint-Méry, vol. 12, f. 147, Ordonnance de M. Hocquart qui fixe l'étendue du Domaine du Roi appelé la Traite de Tadoussac, 23 mai 1733.

[145] Howard H. Peckham, *Pontiac and the Indian Uprising* (Chicago, 1961), 71–3; James Sullivan *et al.*, eds, *The Papers of Sir William Johnson* (Albany, 1921–65), III, 245.

[146] Peckham, *Pontiac*, 282, 285.

[147] Jack M. Sosin, *Whitehall and the Wilderness* (Lincoln, NB, 1961), 66–76.

[148] Peckham, *Pontiac*, 226–7.

[149] See Bernard Knollenberg, 'General Amherst and Germ Warfare', *The Mississippi Valley Historical Review*, XLI (1954–5), 489–94.

[150] Peckham, *Pontiac*, 170. The bacteria spores in the cloth would be released into the air and inhaled by whoever handled the material. I am indebted to Dr H. Velland of the Toronto General Hospital for information on this point.

[151] Sosin, *Whitehall and the Wilderness*, 71–2.

[152] Peckham, *Pontiac*, 282, 285.

[153] Shortt and Doughty, *Documents*, Part 1, 166–7, by the King. A proclamation, 7 Oct. 1763; ibid., 200, Instructions to Governor Murray, Article 60, 7 Dec. 1763.

[154] Sosin, *Whitehall and the Wilderness*, 186, 193.

[155] Ibid., 227–32.

[156] Ibid., 106–23, 135–41, 154–7, 193, 205, 225.

[157] Ibid., 138–9, 252.

[158] Marcel Trudel, *Louis XVI, le congrès américain et le Canada 1774–1789* (Québec, 1949), 130–1, 210–19.

[159] British Museum [now British Library] Additional Mss, 21, 763m, ff. 118–19. (calendared in PAC Report 1886, B 103, Haldimand Collection, I, 32–3, Brigadier General Allan Maclean, Niagara, to General Frederick Haldimand, Que., 18 May 1788).

[160] Clyde A. Milner, II, 'Indulgent Friends and Important Allies: Political Process on the Cis-Mississippi Frontier and its Aftermath', in Howard Lamar and Leonard Thompson eds, *The Frontier in History: North America and Southern Africa Compared* (New Haven and London, 1981), 144.

[161] Between 1830 and 1888 the great herds were reduced from some 75,000,000 to a few hundred. See Frank Gilbert Roe, *The North American Buffalo* (2nd edn, Toronto, 1970), 416–88.

[162] E.E. Rich, *The Fur Trade and the Northwest to 1857* (Toronto, 1967), 141, 164, 194.

[163] René Fumoleau, OMI, *As Long as This Land Shall Last* (Toronto, 1975), Appendix 1.

[164] Ibid., *passim*; D.N. Sprague, 'Government Lawlessness in the Administration of Manitoba Land Claims, 1870–1887', *Manitoba Law Journal*, X, (1980), 415–41; D.N. Sprague, 'The Manitoba Land Question, 1870–1882', *Journal of Canadian Studies/Revue d'études canadiennes*, XV (Autumn 1980), 74–84; Peter A. Cumming and Neil H. Mickenberg, eds, *Native Rights in Canada* (2nd edn, Toronto, 1971).